DUBLIN

THE ROUGH GUIDE

There are more than two hundred Rough Guide titles
covering destinations from Alaska to Zimbabwe and
subjects from Acoustic Guitar to Travel Health

Forthcoming travel guides include

Devon & Cornwall • Ibiza • Iceland • Malta • Tenerife

Rough Guides online

www.roughguides.com

Rough Guide Credits

Text editor: Andrew Tomičić
Series editor: Mark Ellingham
Typesetting: Katie Pringle
Cartography: Ed Wright

Publishing Information

This second edition published January 2000 by
Rough Guides Ltd, 62–70 Shorts Gardens, London, WC2H 9AH
Reprinted April 2001

Distributed by the Penguin Group:

Penguin Books Ltd, 27 Wrights Lane, London W8 5TZ
Penguin Putnam Inc., 375 Hudson Street, New York 10014, USA
Penguin Books Australia Ltd, 487 Maroondah Highway,
PO Box 257, Ringwood, Victoria 3134, Australia
Penguin Books Canada Ltd, 10 Alcorn Avenue,
Toronto, Ontario, Canada M4V 1E4
Penguin Books (NZ) Ltd, 182–190 Wairau Road,
Auckland 10, New Zealand

Typeset in Bembo and Helvetica to an original design by Henry Iles.
Printed in Spain by Graphy Cems.

The publishers and authors have done their best to
ensure the accuracy and currency of all the information
in *The Rough Guide to Dublin*, however, they can accept
no responsibility for any loss, injury or inconvenience
sustained by any traveller as a result of information or
advice contained in the guide.

DUBLIN

THE MINI ROUGH GUIDE

by Mark Connolly,
Margaret Greenwood
and Geoff Wallis

We set out to do something different when the first Rough Guide was published in 1982. Mark Ellingham, just out of university, was travelling in Greece. He brought along the popular guides of the day, but found they were all lacking in some way. They were either strong on ruins and museums but went on for pages without mentioning a beach or taverna. Or they were so conscious of the need to save money that they lost sight of Greece's cultural and historical significance. Also, none of the books told him anything about Greece's contemporary life – its politics, its culture, its people, and how they lived.

So with no job in prospect, Mark decided to write his own guidebook, one which aimed to provide practical information that was second to none, detailing the best beaches and the hottest clubs and restaurants, while also giving hard-hitting accounts of every sight, both famous and obscure, and providing up-to-the-minute information on contemporary culture. It was a guide that encouraged independent travellers to find the best of Greece, and was a great success, getting shortlisted for the Thomas Cook travel guide award, and encouraging Mark, along with three friends, to expand the series.

The Rough Guide list grew rapidly and the letters flooded in, indicating a much broader readership than had been anticipated, but one which uniformly appreciated the Rough Guide mix of practical detail and humour, irreverence and enthusiasm. Things haven't changed. The same four friends who began the series are still the caretakers of the Rough Guide mission today: to provide the most reliable, up-to-date and entertaining information to independent-minded travellers of all ages, on all budgets.

We now publish more than 150 titles and have offices in London and New York. The travel guides are written and researched by a dedicated team of more than 100 authors, based in Britain, Europe, the USA and Australia. We have also created a unique series of phrasebooks to accompany the travel series, along with an acclaimed series of music guides, and a best-selling pocket guide to the Internet and World Wide Web. We also publish comprehensive travel information on our Web site: **www.roughguides.com**

Help Us Update

We've gone to a lot of effort to ensure that this second edition of *The Rough Guide to Dublin* is as up-to-date and accurate as possible. However, if you feel there are places we've underrated or over-praised, or find we've missed something good or covered something which has now gone, then please write: suggestions, comments or corrections are much appreciated.

We'll credit all contributions, and send a copy of the next edition (or any other *Rough Guide* if you prefer) for the best letters. Please mark letters: "Rough Guide Dublin Update" and send to:

Rough Guides, 62–70 Shorts Gardens, London WC2H 9AH, or
Rough Guides, 375 Hudson St, 4th Floor, New York, NY 10014.

Or send email to: mail@roughguides.co.uk
Online updates about this book can be found on
Rough Guides' Web site (see opposite)

The Authors

Mark Connolly graduated from Queen's University Belfast, after which he taught English in Poland, Israel and Japan. He has worked as a radio journalist for BBC Radio Ulster and BBC Radio 5 and is currently based in Dublin.

Since graduating from the University of Kent, **Margaret Greenwood** has worked as a teacher and freelance writer, and has produced books on Ireland and Spain. She's a keen hillwalker and has been visiting Ireland since the early 1980s.

After embarking on more careers than he cares to remember, **Geoff Wallis** now works as a freelance writer. He has been contributing to the Rough Guides since the early 1980s and is currently co-writing *The Rough Guide to Irish Music*. In his spare moments he hunts for rare records and tries to treat his addiction to Nottingham Forest.

Mark Connolly, Margaret Greenwood and Geoff Wallis are also the co-authors of *The Rough Guide to Ireland*.

Acknowledgements

The authors would like to thank: John Lahiffe of Bord Fáilte, Niall Kennedy and the staff at Dublin Tourism, Gráinne Ní Allúin of Dúchas and Valerie Keogh of the National Gallery of Ireland, An Óige, the Independent Holiday Hostels and the Isle of Man Steam Packet Co, Anne Guilhot, Brian McAllister, Shashi and Justin, Heather and Oceana Munro, the Alexander, Killough and Connolly families for their help and support, Sally-Ann Whittaker, Anne Greenwood, Maggie Keenan and Nial and Ger Shanahan. Thanks also to Russell Walton for proofreading.

Readers' Letters

We'd like to thank all the readers who wrote in with comments and updates to the previous edition: Jane Alvarez, Jackie Bayley, Nardene Berry, Rachel Biggs, Rita Binder, Amy Cates, Ann Eskins, Charles Forsyth, Ruth Frost, Emma Gibson, Mike H, Eileen & Phil Hawkins, Tim Jellyman, Kate Kerss, Sophie Latham, David & Lynne Lawrence, Pauline Lee, Joanne Linder, Terry Newell, Richard Overy, Margaret Pallock, Lucy Rutherford, Nicky Thomas, Gary Thomson and Marjorie Threm.

CONTENTS

Introduction

A vibrant and compact city, Dublin has a pace and energy quite at odds with the relaxing image of Ireland as a whole. Prosperity generated by the Republic's economic boom in the 1990s has brought fundamental changes to the life of its capital, reversing the tide of emigration and creating a dynamic cultural centre. Visitors and Dubliners alike are astonished at the rate of transformation; chic bars and restaurants, new exhibitions and trendy shops all signify a major shift in the city's identity, no longer dominated by the insular conservatism of less than a decade ago.

The city's emergence from provincialism is, however, only part of the picture. With the increase in population, Dublin is bulging at the seams, which, of course, brings its problems – spend just a couple of days here and you'll come upon inner-city deprivation as bad as any in Europe. The spirit of Dublin has its contradictions, too, with youthful enterprise set against a deeply embedded traditionalism: the national divorce referendum in 1995 may have gone in favour of reform, but it was a close-run thing. However, the collision of the old order and the forward-looking younger generations is an essential part of the appeal of this extrovert and dynamic city, and, despite the differences, the wit and garrulous sociability for which its inhabitants are famous is a constant feature. In the legendary – and plentiful – bars, the buskers of Grafton Street and the tour guides who ply the streets with visitors in tow, there's an unmistakeable love of banter. Dublin's considerable literary heritage owes much to this trait, and, on either side of the Liffey you'll find reminders of literary personalities who are as intrinsic to the city's character as the river itself – from the bronze plaques in the pavement following the route of Leopold Bloom, hero of James Joyce's *Ulysses*, to the remarkable statue of Oscar Wilde on Merrion Square.

Ireland's tremendous economic growth – an average of nine percent per year between 1994 and 1998 – has given new impetus to just about every facet of the capital's cultural life. Historic treasures are being promoted and displayed in a way previously not possible, from the Millennium Wing of the National Gallery to the new displays of decorative arts at the Collins Barracks, and major periods of social and political history are articulated with flair, both in the plethora of theme-based tours available and the built environment of the city itself. Everywhere in Dublin you'll find evidence of a rich past well worth exploring: exceptional Viking finds excavated at Wood Quay (and now on show in the National Museum); impressive reminders of Anglo-Norman and British imperial power; elegant Georgian streets and squares; and monuments to the violent struggle for independence. The visual arts are enjoying a higher public profile too, with mouthwatering exhibitions in the city's numerous galleries supplemented by the development of a unique design scene, characterized by subtlety and experimentation. Throughout the city there's a palpable sense that Dublin's cultural heritage is coming into its own with striking confidence.

Dublin is, of course, known for its pubs, and, for many, sampling the myriad bars and buzzing nightlife is an integral part of any visit to the city. There's also plenty of music on offer and, while the capital has nothing to match the music cultures of rural Ireland, there's no shortage of traditional, rock and jazz venues. Theatre too has long played a part in the city's cultural life and you can catch plays by O'Casey, Synge and Shaw all year round at the Abbey Theatre, as well as experiencing the vitality of Dublin's continuing dramatic tradition during the Theatre and Fringe Festivals.

For those who want to get out into the surrounding countryside, again there are plenty of options. Dublin is within easy reach of the wild open heights of the Wicklow Mountains, the secluded monastic settlement of Glendalough, a sprinkling of choice stately homes, and some of Europe's most important prehistoric sites, including Knowth and Newgrange.

When to visit

Dublin's warmest months are usually July and August, which are also often the wettest. However, no month is especially hot or cold, and though the climate of Ireland is often damp, this shouldn't be a determining factor in arranging your trip. Obviously the summer is the most popular time, so if you're planning a visit then, you should make sure you've got your accommodation sorted out well before you go – and whatever time you visit, if your stay is going to straddle a weekend, book your room in advance. Before making your decision, you should take a look at the city's calendar of festivals and special events, which range from the parades of St Patrick's Day and the meanderings of Bloomsday (June 16) to blues in Temple Bar in July and the All-Ireland Hurling and Football final in September (see *Sports* and *Festivals & Events* for more).

Dublin's climate

	°F		°C		Rainfall	
	Average daily		Average daily		Average monthly	
	MAX	MIN	MAX	MIN	IN	MM
Jan	46	34	8	1	2.6	67
Feb	47	35	8	2	2.2	55
March	51	37	10	3	2.0	51
April	55	39	13	4	1.8	45
May	60	43	15	6	2.4	60
June	65	48	18	9	2.2	57
July	67	52	20	11	2.8	70
Aug	67	51	19	11	2.9	74
Sept	63	48	17	9	2.8	72
Oct	57	43	14	6	2.8	70
Nov	51	39	10	4	2.6	67
Dec	47	37	8	3	2.9	74

THE GUIDE

Introducing the city

Central Dublin is easy enough to find your way around – it's fairly small, and you're likely to make most of your explorations on foot. One obvious axis is formed by the river **Liffey**, running from west to east and dividing the city into two regions of very distinct character – the **northside**, poorer and less developed than its neighbour the **southside** – each of which has a strong allegiance among its inhabitants. The other main axis is the north–south one formed by Grafton and Westmoreland streets south of the river, running into O'Connell Street to the north. The centre as a whole is rimmed by two canals: the **Royal Canal** to the north, and the **Grand Canal** to the south.

Prices quoted throughout this Guide are in Irish pounds, or punts, which are worth a little less than the pound sterling.

The majority of the famous attractions are south of the river, and, for many visitors, the city's heart lies around the best of what is left of Georgian Dublin – the elegant set pieces of **Fitzwilliam** and **Merrion squares**, with their graceful red-brick houses with ornate, fan-lighted doors and immaculately kept central gardens, and the wide but strangely decorous open space of **St Stephen's Green**. The southside is also the setting for Dublin's august seat of learning, **Trinity College**, with its famous library; **Grafton Street**, the city's upmarket shopping area; **Temple Bar**, the in-place for the arts, alternative shopping and socializing; and most of the city's **museums and art galleries**. Parallel to the river, **Dame Street**, running into Lord Edward Street, strings together a handful of historic monuments: the **Bank of Ireland**, **Dublin Castle** and **Christ Church Cathedral**. The tangle of lanes between here and Wood Quay – Winetavern Street, Copper Alley and Fishamble Street – are remnants of the medieval city. South of Christ Church lies **St Patrick's Cathedral**, while to the west a drab urban scene unfurls, worth exploring nonetheless for the **Guinness Brewery** and, slightly further out, the **Irish Museum of Modern Art** and **Kilmainham Jail**, which are best accessed by bus.

North of the Liffey, the main thoroughfare is **O'Connell Street**, whose key monument, the **General Post Office**, was the scene of violent fighting in the Easter Rising of 1916. Further north is **Parnell Square**, around which you'll find the **Irish Writers' Museum** and **Hugh Lane Municipal Art Gallery**. The inner-city area northeast of O'Connell Street (specifically, east of Gardiner Street) is run-down and certainly at night should be explored with caution, but is nevertheless notable for its literary connections – here you'll find the **James Joyce Centre**. Lodged beside the quays to the east of O'Connell Street stands the impressive **Custom House**, designed by James Gandon. The streets running west of O'Connell Street are busy with a mix of workaday shops and markets, but beyond here are the elegant **Four Courts**, also by Gandon, **St Michan's Church** and **Smithfield**, famous for its monthly horsefair. Further west is the prestigious National Museum at the **Collins Barracks** and **Phoenix Park**, one of the world's largest city parks.

Travel beyond the centre is fairly straightforward. The suburbs, including Glasnevin and Clontarf in the north and Ballsbridge and Donnybrook in the south, are served by regular buses, and the DART line allows easy access to the coastal resorts along the curve of Dublin Bay.

The telephone code for the Dublin area is ℂ01.
Calling Dublin from abroad (or Northern Ireland),
dial ℂ00-353-1, followed by the subscriber's number.

Arrival

The main **points of arrival** are all within easy reach of the city centre, with the bulk of tourist traffic coming in via either the airport, which is just 12km north, or the port at Dún Laoghaire, 14km south.

BY AIR

Dublin Airport arrivals hall has a **tourist office** (daily: July & Aug 8am–10.30pm; Sept–June 8am–10pm), a bureau de change (open for arrivals and departures), various car rental desks and an ATM. For airport information call ℂ704 4222. Buses into town leave from outside the departures exit. Airlink buses (Mon–Sat 6.40am–11pm, Sun 7.05am–11pm) run directly to Busáras (the central bus station), and the thirty-minute journey costs £3, or £3.50 if travelling on to Heuston Station, twenty minutes further along. You purchase your ticket on board. A cheaper alternative (£1.10) is to catch a regular #41 or #41c bus to Abbey Street Lower, near to O'Connell Street. A taxi into

ARRIVAL

the centre should cost about £15, but can be much dearer during rush hour.

BY BUS

Busáras is located off Beresford Place, just behind the Custom House, and is within easy walking distance of O'Connell Street. Buses from all parts of the Republic and Northern Ireland arrive here, along with Airlink buses and coaches from Britain. Busáras has a bureau de change (Mon–Sat 8am–8pm, Sun 10am–6pm) and a left luggage facility (Mon–Sat 8am–8pm, Sun 10am–5.45pm).

BY FERRY

Arriving by ferry from Britain, you will dock at either **Dublin Port**, 3km east of the centre (for Irish Ferries, the Isle of Man Steam Packet Company and Merchant Ferries) or **Dún Laoghaire** (for Stena Line). The former is served by bus #53, which is timetabled to meet ferry services and heads directly for the city centre. Dún Laoghaire is twenty minutes from the centre by the DART (£1.10; see p.10 for more). There is a tourist office at Dún Laoghaire (Mon–Sat 10am–6pm), plus a bureau de change (Mon–Sat 9am–1pm & 1.30–5.30pm, Sun 10am–1pm & 1.30–5.30pm) and an ATM. There's also an interactive video unit available for booking accommodation when the tourist office is closed. Note that some coach passengers from Britain will be driven directly to the city centre.

BY TRAIN

Connolly Station, a couple of hundred yards northeast from Busáras, is the terminus for trains from Belfast and

Sligo to the north and Wexford and Rosslare to the south; it is also on the DART line. Facilities are limited, though there is a left luggage office (Mon–Sat 7.40am–9.30pm, Sun 9.15am–1pm & 5–9pm). **Heuston Station**, its counterpart on the south bank of the Liffey, 4km west of the city centre, is the terminus for trains from Cork, Killarney, Tralee, Waterford, Limerick, Galway, Westport and Ballina. Again, there is a left luggage office (Mon–Sat 7.15am–8.35pm, Sun 8am–3pm & 5–9pm). Bus #90 runs between the two termini. **Tara Street** and **Pearse Street** stations are on the south side of the Liffey and serve DART and suburban train services. For all train information and times call ℗836 6222.

Information and tourist passes

Dublin's **main tourism centre** (July & Aug Mon–Sat 9am–8.30pm, Sun 11am–5.30pm; Sept–June Mon–Fri 9am–5.30pm) is a walk-in centre in a converted church near the western end of Suffolk Street. There are separate desks for information, accommodation, coach trips, bus and rail tickets, theatre bookings, money exchange and car rental. The first two can be incredibly busy and a numbered ticket queueing system operates, so head directly for the dispenser when you enter. The offices at the **airport** and **Dún Laoghaire** (see p.5 and p.6) provide similar facilities, though they stock a less comprehensive range of printed information. You can also email the tourism centre on *information@dublintourism.ie*.

The offices can find you **accommodation** and charge a flat fee of £1 for the service; if they're closed you can also book a room through their interactive video units outside (credit cards only), for which there's no fee. Alternatively, for credit card accommodation booking you can ring ℂ1800/668668 within Ireland, ℂ00800/6686 6866 in the UK, or ℂ353-669/792082 from outside Ireland and the UK, for which there's a £3 charge. For all three services a deposit of ten percent of your hotel or guesthouse bill is required, and you pay the balance at the establishment.

A downtown alternative is the **USIT** discount student travel agency on Aston Quay, opposite O'Connell Bridge (Mon–Wed & Fri 9am–5.30pm, Thurs 9.30am–8pm, Sat 10am–5.30pm; ℂ679 8833), which also has a Web site, *www.usitnow.ie*. USIT can book you a B&B during the summer, and runs its own hotel and hostel. Their notice board is also useful if you're looking for work or a flatshare, and there are flyers for hostels, clubs and other items of interest.

In any of these places, as well as at various bars and cafés around the city, you should be able to pick up a copy of the free *Dublin Event Guide* which provides concise **listings** of gigs, clubs, exhibitions and tourist sites. Information on events in Temple Bar is most readily available by phone (ℂ671 5717); alternatively call in at **Temple Bar Properties**, 18 Eustace St (Mon–Fri 9am–5.30pm), a particularly good source of arts scene info, which also has a Web site, *www.temple-bar.ie*. The other major listings guides are *In Dublin* (£1.95), available at most newsagents, with lots on clubs and style and a longer listings section that also covers restaurants, and *Hot Press* (£1.95), Ireland's witty, iconoclastic rock magazine, which is the best place to find music listings. All three are published fortnightly.

Daily cinema and theatre listings appear in the *Irish Times* (the best national daily newspaper, though on Sundays the *Sunday Tribune* holds sway) and the *Evening Herald* (Dublin's only evening paper).

While the **maps** in this book should suffice for your visit, long-stayers might invest in a pocket-sized *Dublin Street Plan* (£4) of the inner city and suburbs. Small freebie maps of the centre can also be picked up in tourist offices.

If you're planning to visit a lot of attractions in Dublin it may be worth getting a **tourist pass**. Dublin Tourism run eight attractions: Malahide Castle, Newbridge House, the James Joyce Museum and Tower, Dublin Writers Museum, the Shaw Birthplace and Fry Model Railway, and Dublin's Viking Adventure. A **SuperSaver card** (£16, under-18s and over-55s £12.50, children £8.50, concessions £12.50, family £37) covers entry to all, and is valid for one year (though you're limited to one visit only to each attraction). A combined ticket for the Writers Museum and Shaw Birthplace or the Joyce Tower costs £4.50, students £3.80.

Dúchas (✆647 2454), the Heritage Service, take care of Dublin's national parks, monuments and gardens, of which six have admission charges: the Casino at Marino, Kilmainham Gaol, Phoenix Park Visitors Centre, Rathfarnham Castle, St Mary's Abbey and the Waterways Visitors Centre. A **Heritage Card** (£15, over-55s £10, children/students £6, family £36) covers entry to all, and is particularly good if you're planning to travel elsewhere in Ireland. It is valid for one year (you may visit each site as many times as you like) and available at all the sites mentioned.

Transport

The only real way to get to know Dublin is to walk, but to visit the farther-flung sights you'll probably want to use the city's public transport. **Travel passes** come in many forms and are obtainable from Dublin Bus at 59 Upper O'Connell Street, from newsagents displaying the Dublin Bus sign and DART and suburban railway stations. A one-day adult bus pass (£3.30) covers all buses except Nitelink and Airlink, while the bus-and-rail short-hop pass (£4.50) also covers the DART and suburban services. The weekly versions of these tickets are £13 (students £10) and £16 respectively.

BUSES

Buses are the mainstay of public transport, reaching most parts of Dublin, including places beyond the city limits. Regular services operate from 6am; last buses leave the city centre at 11.30pm. Special Nitelink buses run out to the suburbs on Thursdays, Fridays and Saturdays, departing from O'Connell Street, Westmoreland Street and St Stephen's Green at 12.30am, 1.30am, 2.30am and 3.30am. Travel passes are not valid for Nitelink buses, which charge a flat fare of £2.50 (apart from the Maynooth Nitelink, which is a dearer and less frequent service). The price of tickets on regular buses ranges from £0.55 to £1.25; it's prudent to hoard coins as some routes are exact-fare only. For Dublin Bus information call 873 4222. For bus travel beyond the city contact Bus Éireann (836 6111).

DART AND SUBURBAN TRAINS

The other vital service is the Dublin Area Rapid Transport system, or **DART** (Mon–Sat 6.15am–11.20pm,

Sun 9am–11.15pm; ℗703 3504), whose trains link Howth to the north of the city with Bray to the south, via such places as Dún Laoghaire and Dalkey, and connect with suburban services to even further afield. The maximum single fare is £1.60, but if you're considering taking more than one or two trips a day, it may be worth buying some form of travel pass. This advice also applies to some of the **suburban trains** operated by Iarnród Éireann, which use the same tracks as the DART but make far fewer stops en route (Connolly, Tara and Pearse Street stations in the centre, Howth Junction to the north and Dún Laoghaire and Bray to the south). The Northern Suburban service from Pearse Street to Dundalk is the speediest way to make day excursions to Malahide (see p.173), Castletown (see p.185) and Newgrange (see p.188).

TAXIS

Taxis don't generally ply the streets for custom (though it is possible to hail them), but wait in ranks in central locations, such as outside the *Shelbourne Hotel* on St Stephen's Green, in front of the Bank of Ireland on College Green and opposite the *Gresham Hotel* on O'Connell Street; bear in mind though that after 11pm you'll probably have to wait at least an hour. If you want to order a taxi by phone, call Metro Cabs (℗668 3333); **wheelchair-accessible** cabs are available if ordered one hour in advance from Eurocabs (℗844 5844). Other firms with fixed rates, open 24 hours, include Checkers Cabs, 4 Bedford Row (℗834 3434) and Finglas Cabs, at the bottom end of Parnell Square East (℗834 3333). Finding a taxi after midnight on weekends is difficult, so if you know you'll need one, book it.

TRANSPORT

Bus and walking tours

If you're only in Dublin for a short time or just want a quick feel for the city's landmarks, you could take one of the many city tours on offer. The following selection gives a sense of the variety available – the tourist offices have full details. For tours out of town see p.178.

Dublin Bus (☎873 4222) run a couple of Dublin city tours using their fleet of open-topped buses in green-and-white livery, and which depart from the Dublin Bus HQ on O'Connell Street:

The "Dublin City Tour" allows you to hop on and off at any of the twelve different stops including Parnell Square, Trinity College, St Stephen's Green, Dublin Castle, the cathedrals, the Guinness Brewery and Collins Barracks. Tours run every thirty minutes Mon–Thurs and every fifteen minutes Fri–Sun, the first at 9.30am, the last at 4.30pm. Tickets (£7) are valid all day and include discounts to attractions.

The "Grand Dublin Tour" (daily 10.15am & 2.15pm; £10) lasts almost three hours, and includes the Custom House, Kilmainham Jail, the Royal Hospital and Phoenix Park.

Historical Walking Tours (May–Sept daily 11am & 3pm, Sat & Sun also noon; Oct–April Fri–Sun noon; ☎878 0227; £5, concessions £4). History comes alive in this tour with its well chosen locations and witty insights into not only Dublin but Ireland's history, conducted by graduates from Trinity. Tours start at the College gates.

Literary Pub Crawl (Easter–Oct Mon–Sat 7.30pm, Sun noon & 7.30pm; Nov–Easter Thurs–Sat 7.30pm, Sun noon & 7.30pm; ☎670 5602; £6.50, students £5.50). A tour of pubs with literary connections, using professional actors to perform extracts from some of Ireland's greatest works. A great way to spend an evening, elevated by poetry and pints. Starts at *The Duke* on Duke Street.

Musical Pub Crawl (May–Oct daily 7.30pm; Nov & Feb–April Fri & Sat 7.30pm; ✆478 0193; £6, students £5). Another evening roam, or stagger, through Dublin's pubs, this time providing a chance to learn about Irish music. Fun and informative, though as the musicians move with the party you are left in doubt as to the point of changing pubs at all. Kicks off at *Oliver St John Gogarty's* in Temple Bar; arrive early to be sure of a ticket.

BUS AND WALKING TOURS

The Georgian southside

The **Georgian southside** is the richest and most attractive part of the city centre and the focal point for much of Dublin's cultural life. While replete with institutions like Trinity College, the Irish Parliament and the National Gallery, it also fizzes with restaurants and watering-holes, the latest fashions and music, and a confidence that impresses visitors and Dubliners alike. Ireland's economic boom is reflected in the windows of Grafton Street's stores and the shiny new cars parked around Merrion Square, whose elegant terraces are redolent of a previous era of pride and prosperity.

Most visitors gravitate to **College Green**, where the world-famous *Book of Kells* can be seen at **Trinity College**; from here it's a short walk to **Grafton Street**, effectively Dublin's High Street, busy with buskers and tourists. Alleyways off to the west lead to the classy shopping centre of **Powerscourt Townhouse**, a former Georgian mansion; Anne Street and then Molesworth Street to the east takes you up to the splendidly ornate entrance to **Leinster House**, home of the Irish Parliament.

At the top of Grafton Street lies **St Stephen's Green**, once the centrepiece of Georgian Dublin and a place infused with literary and historical associations. The finest examples of Georgian architecture may be found to the east of here, their level of refinement peaking around **Merrion** and **Fitzwilliam** squares. The Wide Streets Commission's (see *History*, p.313) aim to create a European-style capital is most successfully realized in these squares and in the grand thoroughfares of Leeson and Baggot streets, the elegant canal-side Herbert Place, and above all in **Fitzwilliam Street**, the position of which affords an expansive vista leading out to the Wicklow Mountains. Examination of the detail of Georgian interiors is particularly rewarding at **Newman House** (where Joyce studied), off St Stephen's Green, and the nearby **No. 29 Lower Fitzwilliam Street**.

Ireland's cultural treasure-houses are here too – the outstanding prehistoric gold and medieval metalwork on display in the **National Museum** are prime attractions, the fine collection of European art on show in the **National Gallery of Art** is similarly worthwhile and the **R.H.A. Gallagher Gallery** in Ely Place is an important space for contemporary art.

TRINITY COLLEGE

Map 4, E5. Grounds: Mon–Fri 7am–midnight (Sat & Sun, main gate locked at 6pm; use Nassau St gate); free. **Old Library**: June–Sept Mon–Sat 9.30am–5pm, Sun 9.30am–4.30pm; Oct–May Mon–Sat 9.30am–5pm, Sun noon–4.30pm (closed Dec 23 for around ten days); £4.50, students, under-18s and OAPs £4, under-12s free. **Dublin Experience**: late May–early Oct daily 10am–5pm (hourly shows); £3, students/children £2.50. Combined ticket for both £6, students £5.50, family £12.

Dublin's most famous institution and Ireland's oldest university, Trinity College, was founded in 1592 by Queen Elizabeth I to rectify "the barbarism" of the Irish and prevent them from being "infected with Popery" at foreign universities. Admission was restricted to Protestants, but Catholics could get free education by rejecting their faith. Trinity had a formative influence on the Anglo-Irish tradition, as Protestant families sent their sons to be educated here rather than in England, and its alumni made their mark in politics (Edmund Burke, Wolfe Tone, Robert Emmet, Edward Carson, Douglas Hyde), literature (Jonathan Swift, Oliver Goldsmith, Oscar Wilde, Bram Stoker, J.M. Synge, Samuel Beckett) and other fields.

Although religious restrictions were abolished in 1873, its Protestant bias survived after Irish independence, since as late as the 1970s Catholic archbishops forbade their flocks to study at Trinity without first obtaining special permission, on pain of excommunication. Today, seventy percent of its students are Catholic and Trinity is one of three universities in the city: Dublin University (of which Trinity is the sole college); University College Dublin, based near Donnybrook; and Dublin City University, in Glasnevin. However, neither of the others can match Trinity as an architectural set piece that looks like a great university should.

College Green and the university grounds

College Green is something of a misnomer for what is today a heavily trafficked junction outside the College, where a tiny lawn is about as green as it gets. The name commemorates the fact that when Trinity was founded it stood on open common land outside the walled city, including a flat-topped mound, 12m high and 72m in circumference, that had once been the Viking *Thingmount*, or

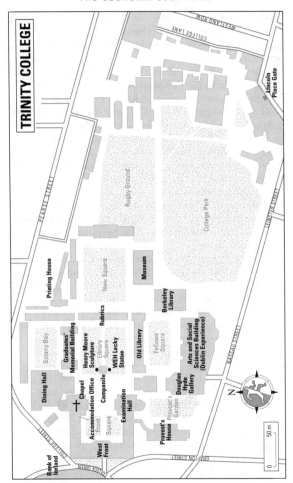

TRINITY COLLEGE

parliament (otherwise known as the *Haugen*, hence College Green's old name, Hoggen Green). In Georgian times the ground was levelled to provide the foundations of Nassau Street, and College Green became the centre of political life, as power briefly diverted from the viceregal seat in Dublin Castle to the Protestant Irish parliament, established here in 1782.

The **West Front**, facing College Green, is flanked by statues of two eighteenth-century graduates, the Tory philosopher and statesman Edmund Burke, and the wit and poet Oliver Goldsmith. Both were sculpted by John Foley, who also did Grattan's statue outside the Bank of Ireland, leading to jokes that he cast the legs of all three from the same mould to save money.

Students meet and lounge against the railings by the entrance gates – the point of departure for **walking tours** of Trinity (mid-March to mid-May Sat & Sun 10.15am and then every 40min until 3.45pm; mid-May to Sept daily same times; £5, including admission to the *Book of Kells*). Although there's nothing to stop you from wandering around by yourself, the sheer number of visitors over summer makes some shepherding essential. Traffic is steered towards the **Dublin Experience** in the Arts and Social Sciences Building, an audio-visual show that takes you through over one thousand years of Dublin history in 45 minutes – a useful introduction if you are unfamiliar with it all and need an overview.

Trinity's main quad is a harmonious composition of eighteenth- and nineteenth-century buildings centred on a thirty-metre-high **Campanile** that's thought to mark the site of the All Hallow's Priory, on whose confiscated land Trinity was built using materials pillaged from other Catholic orders. To the left of the Campanile is a statue of Provost Salmon, who fiercely opposed letting women into Trinity and made good his threat "Over my dead body!" by expiring when they did in 1903. On the lawn behind the Campanile is the Henry Moore sculpture *Reclining Connected Forms*. Mature parkland stretches beyond the main University buildings, providing a quiet green space in the heart of the city centre, open to students and the public alike.

The buildings

If you can get inside, it's worth visiting the Examination Hall and the Chapel on either side of Parliament Square. Both were designed in the 1790s by Sir William Chambers, a Scottish architect who never visited Ireland but executed many commissions in Dublin. The **Examination Hall** (or Theatre) contains a chandelier from the old Irish Parliament and an organ reputedly salvaged from a Spanish ship in 1702. Trinity's **Chapel** is the only one in the Republic shared by all denominations. Its main window is dedicated to Archbishop Ussher, one of the first students at Trinity (which he entered at thirteen), who went on to lecture there, devoting years of study to establishing that God created the world on October 23, 4004 BC.

Beyond the Chapel is a grand **Dining Hall** hung with vast portraits of college dignitaries; it has been much altered since it was built by the German architect Richard Cassels in 1742, and was totally restored after a fire in 1989. The oldest surviving building – dating from 1700 – is the red-brick student dormitory called the **Rubrics**, overlooking Library Square. Behind the Graduates' Memorial Building is an open area known as Botany Bay, so-called because the unruly students living in the vicinity were considered worthy of transportation to Britain's penal colony.

Most tourists make a beeline for the **Book of Kells** (see box, overleaf) in the **Old Library**, entered from Fellows' Square. On the ground floor is a superb exhibition called

The Book of Kells

Created around 800 AD, the **Book of Kells** probably originated at the monastery on Iona, St Colum Cille's (St Columba in English) first Scottish port of call. In 806, Viking raids forced the Columbine monks to move to the monastery of Kells in County Meath – after which the book is named – whence in 1007 it was stolen. It was later found buried in the ground, but its metal shrine or *cumdach* was subsequently looted by the Vikings (who wouldn't have valued the book itself) and some thirty folios (double-page spreads) disappeared. To prevent a worse fate during the Cromwellian wars, the *Book of Kells* was brought to Dublin and given to Trinity by the Bishop of Meath in 1654. Since then it has been jealously guarded, despite the legend that Queen Victoria autographed it during her first visit to Dublin (she actually signed a parchment that was bound into the volume). In 1953 the folios were rebound in four calf-skin volumes, of which two are on display, one showing an illu-minated page, the other text. Both are turned to a new page on a regular basis.

The 340 folios of the *Book of Kells* contain the four New Testament gospels with prefaces and summaries, all in Latin. Opening letters cover an entire page ornamented with arcane symbols and images, and geometric and floral patterns, prob-ably influenced by metalwork such as the Ardagh Chalice and the Tara Brooch in the National Museum. The text is in rounded Celtic script, with human or animal forms at the margins.

"The Book of Kells: Turning Darkness into Light", which sets the book in the context of Irish Christianity and the art of illumination and includes full-scale reproductions of both this and the books from other religious centres – well worth seeing, since on any given day viewing of these texts is limited. Displayed beside the *Book of Kells* in the final room are two of the following four books, rotated at regular intervals: the *Book of Armagh* (807), the *Book of Durrow* (675), the *Book of Mulling* (seventh century) and the *Book of Dímma* (eighth or ninth century).

Upstairs is Thomas Burgh's magnificent library of 1712–32, aptly known as the **Long Room**, to which a second tier of bookcases and a barrel-vaulted ceiling were added in 1860; today it houses 200,000 of the library's oldest books in wonderfully antiquated oak bookcases. As a copyright library, Trinity is entitled to a copy of every book published in Ireland and Britain, so its collection of 3.5 million titles grows by 100,000 per year – the bulk of them being kept in a repository in the suburb of Santry. Also on display in the Long Room is a fifteenth-century **harp** and an original copy of the 1916 Proclamation of the Irish Republic.

Across Fellows' Square stand the 1960s Brutalist-style **Berkeley Library** and Arts and Social Sciences Building. The library is named after Kilkenny-born George Berkeley, who studied at Trinity when he was fifteen; a philosopher and educationalist whose influence spread to the American colonies, Berkeley contributed to the foundation of the University of Pennsylvania in 1740 (California's Berkeley University bears his name). The arts block contains a theatre, a coffee bar and the **Douglas Hyde Gallery** (Mon–Wed & Fri 11am–6pm, Thurs 11am–7pm, Sat 11am–4.45pm; free), an experimental art venue that's usually worth checking out; it also has a well-stocked bookshop.

Just beyond the Berkeley Library, the School of Engineering occupies a **Museum** designed by Benjamin Woodward (who raised the height of the Old Library) and carved with monkeys, owls and parrots by the O'Shea brothers, whom Woodward invited to carve freely like medieval artists, but then fired after the College authorities expressed displeasure with their work. It's worth looking inside the entrance hall to view the skeletons of a pair of giant Irish deer that were found at Lough Gur, County Limerick (the species became extinct 11,000 years ago). To the north of New Square is Cassels' first building in Dublin, a **Printing House** resembling a Doric temple, which now houses the departments of microelectronics and electrical engineering.

THE BANK OF IRELAND

Map 4, D5. House of Lords Tours Tues 10.30am, 11.30am & 1.45pm; free. **Story of Banking** Tues–Fri 10am–4pm; £1.50, students £1.

Across the road from Trinity the massive **Bank of Ireland** flanks the curve into Dame Street. It was here that the Anglo–Irish Ascendancy's efforts towards self-government culminated in the **Grattan Parliament** of 1782, where Henry Grattan – whose statue stands outside – declared "Ireland is now a nation." Work on a suitable building began as early as 1729, when Sir Edward Lovett Pearce designed a bicameral house with a colonnaded forecourt facing College Green. The Corinthian portico on Westmoreland Street was added by Gandon in 1785, as the Lords' entrance (they objected to sharing a door with MPs). Like the Ionic portico on Foster Place, it is linked to Pearce's building by a curved screen wall.

Grattan's Parliament was short-lived: by patronage and bribery, Britain induced a majority to pass the Act of Union (1801), which subsumed their authority in Westminster. Bereft of a function, the building was sold to the Bank of Ireland for £40,000, after the House of Commons chamber had been demolished to prevent it from being used again as a parliament.

The real attraction is the old **House of Lords**, with its vaulted ceiling, 1233-piece crystal chandelier, and tapestries depicting the Protestant victories of the Siege of Londonderry (1689) and the Battle of the Boyne (1690). Though its long table seems authentic, the Lords actually sat back-to-back around the walls for debates, with the Lord Chancellor on a woolsack. The stuccoed **Cash Hall** looks like part of the House of Commons but is quite unlike the original, which had galleries for some seven hundred spectators; parliamentary debates were a fashionable entertainment at that time. Around the corner on Foster Place, an armoury added during the Napoleonic wars now serves as an arts centre where concerts are often held, and as the venue for the **Story of Banking**, a film "narrated" by David La Touche, the bank's founder, and an exhibition including the silver-gilt **mace** that belonged to the House of Commons. Sold by Speaker Foster's descendants, it was bought back from Christie's in London by the bank in 1937.

GRAFTON STREET AND AROUND

Running uphill from College Green to St Stephen's Green, **Grafton Street** is the best place to catch street entertainers – and there are plenty to choose from, ranging from string quartets to groups of guitar-playing eight-year-olds with as many chords as years. Here too, you may catch the peculiarly Irish phenomenon of street poetry, the performers of which are said to be descended from the Celtic bardic tradition. The famous **Molly Malone statue** (by Jean Rynhart) at the bottom of the street is nicknamed the "tart with the cart" due to its brazen décolletage and what Molly reputedly got up to while wheeling her barrow of cockles and mussels through streets broad and narrow. It is thought that she died in 1734 and was buried near St Werburgh's Church (see p.79). At that time, Grafton Street was a fairly rudimentary lane which led to the execution grounds and common that was then St Stephen's Green. Today it boasts malls and department stores, a handful of places to eat and some famous pubs on its side streets (there are none on Grafton Street itself).

Duke Street, on the east side of Grafton Street, is home to **Davy Byrne's**, the "moral pub" where Leopold Bloom had a Gorgonzola-and-mustard sandwich and a glass of Burgundy in *Ulysses*. *The Duke* across the way is the starting point for "Dublin's Literary Pub Crawl" (see p.12).

For more on Davy Byrne's see p.246.

Detouring in the other direction off Grafton Street you'll find the **Powerscourt Townhouse** (Mon–Sat 9am–6pm, Thurs till 8pm, Sun noon–6.30pm, see *Shopping* on p.286), an imaginative conversion of an eighteenth-century mansion built for Viscount Powerscourt, using granite from his estate in County Wicklow (see p.179). Its grand entrance on William Street South opens into a hall, with a staircase leading to the finest surviving reception room on the top floor; others have been converted into shops. Like the Georgian Room on the floor below, it was executed by Michael Stapleton, who was responsible for the plasterwork at Trinity. Saturdays see **concerts** of light music and jazz in the atrium, which was once the mansion's inner courtyard (see p.256).

While in the vicinity, check out the **Dublin Civic Museum** (Tues–Sat 10am–6pm, Sun 11am–2pm; free) at 58 South William Street. Though it's mainly devoted to temporary exhibitions on anything from barges to coal-hole covers, you can be sure of seeing a number of permanent features, including the head of the statue of Nelson that stood on O'Connell Street till it was blown up in 1966, and the 1877 bylaws of St Stephen's Green, denying entry to persons "in an intoxicated, unclean or verminous condition" and "any dog which may be reasonably suspected to be in a rabid state". Castle Market, the narrow street over the road, leads to the Market Arcade, which comes out on to South Great George's Street (see p.88).

For more on Bewley's see p.222.

Returning to Grafton Street, you can't miss the Egyptian mosaic facade of **Bewley's Oriental Café**. *Bewley's* is a Dublin institution where all classes mingle over tea, coffee, all-day fried breakfasts, cakes and sticky buns. Founded by the Quaker Bewley family in the 1840s, it almost folded in 1986, provoking such a national outcry that the government had to step in until a buyer was found. There are other branches of *Bewley's* on Westmoreland Street and South Great George's Street.

Further on, at the top of Grafton Street, looms the **St Stephen's Green Shopping Centre**, a 1980s extravaganza whose frothy white "Mississippi Steamboat" facade mimics the Georgian frontages overlooking the Green.

DAWSON STREET AND MOLESWORTH STREET

There are some quieter streets to the east of Grafton Street that are nice to wander around. **Dawson Street** is notable for its swanky pubs and restaurants, bookshops, and two august institutions. Originally built for the aristocrat Joshua Dawson (after whom the street is named), the **Mansion House** has been the residence of Dublin's Lord Mayor since 1715 – its stucco facade and porte-cochere were added in Victorian times. It was here that Dáil Éireann (the Irish parliament) adopted the Declaration of Independence in 1919 and where the truce that ended Anglo-Irish hostilities was signed in 1921. Though you can't enter the Mansion House, it's possible to visit the **Royal Irish Academy Library** next door (Mon–Fri 9.30am–5.30pm; closed bank holidays and the last three weeks of Aug), which houses a large collection of ancient Irish manuscripts and printed works. Beside the library stands **St Ann's Church**, whose interior dates back to the early 1700s. The shelves behind the altar were used for storing bread to be distributed to the poor of the parish under the terms of a bequest. Past parishioners include Wolfe Tone (who was married here in 1765), Bram Stoker and Douglas Hyde, and the graveyard contains the tomb of the poet Felicia Hemans, who wrote "The boy stood on the burning deck . . ." and lived at no. 21. It's also worth calling in to the church for the lunchtime concerts of classical music held here (most Wed & Thurs, 1.15pm; call ℗676 7727 for details).

Molesworth Street, running towards the eighteenth-century grandeur of Leinster House, retains three Huguenot-style gabled houses from the mid-eighteenth century. At no. 17 is **Freemasons' Hall**, the headquarters of Ireland's Grand Lodge, which runs guided tours (second week in June–Aug Mon–Fri 11.30am & 2.30pm; £1). Its interior combines every style of Victorian architecture from Egyptian to Roman and Gothic, all wildly over the top. There's also a museum of Masonic regalia and a library of works on mysticism and secret societies. Visitors are solemnly assured that what little influence the Freemasons have in Irish society is only for the good.

LEINSTER HOUSE

Kildare Street, at the top of Molesworth Street, is the heartland of Dublin's establishment. Its centrepiece is **Leinster House**, which houses the Irish Parliament, flanked to the north by The National Library, The Royal

The Irish Parliament

Few legislatures have been so hard won – and divisive – as the **Irish Parliament** (*Oireachtas na hÉireann*). Its basic form was hammered out in the London negotiations that established the Irish Free State (a title reflecting Britain's objection to the term "Republic"). Under the Anglo–Irish Treaty it had to vow loyalty to the British monarch and accept Ireland's partition into a 26-county Free State and a 6-county Northern Ireland.

Both conditions split the Nationalists down the middle, with the anti-Treaty side initiating a bitter Civil War (1922–24) with the Free-State forces. Both sides claimed to be the rightful heirs of *Dáil Éireann*, the Irish shadow parliament of 1919 to 1921, whose own legitimacy derived from the Proclamation of the Republic during the Easter Rising. Not until 1927 did de Valera and his Fianna Fáil party grudgingly recognize the Free State and enter parliamentary life "with guns under their coats". In 1937, citizens voted to accept a new constitution formulated by de Valera, which is the basis for the present system of government of the Republic of Ireland.

While the president is the head of state, legislative and executive powers are vested in parliament, which has two chambers: *Dáil Éireann* (House of Representatives) and *Seanad Éireann* (Senate). The Dáil (pronounced "Doil") has 166 representatives (*Teachtaí Dála* or TDs), elected by proportional representation, whereas the sixty senators are appointed by various authorities including the Prime Minister or *Taoiseach* (pronounced "Tee-shuck") and the universities. Critics say that the system encourages cronyism and corruption – as evinced by a stream of scandals involving nearly every party and government since the 1970s.

College of Physicians (closed to the public) and the former Kildare Street Club, and to the south by the National

Museum. The area was developed by James Fitzgerald, Earl of Kildare, who in 1745 bought some cheap land on the edge of town and commissioned Richard Cassels to build a mansion on it. Asked if he regretted leaving the fashionable northside, the Earl replied, "they will follow me wherever I go" – and he was right, for Lord Fitzwilliam then laid out Merrion Square, starting a development boom on the southside.

The Earl's mansion was designed so that the facade facing town resembles a townhouse, and the side on what is now Merrion Square looks like a country residence – it's thought to have been a model for the White House in Washington. Approached from Kildare Street, its imposing pedimented facade sits behind elaborate ornamental railings beyond a wide courtyard. Its present name, Leinster House, honours the elevation of the Earl to Duke of Leinster. One of his sons, Lord Edward Fitzgerald, escaped arrest here by the British after spies betrayed his preparations for the 1798 Rebellion.

The mansion was converted into the **Irish Parliament** in 1922 after the establishment of the Irish Free State. Despite calls to fulfill Daniel O'Connell's dream of restoring the former Grattan Parliament (see p.22), the provisional government at the time deemed Leinster House easier to defend. Beset by enemies at home and abroad, they felt, as Kevin O'Higgins confessed – like "eight young men standing amidst the ruins of one administration with the foundation of another not yet laid, and with wild men screaming through the keyhole".

Parliament generally sits from mid-January to July, breaking for Easter, and mid-September until Christmas, on Tuesdays at 2.30pm, and Wednesdays and Thursdays at 10.30am. Visitors wishing to visit Leinster House should telephone the Captain of the Guard, preferably two weeks in advance (©618 3296); tours are then arranged subject to the number of people wishing to visit at any given time and the political diary. Irish citizens need to be sponsored by their TD to gain

LEINSTER HOUSE

admittance. The sedate Senate meets in a semicircular blue salon in the north wing – the Dáil sits on the other side of the building and is more of a bear-pit. Visitors are guided from one chamber to the other by frock-coated ushers.

THE NATIONAL LIBRARY AND HERALDIC MUSEUM

The **National Library** (Mon–Wed 10am–9pm, Thurs & Fri 10am–5pm, Sat 10am–1pm; free) was built in the late nineteenth century, along with the National Museum, to flank Leinster House. Less of a crowd-puller, it's chiefly worth visiting for its associations – almost every major Irish writer from Joyce onwards has used it at some time. Temporary exhibitions in the foyer feature anything from old Irish maps to the diaries of Joseph Holiday, describing Dublin's theatrical life. Ask for a visitor's pass to enter the stately domed Reading Room on the first floor, scene of one of the great set pieces of *Ulysses* – Stephen's extravagant speech on Shakespeare. If you want to trace your ancestors, visit the Family History Room (same times) where two professional genealogists are on hand to give you advice about how to access the parish, land and state records held here and elsewhere in the city.

The former **Kildare Street Club** stands at the bottom of Kildare Street, a Venetian-Gothic red-brick edifice with whimsical figures carved on its pillars – including monkeys with billiard cues and a mole with a lute. Once a bastion of Anglo-Irish conservatism, it was described by novelist George Moore in 1886 as "a sort of oyster-bed into which all the eldest sons of the landed gentry fall as a matter of course. There they remain spending their days drinking sherry and cursing Gladstone in a sort of dialect, a dead language which the larva-like stupidity of the club has preserved." It now houses the Alliance Française and the **Heraldic Museum** (Mon–Wed 10am–8.30pm, Thurs &

Fri 10am–5pm, Sat 10am–1pm; free), which contains such items as Sir Roger Casement's Order of St Michael and George, the Lord Chancellor's purse and mantle, and the insignia of the Order of St Patrick.

THE NATIONAL MUSEUM

Map 4, F7. Tues–Sat 10am–5pm, Sun 2–5pm; free.

With its prehistoric gold, medieval treasures and Viking finds, as well as material covering the period 1916–21 and a small but impressive Egyptian collection, the **National Museum** is one of the city's essential sights. Occupying part of a building raised in the late 1880s to accommodate both the museum and the National Library, the core of the collection was acquired in 1891, as a donation from the Royal Irish Academy (or Royal Hibernian Academy), a society founded in 1785 by the Earl of Charlemont. The collection has grown a great deal since then, and in 1994 the museum acquired the Collins Barracks (see p.142) which now houses artefacts covering social, political and military history and the decorative arts.

> **Times for guided tours (40min, £1) of the National Museum vary – they're posted up at the entrance each day.**

Below are listed just the highlights, and by focusing on these you could see the best of the museum in an afternoon. The numbers in the text correspond to the floor plans on pp.31 and 35.

Ór – Ireland's gold

The museum's stunning collection of prehistoric gold (*ór*) occupies the sunken main hall; less glamorous artefacts from

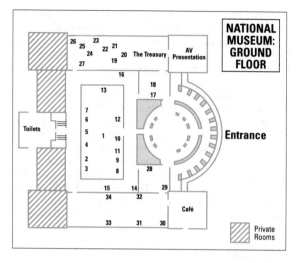

the same era are ranged around the raised perimeter – and all is made eminently accessible to the non-specialist. A central display section [1] explains how gold was extracted in ancient times and why peat bogs have yielded so many treasures during turf-cutting or ploughing, when so few have been found at excavations of inhabited sites.

In the Early Bronze Age (c. 2200 BC) goldsmiths created **lunulae** [2] – crescent-shaped collars made from thin sheets of beaten gold – and decorated them with chevrons or stripes, incised on the front or hammered out from behind, by the technique known as repoussé. Sun discs and basket-shaped ear- or hair-rings (it's not known which) [3] show evidence of the same techniques. During the mid-Bronze Age, sheet-gold was beaten into armlets, earrings and neck-laces – as in the **Derrinboy Hoard** [4] – or twisted into **torcs**; one from County Antrim is as chunky as an industrial

THE NATIONAL MUSEUM

drill [5]. From c. 1200 BC, twisting became the favoured technique and torcs grew much larger, suggesting that a new source of gold had been found. Note three for the waist, with different kinds of fasteners [6]. Gold beads were also combined with chunks of amber, to form lustrous necklaces [7].

Despite scant evidence for goldworking at the start of the late Bronze Age (1000–500 BC), after 850 BC came a period of prolific production using various techniques. Cast or hammered-bar goldwork gave rise to bracelets and dress- or sleeve-fasteners with cupped terminals, decorated with incised whorls [8]. Applying gold foil to base metal objects (termed *bullae*) produced purse-shaped artefacts and so-called ring money [9]. The **Tumna Hoard** [10] of nine hollow gold balls the size of doughnuts is flanked by two sunflower pins from County Laois [11] and the **Banagher Hoard** [12] of an amber necklace, a gold bracelet and dress-fastener and two bronze rings – all dating from 800–700 BC.

From the same period come the magnificent **Gleninsheen Gorget** (one of several gold collars with roundel fastenings attached by gold wire) and the **Mooghaun Hoard** [13]. The latter was found by navvies digging the West Clare Railway in 1854.

Prehistoric Ireland

Less dazzling prehistoric material includes a life-size reconstruction of a late Neolithic (3400–2800 BC) **passage tomb** [14] and the astonishing **Lurgan Logboat** [15], which is made of hollowed-out oak trunks, over fifteen metres long (c. 2500 BC). The **Lissan Rapier** and the bronze spearheads and shields of the **Dowris Hoard** [16] date from the final phase of the Irish Bronze Age (900–500 BC).

The Treasury

The Treasury is where you'll find the most well-known ecclesiastical objects in the collection, dating from the Iron Age to the late Middle Ages. Enough remains of the fragmented **Petrie Crown** to recognize the sumptuous, fluid curves of La Tène-influenced metalwork, a Celtic style which came from continental Europe [**17**]. The crown was found along with a gold collar and miniature sailing boat with oars [**18**], beautiful pieces from the **Broighter Hoard** (first century BC) discovered in County Derry in 1896.

The **Derrynaflan Hoard** [**19**] found in 1980 in County Tipperary contains a silver-filigreed paten and fine chalice dating from the eighth and ninth centuries, though they are somewhat overshadowed by the more elaborate chalice from the **Ardagh Hoard** [**20**], also from the eighth century. Perhaps the finest example of Irish metalwork is the **Tara Brooch** [**21**] found on the shore near Bettystown in 1850, both sides of which bear intricate patterns that may have inspired those in manuscripts such as the *Book of Kells*. Such "knot" designs also appear on the shaft of a stone **cross** from County Offaly, depicting a horseman and a stag [**22**].

During the Middle Ages, elaborate reliquaries were made to hold holy relics or texts. **St Patrick's Bell Shrine** [**23**] contains a bell reputedly owned by the saint. Adorned with gold wire upon a silver backplate, it was created in the early twelfth century and handed down through generations of the Mulholland family until the late 1770s. In the same case is the bronze **Shrine of St Lachtin's Arm**. Odder still are the **Shrine of St Bridget's Shoe** – the size of a child's foot – and the **fiacail Pádraig**, containing the tooth that fell from St Patrick's head at Killespugbrone, which share a case with the house-shaped shrine called the **Breac Moedóic** [**24**] and its original leather satchel. Book-shrines decorated with repoussé saints include the **Stowe Missal**, the **Cathach** and the **Soiscél Molaise** [**25**].

Incongruously surrounded by processional crosses of English manufacture, the ivory **Kavanagh Charter Horn** [**26**] was for centuries one of the symbols of the Kings of Leinster. As you head back into the main hall, you'll find a couple of **Sheela-na-Gigs** [**27**] either side of the door, enigmatic female figures that appeared on many early Irish churches despite their pagan antecedents and their overt sexuality. Before you leave, it's worth catching the twenty-minute **AV presentation** at the other end of the Treasury, which takes you through the history of Celtic art at a swift pace and includes enticing shots of ancient sites around the country.

The Road to Independence

The final exhibition on the ground floor relates the struggle for Irish independence, but lacks the space to do justice to its subject and will eventually be moved to the Collins Barracks. Meanwhile, the first room covers events ranging from the abortive uprising of Robert Emmet (whose sword and death mask [**28**] are displayed) to the activities of the Fenians in America, before returning to Ireland and the campaigns of O'Connell and Parnell. After both failed to achieve reform through Britain's parliament, a new generation sought to revive and promote Irish culture through the Gaelic League, founded by Douglas Hyde, whose bust shares a display case with the first Gaelic typewriter [**29**].

The main section is devoted to the Easter Rising and the War of Independence. You'll see the uniforms of the Irish Volunteers and the Citizen Army that fought in 1916 [**30**]; Sir Roger Casement's dress suit and a sword-stick and barrister's gown belonging to Pádraig Pearse [**31**]; the pistols fired by Countess Markievicz [**32**]; a uniform of the hated

British Black and Tans [**33**]; and one worn by Michael Collins as Commander-in-Chief of the Irish Republican Army [**34**]. There's a video-wall at the far end which gives a brief account of the Easter Rising using contemporary newsreel footage.

Viking-age Ireland

Upstairs, the exhibition on Viking-age Ireland (800–1200 AD) overlaps chronologically with the Treasury on the floor below and proves a worthwhile contrast. While the ecclesiastical treasures on the ground floor illustrate the richness of life emanating from Irish religious foundations, the Viking exhibits mark a very different culture with artefacts of conquest, international trade and the beginnings of urban Dublin.

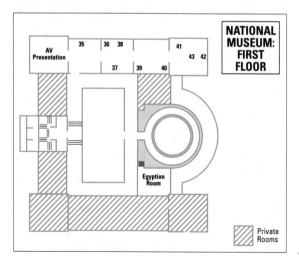

The early Viking invasions are represented by artefacts from burial grounds at Islandbridge and Kilmainham, including the **skeleton of a warrior** [**35**] with a long sword. It was partly due to the Viking threat that the *crannog* or lake-dwelling persisted for so long in Ireland; one from County Westmeath has yielded a wooden bucket and gaming board, and antler combs [**36**]. While the Vikings appreciated the skills of Irish jewellers – as evinced by penannular and "thistle" **brooches** [**37**] – others were liable to be enslaved or killed, like the man whose hacked-about **skull** was found with a gruesome iron slave-chain [**38**]. The adjacent room shows films relating to the Vikings in Ireland and the excavation of sites.

The next section covers **Viking Dublin**, with **models** of a house and the layout of Fishamble Street [**39**], accompanied by a host of finds from excavations on Winetavern Street and Wood Quay, ranging from loom weights to ironworkers' tools. Notice the finely carved **deer-antler combs** [**40**] that the Vikings used as money as well as for taming their hair. (For more on Viking Dublin see pp.72 and 309.)

The final room displays Christian artefacts from Viking times, including some of the museum's most famous possessions. The **Tau Crozier** [**41**] is the only surviving one with a T-shaped head, though they were often depicted in early manuscripts, while the exquisite **Crozier of St Tola** follows the familiar form of a shepherd's crook [**41**]. Iron and bronze bells (often hand-held rather than hung in belfries) presage **St Manchan's Shrine** [**42**], a mid-twelfth-century masterpiece elaborately decorated with repoussé saints. Finally, there's the famous **Cross of Cong** [**43**], made to enshrine a fragment of the True Cross given by Pope Calixtus II to the King of Connaught in 1123 but which was later lost.

Finally, tucked away off the upper gallery you'll find the tiny, but very worthwhile, **Egyptian Room**, highlights of which include Egyptian hieroglyphic scripts and material on how to read them, some splendidly decorated mummies and a wonderfully detailed wooden model of a Nile boat, complete with rowers and armed guard.

ST STEPHEN'S GREEN

Map 4, E8. Mon–Sat 8am–dusk; Sun & bank holidays 10am–dusk.

While **St Stephen's Green** is the largest – and perhaps the most famous – of Georgian Dublin's squares, the Green itself is the least Georgian in character. A central floral display, herbaceous borders and jubilee bandstand all mark its identity as essentially Victorian; Lord Ardilaun (Sir Arthur Guinness) funded the present layout in 1880, and a statue of its benefactor faces west out of the Green. It's such a pleasant public space today that it's difficult to imagine it as anything else. Originally an open common in the vicinity of a lepers' hospital, the Green was surrounded by buildings by the late seventeenth century but nonetheless remained a dangerous spot, with footpads lurking on every corner. Public hangings occurred here until the eighteenth century, and as late as 1800 the Green was surrounded by a fetid ditch clogged with dead cats and dogs. To try and improve matters, railings and locked gates were installed in 1814 and an annual fee of one guinea was levied on users, but it was only when Lord Ardilaun bought the property, paid for its new layout and donated it to the people of Dublin that true bourgeois respectability was attained.

As well as being a fine place to take a break from the rigours of the city centre, St Stephen's Green is worth visiting for its great range of **statues**, which bear testimony to the city's varied history and cultural life; maps pinpointing the location of each are situated at the Green's main entrances. "Crossing Stephen's that is my green" is inscribed beneath a keenly-fashioned bust of **Joyce** towards

Countess Markievicz

A confirmed feminist and ardent socialist, Constance Gore-Booth was one of Ireland's most remarkable women, whose dynamic role during the upheavals in Dublin at the beginning of the century marks her as one of the great figures of twentieth-century Irish political history.

Born into the Anglo-Irish aristocracy in 1868, she spent much of her childhood in Lissadell, County Sligo, and, after studying art in London, moved to Paris in 1898, where she met and married Polish Count Casimir Markievicz. On her return to Ireland her nationalistic sentiments began to evolve and she joined Sinn Féin, where she quickly made her mark by founding na Fianna Éireann, the Sinn Féin youth movement in 1909. Influenced by the socialism of Connolly and Larkin, she became involved in class politics, working with the poor and organizing soup kitchens during the 1913 lockout (see p.316).

Having joined the Irish Citizen Army Countess Markievicz was second-in-command at St Stephen's Green in the 1916 Easter Rising (see p.110) – the death sentence she received for her involvement was commuted on the grounds of her sex (an inequality which disgusted her). She went on to become president of the Women's Volunteers and the first woman to be elected to Westminster, though as a member of Sinn Féin she boycotted parliament and instead became the Minister for Labour in the first Dáil Éireann in 1919. During the War of Independence the Countess was jailed twice and in 1922 was firmly on the anti-Treaty side, boycotting the post-treaty Dáil with other anti-Treaty republicans; however, when de Valera formed Fianna Fáil in 1926, she joined and was elected to the Dáil shortly before her death in 1927.

the southside; an abstract bronze of **W.B. Yeats** by Henry Moore conveys something of the spirituality of the poet (take care here as this secluded spot can be dangerous) and the Green's more violent history is remembered in a bust of **Countess Markievicz** (see box, opposite) who, along with Commandant Mallin, led the insurgents occupying the Green during the Easter Rising. For further evidence of this take a look at the Royal College of Surgeons on the west side of the Green, whose pillars are still scarred with bullet-marks; the insurgents, having failed to seize the *Shelbourne*, were forced to retreat into the building when pinned down by snipers. At the northwest corner of the Green the **Fusiliers' Arch** honours the 212 Royal Dublin Fusiliers killed in the Boer War, and is still known to some as "Traitor's Gate" – enlistment or conscription into the British army being a long-standing *bête noire* of Nationalists. A **monument to Wolfe Tone** (see box, p.92), nicknamed "Tone-henge" for its granite slabs, is situated at the northeast corner; behind that lies one to commemorate the **Great Famine**; near the Leeson Street exit you'll find Joseph Wackerle's **Three Fates** fountain, presented by the German people in gratitude for help given by the Irish to World War II refugees; and finally a statue of **Robert Emmet** stands on the pavement opposite the Royal College of Surgeons, looking across to the site of his birthplace at nos. 124–5, now demolished.

St Stephen's Green North and West

Aside from its memorial role, the Green is an important point of orientation and its sides, designated as North, South, East and West, retain a number of important Georgian buildings. Once known as "Beaux Walk" after the dandies who promenaded there in the eighteenth century, **St Stephen's Green North** still reeks of money, with pedestrians gabbling into their mobiles as they stride towards the **Shelbourne Hotel** (see p.202 and p.248). The *Shelbourne* boasts of having "the best address in Dublin" and has been a meeting place for the upper echelons of society since it was founded in 1824. Non-residents can wander in for a drink and something to eat in the lobby at any time of day. Afternoon tea (from 3pm) is popular, but the lobby and bar really come alive in the evening, when the hotel is great for celebrity spotting. Just past the hotel look out for the small **Huguenot Graveyard** at the start of Merrion Row, established in 1693 for the French Protestant refugees who settled in Dublin's Liberties (see p.90). Only a few simple tombs are left, but this seems a fitting tribute to their quietly industrious way of life.

St Stephen's Green West is dominated by the extravagantly decorative facade of the St Stephen's Green Shopping Centre and, midway down, **The Royal College of Surgeons**, an early nineteenth-century classical building topped by figures representing Medicine and Health.

Newman House

Map 4, D9. Hourly guided tours only: June–Aug Tues–Fri noon–5pm, Sat 2–5pm, Sun 11am–2pm; £2, students, unemployed and senior citizens £1.

On **St Stephen's Green South** nos. 85–86 are collectively known as **Newman House**, named after John Henry Newman, first rector of the Catholic University of Ireland. Founded in 1854 to provide a Catholic equivalent to Trinity College, the institution provided education for generations of Catholics who would otherwise have been obliged to study abroad or submit to the Protestant hegemony of Trinity; James Joyce, Pádraig Pearse and Éamon de Valera were among its alumni. The university later moved out to Belfield, changing its name to University College Dublin (UCD) along the way.

Newman House is fabulously decorative. **Number 85** was originally Clanwilliam House, a miniature Palladian mansion built by Cassels in 1738 for Captain Hugh Montgomery to entertain while in town for the "Season". Inside, superb stucco work by the Swiss-Italian Francini brothers decorates the **Apollo Room** on the ground floor, including nine muses on the walls, a rabbit and two putti over the doorway, and a fine figure of the god himself above the fireplace.

Upstairs is the **Saloon**, with its coffered ceiling and allegorical relief of good government and prudent economy. When the Jesuits acquired the building in 1883, they covered the naked female bodies on the ceiling with what look like furry bathing costumes, to protect the morals of their students; the garments were removed when the house was restored in the 1980s, but one was left *in situ* to show how bizarre they appeared. At the back of the house is an extension in the Gothic style, used as a **Physics Theatre**, where Joyce once lectured to the "L & H" (Literary and Historical Society).

Number 86 is a larger house built in 1765 for Richard "Burnchapel" Whaley, a virulent anti-Catholic who earned his sobriquet by torching chapels in County Wicklow. His son, Buck Whaley, was a founder of the Hellfire Club (see box, p.64). The saloon has flowing Rococo plasterwork by Robert West and is known as the **Bishop's Room**, having been used for meetings of the university's committee. On the top floor are the **classroom** where Joyce studied from 1899 to 1902 and the **bedroom** of the poet Gerard Manley Hopkins, who was Professor of Classics from 1884 until his death in 1889, a miserable period during which he wrote what are called the "Terrible Sonnets".

Beside Newman House stands the Byzantine-style **University Church**, whose opulent interior is adorned with marble quarried from five different sites in Ireland (definitely worth seeing) and regarded as a chic location for weddings. **Iveagh House**, further along, was the first

building that Cassels designed in Dublin, a stately pedimented building which now houses the Department of
Foreign Affairs.

Harcourt Street and the Iveagh Gardens

Harcourt Street, leading off from the southwest corner of
the Green, is a well-preserved Georgian street, laid out in
1775, and one that has its fair share of noteworthy addresses
– no. 6 was formerly the headquarters of Arthur Griffith's
Sinn Féin; Sir Edward Carson, a staunch opponent of
Home Rule who founded the Ulster Volunteers, was born
next door; and George Bernard Shaw once resided at no.
61. The former Harcourt Street railway station now houses
the wonderful *Odeon* bar and alongside you'll find the
exclusive *POD* nightclub (see p.250 and p.262 respectively).
Here, too, are **Findlaters** wine merchants, established in
1823, and you can visit their small **museum** in the vaults
with its interesting memorabilia of assorted bottles, advertisements and news clippings related to the history of the
wine trade (Mon–Fri 9am–6pm, Sat 10.30am–5.30pm;
free).

Whilst in the vicinity, visit the secluded **Iveagh
Gardens** (Mon–Sat 8am–dusk, Sun 10am–dusk; free) off
Clonmell Street. With its own grotto, cascade and rosari-
um, it formed the back garden to Clonmell House, formerly home to a Lord Chief Justice whose jailing of the
owner of the *Dublin Evening Post* resulted in a devious act
of revenge. The *Post* advertised a "Grand Olympic Pig
Hunt" near the judge's country estate in Blackrock, gave
whiskey to everyone who turned up and invited them to
catch soaped pigs, which fled into the estate pursued by
thousands of tipsy Dubliners – causing the judge to rush
off to Dublin Castle telling the viceroy that Blackrock was
in a state of insurrection.

The garden's far exit brings you out on to Earlsfort Terrace near the **National Concert Hall** (see p.256), Dublin's premier classical music venue. An imposing building constructed for the Great Exhibition of 1865, it subsequently became the centrepiece of University College Dublin, before being inaugurated as the National Concert Hall in 1981.

EAST OF ST STEPHEN'S GREEN

The area to the **east of St Stephen's Green**, bound to the east by Wilton Terrace and to the south by Leeson Street, constitutes one of the finest areas of **Georgian Dublin**. A product of the immense prosperity generated during the eighteenth century, when the Wide Streets Commission gave speculators carte blanche to buy up greenfield sites on both sides of the Liffey (see *History*, p.313), this whole district well repays exploration on foot. Starting in **Leeson Street,** which was originally devised as a grand approach to St Stephen's Green from Donnybrook, turn into Pembroke Street, whose rows of ornamental balconies and elegant fanlights lead off to the private green lawns of **Fitzwilliam Square**. Occasional gaps between the mature beech, laurel and holly trees afford a glimpse of the well-tended privilege enjoyed by the Georgian gentry. Laid out between 1791 and 1825, the square was the last and smallest to be developed by the Fitzwilliams and is a fine example of Georgian Dublin at its most intimate. It retains, too, a sense of the vigorous cultural life long generated in this part of the city: W.B. Yeats resided at no. 42 between 1928 and 1932, his brother Jack, the painter, lived just around the corner at no. 18 Fitzwilliam Place, and the adjacent building to no. 19 on the square itself was the home of Robert Lloyd Praeger, eminent naturalist and author.

Either the north or the south side of the square will bring you to **Fitzwilliam Street Upper** which, along with Merrion Square and Fitzwilliam Place, once formed the longest stretch of uninterrupted Georgian housing in Europe. Despite the demolition of 26 houses in the 1960s, it still affords a marvellous perspective on the planners' ambitions to bring the wild grandeur of the hinterland into the heart of the city. (It's also worth pausing here to admire the view south as the street opens out to a spectacular vista of the Wicklow Mountains.) Continuing north, Fitzwilliam Street crosses a number of fine Georgian streets, and at the top of Mount Street Upper you will see the delightfully poised pepperpot church of St Stephen's, a Neoclassical work dating from 1824.

No. 29 Lower Fitzwilliam Street

Map 4, H8. Tues–Sat 10am–5pm, Sun 2–5pm, closed two weeks prior to Christmas; guided tour £2.50, students, unemployed and senior citizens £1, children free.

Once the home of the Beatty family, this assiduous reconstruction of a Georgian townhouse is well worth visiting. An engaging and informative **guided tour** explains the kind of society developed by the political and merchant classes of eighteenth-century Dublin and the minutiae of bourgeois life, starting in the basement, where water was filtered for drinking and coal and wine were stored in the cellar. Next door to the pantry the housekeeper's room has a small window, through which she could keep a close eye on light-fingered servants (who slept in slums elsewhere). Gracious living began upstairs, where you'll see such contraptions as a lead-lined cooler and a pneumatic exercise machine – for days when Master hadn't time to go riding. The nursery contains a giant doll's house and a bed for the governess, who was hired to instruct the daughters (boys went to boarding school) in such ladylike arts as embroidery; the needlework samplers on the wall were the Georgian equivalent of a curriculum vitae.

Back outside, the building you can see at the bottom of Fitzwilliam Street Lower is the **National Maternity Hospital**, founded in 1894, but the real attraction here is Merrion Square.

Merrion Square

Merrion Square marks the zenith of Georgian town-planning and was laid out by Lord Fitzwilliam of Merrion in the 1770s. Its spacious terraced houses have belonged to diverse famous citizens, and a stroll past their commemorative plaques gives a marvellous sense of the cultural legacy of the place. Though most of the houses now serve as offices, enough people still live here for the square to retain a residential feel.

Like St Stephen's Green, **the north side** of the square was once the most fashionable. The Wildes lived at no. 1; their son Oscar was born at nearby 21 Westland Row. However, **Merrion Square South** has the greater concentration of eminent ex-residents. Daniel O'Connell bought no. 58 in 1809, to the dismay of his frugal wife Mary, who lamented, "Where on earth will you be able to get a thousand guineas?". The Austrian physicist Erwin Schrödinger, co-winner of the 1933 Nobel Prize, occupied no. 65; the poet, mystic and painter George Russell (AE) worked at no. 84, and in 1922 W.B. Yeats moved into no. 82, having previously lived at 52 Merrion Square East. There's nothing to recall the British Embassy at no. 39, burnt out in 1972 by a crowd protesting against the Bloody Sunday massacre in Derry. On weekends during the summer, the park railings offer a splendid array of paintings as artists gather to sell their work.

Oscar Wilde

Oscar Fingal O'Flahertie Wills Wilde was born in 1854, his mother a literary hostess and sometime poet, his father an eye specialist. A star at Trinity College, Wilde won a scholarship to Oxford, where he immersed himself in aestheticism and gained his reputation as a brilliant conversationalist – making him the essential party guest. While his outlandish dress sense and incisive repartee made him many enemies, this did not seem to bother him – his belief being that "there is only one thing in the world worse than being talked about and that is not being talked about" – and he went on to write dazzling satires such as *Lady Windermere's Fan* and *The Importance of Being Earnest*, ensuring his success as a dramatist.

Although he was heterosexual in his youth and married Constance Lloyd in 1884, Wilde began to have homosexual relationships from 1886, finally falling in love with Lord Alfred Douglas, the son of the Marquis of Queensbury. The Marquis' wrath over Wilde's involvement with his son resulted in the famous court case, when he was prosecuted by his erstwhile friend Edward Carson for indecent acts. He was jailed for two years hard labour and whilst in prison wrote his famous poem *The Ballad of Reading Gaol*, containing the line "each man kills the thing he loves". Imprisonment broke his spirit in many ways. His long-suffering wife died in 1898 and Wilde, living the life of a social pariah in Paris, was abandoned by his "beloved Bosie" – Lord Douglas. He died alone in 1900, heartbroken and impoverished.

A trio of fine public buildings occupy **Merrion Square West** and **Merrion Street Upper** – The National Gallery of Ireland (see opposite), The Natural History Museum (see p.57) and Leinster House (see p.26), the entrance to which faces onto Kildare Street. The obelisk on Leinster Lawn is dedicated to Michael Collins, Arthur Griffith and Kevin O'Higgins, the architects of the Free State.

Merrion Square itself is a real pleasure to walk through, with its thickets of low-flowering shrubs, tulip-filled borders and bluebells. At the centre are perfectly manicured lawns from which the upper storeys of fine Georgian houses are visible above the treetops. It was from here in 1785 that Richard Crosbie from County Wicklow, attired in a fur-lined silk robe and a leopard-skin cap, made Ireland's first balloon ascent. Flamboyance, however, was not confined to the eighteenth century, and a remarkable statue of Oscar Wilde (see box) languishes against a rock near the junction of Merrion Square West and North, in a pose of outrageous insouciance. Before him stand the figures of a pregnant woman, representing his wife Constance expecting their second child, and a male torso; the columns on which they rest are inscribed with Wildean epithets, from the witty "Only dull people are brilliant at breakfast", to the poignant "Who, being loved, is poor?" Before leaving the park look out too for the bust of Michael Collins and that of Bernardo O'Higgins, liberator of Chile.

THE NATIONAL GALLERY

Map 4, G7. Mon–Sat 10am–5.30pm, Thurs until 8.30pm, Sun 2–5pm, closed on Good Friday and Dec 24–26; free.

The National Gallery houses a fine collection of European art dating from the fifteenth century to the present day. The **Lower Levels** are chiefly given over to the development of Irish painting from the seventeenth century onwards, including a marvellous Yeats Museum, as well as seventeenth- and eighteenth-century British painting. Highlights of the **Upper Levels** include a small but choice selection of works from the Early Renaissance, superb paintings by Caravaggio, Goya and Velázquez, seventeenth-century Dutch and Flemish landscapes and interiors, and an excellent group of French Impressionist pieces.

The collection grew out of an enthusiastic public response to the Fine Art Hall of the Irish Industrial Exhibition of 1853, organized by the railway magnate William Dargan. Dargan was so impressed that he donated his profits to fund the National Gallery. Since its inauguration in 1864, the gallery's collection has grown from 125 paintings to more than 10,000 pictures and sculptures, partly thanks to bequests by the likes of the Countess of Milltown (who gave almost 200 paintings from Russborough House) and George Bernard Shaw (who left one third of his residual estate to the "cherished asylum" of his youth).

Besides free **guided tours** on Saturdays (3pm) and Sundays (2.15pm, 3pm & 4pm), the gallery offers a range of **lectures** and **workshops**, some of them intended for children and the visually impaired (as detailed in the monthly *Gallery News*, available in the foyer). The **Millennium Wing** on Clare Street will open towards the end of the year 2000 and will include a national and international exhibition space, a centre for the study of Irish art and an excellent **multimedia gallery**, in which background material to paintings in the collection is readily accessible (currently in Room 7). Disruption to the National Gallery's collection as a whole will be minimal during construction, but key paintings from the Dutch, Spanish, French and Italian collections have been moved to Room 25 while work is in progress. It is possible to check whether particular paintings that you wish to see are on display by telephoning ©661 5133.

Lower Levels: The Milltown Wing

The ground-floor **Milltown Wing** (Rooms 1–6) cover **Irish art**, beginning with the eighteenth century, a period

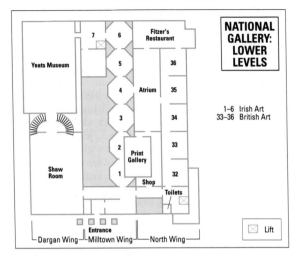

when many Irish painters found employment in England. Notable among the exiles was **Nathaniel Hone** the Elder, who spent most of his life there and became a founder member of the Royal Academy – his most famous painting, *The Conjurer*, is a satire of the academy's president, Sir Joshua Reynolds. In the late eighteenth and early nineteenth centuries the emotionally charged extravagances of Romanticism emerged in pictures such as James Arthur O'Connor's *A Thunderstorm: The Frightened Waggoner*, with its wind-tossed trees and dramatic lighting, and in the pyrotechnic excesses of *The Opening of the Sixth Seal* by **Francis Danby** (Room 3), an apocalyptic vision based on the Book of Revelations. An interest in individuality becomes increasingly apparent as painters began to take people from all social strata for their subjects: in William Mulready's *The Toy Seller* (Room 3) the artist's interest

THE NATIONAL GALLERY

clearly lies in the racial interaction between a black toyseller and a wealthy white woman; A.N. Burke places a barefoot peasant at the centre of his *A Connemara Girl*, and *The Sick Call*, by **Matthew James Lawless**, makes oblique reference to the misery of the Irish people in the years after the Famine.

Some artists of the second half of the nineteenth century drew their inspiration from France and Impressionism – a development exemplified by **Walter Osbourne** and **Roderic O'Conor** in paintings such as O'Conor's wonderful *La Jeune Bretonne*, a warm study of a Breton girl, and in his vibrant country scene *Farm at Lezaven Finistère* (for more on O'Conor visit the Hugh Lane Gallery; see p.118). Osbourne's work is particularly well represented. Paintings such as *Apple Gathering at Quimperlé* and *A Cottage Garden at Uffington* demonstrate his preoccupation with atmospheric light and colour and love of simple rustic settings; further demonstrated in *In a Dublin Park*, with its oppressed working-class Dubliners bathed in dappled light, and in *Near St Patrick's Close, an old Dublin street,* where for all its carts, dogs and paupers, the eye is led to the pale light gathering behind the shifting clouds (Room 4).

Paintings from the early twentieth century in rooms 5 and 6 show a more direct approach to the representation of the lives of ordinary people. Garish and confrontational, **William Orpen's** satirical *The Holy Well* depicts villagers of the west tearing off their clothes to seek succour at the well; a lone figure derides their faith, bestriding the well in a posture of defiance. Orpen's *Knackers' Yard*, painted in 1909, conveys a graphic sense of the brutality of that trade, an eery precursor of his role as official war artist in World War I. The landscapes of the west of Ireland are memorably realized in the much-loved paintings of **Paul Henry**, while the bold colour of his *The Potato Diggers* suggests the influence of the post-Impressionists. In Room 6 *The Artist's*

Studio, a strangely busy painting of Hazel Lavery by her husband **Sir John Lavery**, reflects something of the turmoil that this beautiful woman created around herself.

Lower Levels: The Dargan Wing

The grandiose **Shaw Room** sports a collection of full-length paintings of the seventeenth- and eighteenth-century aristocracy – perhaps the most interesting of which is **Charles Jervas**'s *Lady Mary Wortley* dressed in a broodingly sensual rich black gown. The gigantic *Marriage of Princess Aoife of Leinster and Richard de Clare* by **Daniel Maclise** depicts the consummation of the alliance between the King of Leinster and the Norman warlord Strongbow, which took place on the battlefield after the capture of Waterford in 1170 (hence the corpses in the foreground). Nearby a splendid statue of Shaw by **Paul Troubetzkoy** stands taut with intellectual rigour as he casts a critical eye down the length of the gallery. **Mark Shields**' portrait of the first female President of Ireland, Mary Robinson, with her husband Nicholas, is framed by the twin staircases which lead to the Yeats Museum.

The **Yeats Museum** is dedicated to the work of **Jack B. Yeats**, but also covers some of the work of the talented family from which he came, including portraits of family members by his father, **John Butler Yeats**, and pieces by his sisters **Lily** and **Elizabeth Corbet**, founder members of the Irish Arts and Crafts Movement. However, it's the paintings by Jack B. Yeats that really steal the show. The early work on view here shows his preoccupation with everyday scenes, and yet *The Double Jockey Act* gives a tantalizing glimmer of the raw energy that was to characterise his later, more abstract paintings. The Dublin pictures of the 1920s display Yeats's passionate interest in the life of Ireland; *The Liffey Swim* generates all the gritty excitement of the

Jack B. Yeats

The art and politics of Jack. B. Yeats were profoundly affected by the happy years he spent living with his grandparents in County Sligo from the age of eight to sixteen. During this time he developed a deep love of the country and its people and acquired a pool of memories that were to sustain him throughout his adult life in England and Dublin – the immediacy of his paintings is often deceptive since many were produced retrospectively rather than by direct observation. Born in 1871, Yeats lived in England until he was eight, and then again from 1887 to 1910, first studying art in London and then settling in Devon, supporting himself and his wife through painting and illustration. In 1905 he made a tour of the west of Ireland with J.M. Synge, producing illustrations for the *Manchester Guardian*. The trip renewed his connection with the landscapes of the west and this, along with his subsequent association with Synge, fuelled a desire to return.

On his relocation to Ireland in 1910, where he was to live until his death in 1957, he learnt Irish and attended Sinn Féin meetings. War, however, appalled him, and he was greatly distressed by the events surrounding the 1916 Rising. While W.B. Yeats became a senator in the Irish Free State, Jack remained a more idealistic patriot, whose belief in the dignity of ordinary Irish people is evident in his numerous paintings of farm workers, jockeys, tinkers and sailors. However, as he moved away from illustration, Yeats's art became increasingly more abstract, and the later paintings show a free expressivity as he communicates the spirit of the individual in landscapes of chaos and wild beauty.

Dublin crowd as they watch the contestants surge along the river. As the paintings progress, the tension between Yeats's urge to portray the contemporary scene with all its life and colour and a desire for more abstract creativity becomes increasingly apparent. Even as early as 1930 he conjures up a tremendous sense of freedom and light in the minor landscape painting *Power Station*. The 1940s collection sees a series of pictures in which a foregrounded single figure appears to communicate with the abstract colour and form of a landscape. Both *The Gay Moon* and *And so my brother, hail and farewell for evermore* offer an evocation of turbulent inner lives imaged through nature. The height of Yeats's expressivity is reached in pictures such as *The Singing Horseman* and *For the Road*, spirited paintings in which the subject appears to be trying to break free from the canvas, and *Grief*, a chaotic abstraction of anguish.

Lower Levels: The North Wing

Portraits of figures from Irish public life occupy Room 32 in the North Wing. **Jacques Blanche**'s famous portrait of Joyce is here and nearby hangs **Augustus John's** marvellously animated Seán O'Casey. **Robert Ballagh**'s fittingly iconic portayal of Dr Noel Browne, Ireland's great socialist minister, hangs alongside his political enemy Archbishop McQuaid, by **Simon Elwes**, in a classic piece of gallery diplomacy.

Beyond here the North Wing is largely devoted to **British art**, mostly of the eighteenth century, including numerous paintings by **Sir Joshua Reynolds**, whose *Parody of Raphael's "School of Athens"* is a caricature of the Earl of Charlemont and his circle, and their obsession with ancient Rome and Greece. A series of superb full-length portraits represent the work of **Gainsborough**, Reynolds' great rival. Other notable works include portraits of the aristocracy by **Francis Wheatley**, which constituted his bread-and-butter until debts and a scandalous love affair forced him to seek refuge in Ireland, where he painted *The Dublin Volunteers on College Green* (showing how much College Green has changed since then). There's also a delightful portrait of *The Mackinen Children* by **Hogarth**.

Room 35 gives access to an atrium with stairs ascending to the **Print Gallery** (Mon–Fri 10am–1pm) where the collection includes **James Malton**'s watercolours of Georgian Dublin. Various temporary exhibitions are held throughout the year and watercolours by **Turner**, including views of Rhineland castles and the Doge's Palace in Venice, are exhibited every January.

Upper Levels: The North Wing

A good selection of altarpieces and paintings of the Early Renaissance occupy Rooms 23 and 24. A moving portrayal of the *Annunciation* by **Jacques Yverni** is here, a product of the fifteenth-century Avignon school which developed around the papal court during the Great Schism. *SS Cosmas and Damian*, a panel by **Fra Angelico**, the fifteenth-century Florentine master, hangs near **Filippo Lippi**'s lively *Portrait of a Musician*, and there's a fine Sienese triptych, *The Virgin and Child with SS Mary Magdalen and Peter*, by **Giacomo Pisano**. The early Italian master **Paolo Uccello**'s obsession with perspective is evident in his *Virgin and Child*, which shows an animated baby Jesus trying to scramble away from Mary's hands and out from the plane of the picture.

Room 25 is currently being used to display key paintings temporarily displaced by the building of the Millennium Wing. Rooms 26 to 30 contain **Flemish, German and Dutch art** from the fifteenth century onwards. Some of the finest works are in Room 26, such as the lively *Peasant Wedding* by **Brueghel the Younger**, *St Francis of Assisi* by

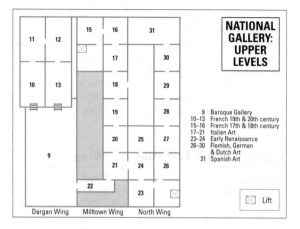

NATIONAL GALLERY: UPPER LEVELS

9 Baroque Gallery
10–13 French 19th & 20th century
15–16 French 17th & 18th century
17–21 Italian Art
23–24 Early Renaissance
26–30 Flemish, German & Dutch Art
31 Spanish Art

⊠ Lift

Dargan Wing   Milltown Wing   North Wing

Rubens and *A Boy Standing on a Terrace* by his most talented pupil, **van Dyck**. Room 27 features two works by the sixteenth-century German portraitist **Conrad Faber**, and *The Descent into Limbo* by an anonymous follower of Hieronymous Bosch. *Rest on the Flight into Egypt* by **Rembrandt** hangs in Room 29, along with *David's Dying Charge to Solomon* by his leading pupil, **Ferdinand Bol**, and *The Castle of Bentheim* by **Jacob van Ruisdael**. *A Young Fisherman* by **Frans Hals** and **Vermeer**'s exquisite *Lady Writing a Letter* can be found in Room 30. The latter has been stolen and recovered twice – first by Bridget Rose Dugdale in 1974, in order to raise money for the IRA, and again in 1986 from Russborough House.

The lion's share of the gallery's collection of **Spanish art** is usually on display in Room 31, although it's worth checking this with enquiries during the construction of the Millennium Wing. This includes three works by **Goya**: *Lady in a Black Mantilla*, *Doña Antonia Zárate* and *El Sueño*,

THE NATIONAL GALLERY

an unusual picture of a sleeping woman somewhat reminiscent of the *Majas* paintings. The spiritual *St Francis Receiving the Stigmata* by **El Greco** is also here, while **Murillo** is represented by *The Holy Family* and *The Penitent Magdalene*. Another highlight here is **Velázquez'** *Kitchen Maid with the Supper at Emmaus* – Christ and his disciples are in the background and attention is focused on the Moorish maid, her startled pose perhaps suggesting that she too might convert to Christianity.

Upper Levels: The Milltown Wing

Entering the Milltown Wing from Room 24 takes you straight to **Italian painting** from the fifteenth to eighteenth centuries. A poignant, glowing *Pietà* by **Perugino** hangs in Room 21, along with some interesting Renaissance portraiture and a superb small monochrome by **Mantegna**, *Judith with the Head of Holofernes*. **Titian's** stupendous *Ecce Homo* shares Room 20 with a couple of other grand Venetian paintings: a *Portrait of an Elderly Senator* by **Tintoretto** and *Saints Philip and James the Less* by **Paolo Veronese**. **Caravaggio's** *The Taking of Christ* is the highlight of Room 19, with all the dynamic violence of the act conveyed in the powerful movement of the soldiers' gestures, with Christ a figure of spiritual stillness at the centre of it all. Beyond here are two fine views of eighteenth-century Dresden by **Bernardo Belloto**, Canaletto-like vistas of Rome by **Giovanni Paolo Panini**, and **Tiepolo's** *Allegory of the Immaculate Conception and the Redemption*.

At the end of the Milltown Wing rooms 15 and 16 are given over to major French artists of the seventeenth and eighteenth centuries. **Poussin**, the French classical painter par excellence, is represented here by *Acis and Galatea*, *The Holy Family* and the strangely lyrical *Lamentation over the Dead Christ*. Paintings by **Claude Lorraine**, Poussin's contemporary and compatriot, include *Hagar and the Angel* and *Juno Confiding Io to the Care of Argus*. With the exception of Watteau, the gallery owns something by every major French artist of the eighteenth century, two especially fine examples being *Venus and Cupid* by **Fragonard** and *The Funeral of Patroclus* by **David.**

Upper Levels: The Dargan Wing

The **Baroque Gallery** in Room 9 is a slightly less opulent counterpart to the Shaw Room on the floor below, hung with enormous paintings chiefly by artists who are little known today. However, there are three by old masters that are too large to include in their respective national sections – *The Annunciation* and *St Peter Finding the Tribute Money* by **Rubens**, and *The Finding of Cyrus* by **Castiglione**.

The gallery owns some fine work by pivotal **Impressionists**, the best of which hang in Room 10, including *A River Scene: Autumn* by **Monet**, **Sisley**'s *The Canal du Loing at Saint Mammès*, and paintings by **Bonnard** and **Pissarro**. The prolific German Expressionist **Emil Nolde**'s *Two Women in a Garden* is also here, along with a wonderfully vibrant *Still-life with Mandolin* by **Picasso**.

Adjacent rooms 11 to 13 include minor works by major painters of the French Barbizon school, including **Corot**, **Millet** and **Courbet**.

THE NATURAL HISTORY MUSEUM

Map 4, G8. Tues–Sat 10am–5pm, Sun 2–5pm; free.
Across the Leinster Lawn from the National Gallery stands the **Natural History Museum**, which preserves the essence of Victorian museums like a fly in amber, being virtually unchanged since the explorer and missionary Dr David Livingstone delivered its inaugural lecture in 1857. A

statue of a rifle-toting naturalist on the lawn presages an orgy of the taxidermy and taxonomy within. The ground-floor Irish Room opens with three skeletons of the giant Irish deer, which became extinct 11,000 years ago, and ends with a section on endangered wildlife, so the mood is sombre. Upstairs, the World Collection has rhinoceroses, pandas and other appealing creatures, plus the skeletons of two humpback whales stranded on Irish shores. The top gallery displays the amazing Blaschka collection of glass models of marine plants, masterpieces of the glassmaker's art.

THE GOVERNMENT BUILDINGS AND AROUND

Map 4, F8. Sat 10am–12.30pm & 1.30–4.30pm; guided tours only (maximum 16 people, last tour 3.30pm). Free tickets from the National Gallery.

Beyond the Natural History Museum looms the Edwardian colossus of the **Government Buildings**. The last great edifice erected by the British, its domed centrepiece was inaugurated by George V as the Royal College of Science in 1911, and lectures proceeded despite eleven more years of noisy construction work. No sooner was it finished than the north wing was occupied by the Free State government, whose ministers lived and worked there during the Civil War, for fear of assassination. (Kevin O'Higgins was nearly killed by a sniper when he went onto the roof at night to smoke.) After the Royal College vacated in 1989 the whole complex was refurbished to suit the government. Besides the stylish decor, it's fascinating to see the lair of the powers-that-be, with their odd perks and quirks, in a forty-minute **guided tour** shadowed by a gimlet-eyed security man.

You'll start by mounting the **Ceremonial Staircase** – the square holes in the balustrades are a trademark of Angela Rolf, who designed much of the furniture. Though Charles Haughey vetoed moving Cabinet meetings into the

Sycamore Room, he was happy with the **Taoiseach's Office**, complete with a private lift to a rooftop helipad and a basement limo. The historic **Cabinet Room** is the only part of the building that's still in old-fashioned style, hung with portraits of Wolfe Tone, Parnell, Markievicz and other Irish heroes.

That most English of Irishmen, Arthur Wellesley, Duke of Wellington, may have been born across the road at no. 24 Merrion Street Upper (now a hotel) – though evidence also points towards Trim in County Meath. The Duke was reticent about his Irish origins – on one occasion when reminded, he retorted, "Being born in a stable doesn't make one a horse."

The RHA Gallagher Gallery

Map 4, F9. Tues–Sat 11am–5pm, Thurs until 9pm, Sun 2–5pm; free Cross Baggot Street at the top of Merrion Street Upper and you find yourself in **Ely Place**, a charming Georgian residential laneway. Here, while completely at odds with the Georgian houses that surround it, stands **The Royal Hibernian Academy of Arts Gallagher Gallery**. The Royal Hibernian Academy of Arts was established in 1823 and its annual exhibition soon became an important feature of the city's cultural calendar. Although the Academy's buildings in Lower Abbey Street were destroyed during the 1916 Rising, it continued to hold its annual exhibition at alternative venues. Former academicians include Nathaniel Hone, Walter Osbourne, John Butler Yeats, Jack B. Yeats and Charles Lamb. The Gallagher Gallery, built for the RHA in 1988, is a discrete modern building providing an excellent airy space for viewing painting and sculpture. It's one of Ireland's most important galleries for modern art, hosting several major Irish and international contemporary shows each year.

Temple Bar and the old city

Nowhere is Dublin's economic transformation over the last decade more evident than in **Temple Bar**, the area sandwiched between Dame Street and the Liffey. Marketed as Dublin's "Left Bank", Temple Bar gained a name as the city's artistic quarter in the early 1980s, when it was redeveloped in a way that was intended to retain much of Temple Bar's unique character. However, the bullish 1990s saw Dublin property prices soar, especially here, resulting in a change of emphasis from culture to entertainment. Nowadays Temple Bar has the city's greatest concentration of restaurants, galleries, pubs and clubs, but outsiders rather than Dubliners provide the majority of customers. Indeed, such has been the proliferation of alco-tourists packing its pubs, that hen and stag parties have been banned from licensed premises within Temple Bar, in an attempt to reverse its reputation as a bacchanalian rather than a bohemian centre.

You'll see building work everywhere in Temple Bar – swanky new cybercafés, spartan coffee houses, shops and restaurants seem to be opening on a daily basis and apartments are being built or refurbished in old warehouses all over the place in an effort to bring people back to the city centre. As property prices continue to rise and its cobbled streets become ever more crowded, the tide of development has swept westwards towards Wood Quay, where the hugely controversial civic offices stand, locally known as "the bunkers". Underneath its concrete slabs rests the origins of **Viking Dublin**, while this period in the city's history is re-created on Essex Street West in **Dublin's Viking Adventure**.

The **historic core** of the city lies to the west and south of Temple Bar and is roughly triangulated by Dublin Castle and the cathedrals of Christ Church and St Patrick's. Although few old buildings remain, many streets in this area follow contours as staked out by the Vikings in the ninth century, when a main axis ran east–west along the ridge (now Castle Street, Christchurch Place and High Street) and lanes divided by wattle fences descended to the quays. The Anglo-Normans took and fortified this area in the early thirteenth century, building the castle and enclosing Dublin with walls, towers and gateways and founding both **Christ Church** and **St Patrick's Cathedral**.

From nearby Cook Street you can see a massive section of the Norman city walls, and, if you can get inside, there are curios to be found in **St Werburgh's** and **St Audoen's** churches. **Marsh's Library**, near St Patrick's, is a wonderfully archaic scholar's den from the time of Jonathan Swift, who was dean of the cathedral for many years. If pubs, restaurants and market stalls are more your thing, head for South Great George's Street, running 100m or so from Dame Street.

Near the end of Dame Street stands **Dublin Castle**, the former centre and symbol of British authority and the seat of the viceroy. Only since independence have Dubliners been able to enjoy its architecture and tour the State

Apartments where the viceroys once held court. Today the castle is still used for state ceremonies and diplomatic summits.

TEMPLE BAR

Until the dissolution of the monasteries in 1537, the land on which Temple Bar stands was the property of the Augustinian order. It owes its name not to the friars, however, but to Sir William Temple, who bought the plot in the late sixteenth century. During the eighteenth century, this area was a centre for Dublin's lowlife, while in the nineteenth it attracted small businesses and traders.

The land was acquired in the 1960s by CIE (the state transport company at the time), whose aim was to build a new central bus terminal to replace the one on the other side of the river. As CIE procrastinated and uncertainty over the future of the area grew, small shops, studios and offices took on cheap short-term leases in Temple Bar. In the 1980s a movement to preserve the district gained momentum and under pressure from politicians, most notably Charles Haughey, CIE abandoned its plan. With Dublin lobbying to become European City of Culture in 1991, the development of Temple Bar moved into top gear.

In this section are highlighted some of the major galleries and exhibitions in the area, but for a comprehensive list of what's on where, check the Listings section of this guide. It's also worth dropping in to the **Temple Bar Properties** (see p.65) at no. 18 Eustace Street; their free quarterly *Temple Bar Guide* comes with a useful map.

For details of the best places to drink in Temple Bar, see Drinking; for restaurants see Eating; for music venues see Live music and clubs.

If you're approaching Temple Bar from the Ha'penny Bridge, you enter through **Merchant's Arch**, a dark alley-way that gives you an idea of how Dickensian Temple Bar must have looked a century ago, when many of the streets beside the quays had such archways. Straight ahead of you is **Crown Alley**, which leads to the Central Bank on Dame Street. About halfway down to your right is the *Bad Ass Café*, where Sinéad O'Connor (aka Mother Bernadette Mary) once worked as a waitress while singing with Ton Ton Macoute.

Dublin's financial centre since the eighteenth century, **Dame Street**, lies at the opposite end of Crown Alley to Merchant's Arch. The street was named after a dam which linked the hilltop Viking settlement to the outlying *Thingmount* (see p.16), and has a flush of Victorian banking houses now trumped by the **Central Bank**. Designed by controversial architect Sam Stephenson in 1978, the bank is an outsized stack of concrete slabs whose plaza has been colonized by rollerbladers, skateboarders and, on weekends, percussionists. Plans are afoot to create a closed space in front of the bank, a project that may provoke a somewhat ambivalent reception amongst Dubliners – in a recent architectural survey, the Central Bank was voted one of the most hated as well as one the most loved buildings in the city.

The heart of Temple Bar

You won't have to wander far to find an arts centre of some kind in Temple Bar. Ultramodern **Curved Street**, off Temple Lane (once known as Dirty Lane), is flanked by the **Arthouse**, centre for the Artists Association of Ireland (AAI), the representative body for professional visual artists in Ireland, and the state-of-the-art **Temple Bar Music Centre**, home to recording and television studios and organizations

TEMPLE BAR

The Eagle Tavern and the Hellfire Club

Before it was demolished by the Wide Streets Commission in 1757, the **Eagle Tavern** was among the foremost roistering spots of Georgian Dublin. Standing beside the equally popular *Lucas Coffee Shop*, it allowed gentlemen-about-town to spend day and night in dissipation without having to walk far. It was at the *Eagle* that the notorious **Hellfire Club** was founded in 1735 by the Earl of Rosse, Buck Whaley, Colonel St Leger and the artist James Worsdale. Dedicated to gambling, whoring and profanity (they walked all the way to Jerusalem and played handball against the Wailing Wall to win a bet of £15,000) rather than black magic *per se* – though the Devil is said to have appeared at one of their parties – their main meeting place was outside Dublin at Speaker Connolly's hunting lodge on Montpelier Hill. The scandal they caused eventually forced them to quit Ireland, but in 1755 the Club was re-established in England by Sir Francis Dashwood, at Medmenham Abbey. Though he was later to become Chancellor of the Exchequer he made such a hash of it that he was retired to the Lords, and the Hellfire Club languished as its members succumbed to bankruptcy or cirrhosis.

Sadly, for those seeking any relic of the Club in Dublin, the location of the tavern is uncertain, due to a missing portion of the original surveyor's map. Although a plaque on the wall of Eustace Street states that it occupied the site of the Quaker meeting-hall where Wolfe Tone later founded the Dublin United Irishmen, most sources place the tavern on Cork Hill, where much was levelled to create Parliament Street and City Hall, so *Thomas Read* pub or *Da Pino* restaurant may be closer to the mark.

supporting the development of the Irish music industry. A passageway links to **Eustace Street**, where you'll find the

Information Centre and, further up, the coolly minimalist **Irish Film Centre** (see p.249 and p.267). Its two screens show art-house and special-interest films, and its bar and restaurant attract a trendy crowd.

On the other side of Eustace Street, Dublin's unique outdoor performance venue, **Meeting House Square** (named after a former Quaker meeting-hall), hosts a wide variety of events throughout the summer, including outdoor screenings of films and concerts and an outdoor food market (see *Shopping*, p.283). Nearby are the **Gallery of Photography** and Ireland's premier drama school, the Gaiety School of Acting. Facing the stage at Meeting House Square is **The Ark**, which is dedicated to artwork by and for children.

At the top of Eustace Street, turning right into Temple Bar will take you to the **Original Print Gallery**, where you can see a wide selection of the best work of emerging and established Irish and international printmakers, and slightly further, on the corner opposite Temple Bar Square, stands **Temple Bar Gallery and Studios**, the largest of its kind in Ireland, with thirty artist studios and two exhibition spaces. South of here, in a small alley off Cope Street, the word "Art" flashes on a neon sign outside a converted warehouse, home of the **Graphic Studio Gallery**, the best commercial art gallery in the area. If you turn left at the top of Eustace Street, along Essex Street East, you'll find the **DESIGNyard** (see p.274), a showcase for contemporary Irish jewellery, furniture and interior design. Further up on the same side of the street, U2 spent millions on *The Clarence Hotel* (see p.199) and have turned it into Dublin's coolest establishment, with a rooftop penthouse used by the likes of Björk and Jack Nicholson. Before the Custom House moved downriver in the 1780s, this was the site where a crane used to unload ships – hence Crane Lane, nearby.

TEMPLE BAR

Broad **Parliament Street** was the first of the new roads cut through the old city after the formation of the Wide Streets Commission in 1757. Despite the results it achieved within a decade, the Commission was widely hated at the time, since tenants who ignored its compulsory purchase orders had their roofs removed overnight to force them to quit. Fortunately, it spared what is now Dublin's oldest shop, at no. 4. Thomas Read has been a cutlers since 1670 and contains its original display cabinets and furniture (the *Thomas Read* pub is next door).

On the corner of Parliament Street which faces Grattan Bridge stand the Sunlight Chambers, whose filthy exterior has a beautiful bas-relief frieze of men making their clothes dirty through honest toil, and women washing them. Its unusual theme is explained by the fact that Sunlight was the brand of soap manufactured by Lever Brothers (now the Unilever conglomerate), who commissioned the building at the turn of the century.

CITY HALL AND THE OLYMPIA

Parliament Street slopes slightly uphill towards the **City Hall** on Dame Street. Built in 1769 as the Royal Exchange, it's been occupied by the Dublin Corporation since 1825. You can walk in to view its rotunda, which contains statues of O'Connell and other worthies in Roman garb; among the murals is one depicting Lambert Simnel being carried through the streets (see p.77). The civic coat of arms on the floor shows three burning bastions, symbolizing resistance to invaders, but the motto *Obedientia Civium Urbis Felicitas* ("Happy the City whose Citizens Obey") suggests that rebellion was a greater worry for Dublin's rulers. During the Easter Rising, City Hall was seized by the insurgents, who sniped at British forces in the castle from its roof.

Diagonally opposite the City Hall, behind a stained-glass porte-cochere, is the **Olympia Theatre** (see p.266). Since opening as the "Star of Erin Music Hall" in 1749, it has played host to many great Irish and international entertainers and features gigs by local bands on Friday and Saturday nights.

DUBLIN CASTLE

Map 4, B6. Tours of state apartments Mon–Fri 10am–5pm, Sat, Sun & bank holidays 2–5pm; £3, students/children £2, family £5. It is advisable to ring ahead, as the tours do not run on state occasions (℮677 7129).

For seven hundred years, **Dublin Castle** embodied English rule as the headquarters of the viceroy. Built by the Anglo-Normans in the early thirteenth century, it was the key element of their walled city and served their successors well, withstanding all attempts to take it by force.

Its gravest test was in 1534, when besieged by Silken Thomas Fitzgerald, Henry VIII's Lord Deputy, who had renounced his allegiance to the English crown. The castle was formally handed over to Michael Collins and the Irish Free State on January 16, 1922. The story goes that the last viceroy complained, "You're seven minutes late, Mr Collins", to which he replied, "We've been waiting seven hundred years, you can have the seven minutes." Today, denuded of menace, it could be mistaken for a private college. Its palatial interior is revealed only on guided **tours** of the State Apartments, though you can look around the courtyards and the Chapel Royal for free.

Above the main gate is a **figure of Justice** that turns her back on Dublin – an apt symbol of British justice, Dubliners said. Moreover, the scales of Justice tilted whenever it rained, till the authorities ensured even-handedness by drilling holes in the scale-pans. The nearby

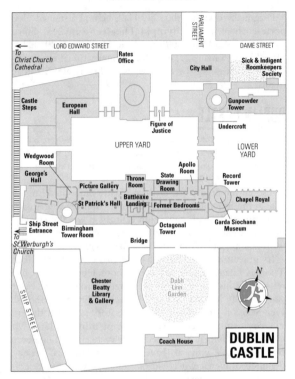

Bedford Tower is an eighteenth-century clock tower built upon the base of a Norman gate-tower. It was from here that the Irish "Crown Jewels" – a diamond St Patrick Star and Badge, together with other insignia – were stolen shortly before the state visit of Edward VII in 1907. Nobody was ever caught and the jewels have never been recovered.

The **Upper Yard** marks the extent of the original medieval castle, which was ravaged by fire in 1684. Surveyor-General Sir William Robinson took the opportunity of creating a larger complex of residential and administrative buildings, the arcaded appearance of which closely resembles his design for the Royal Hospital, Kilmainham (see p.99). It's hard to imagine the same place heaped with the bodies of rebels, brought into the city on carts after the British crushed the Rebellion of 1798 – or the castle's defenders being slain and buried here in shallow graves during the Easter Rising.

The State Apartments

You'll begin your tour of the **State Apartments** by ascending a grand staircase leading to the Battleaxe Landing, where the viceroy's ceremonial bodyguards stood. During World War I the **bedrooms** served as a Red Cross hospital – the wounded James Connolly was held here before his execution at Kilmainham Jail. Famous names like Nelson Mandela, Chancellor Kohl and Mrs Thatcher (who insisted cable TV be installed) have slept in Her Majesty's Bedroom. Across the corridor, the **Apollo Room** has a gorgeous ceiling from another house, featuring symbols of hunting, farming, war and music. The Drawing Room was also reconstructed after a fire in 1941, and contains a mirror bought for £5 by a farmer who used it for a headboard for 25 years; it's now valued at £100,000.

In the **Throne Room**, the Act of Union is embodied in a chandelier combining the rose, shamrock and thistle, and in a throne belonging to William of Orange. Viceregal portraits line the gallery-cum-dining room, with Cornwallis (who lost the American colonies) hung in disgrace behind the door. After dinner, men would play billiards in the **Wedgwood Room**, which is decorated with four plaques

DUBLIN CASTLE

in that style and roundels of Day and Night. The circular **Birmingham Tower Room** is an eighteenth-century conversion of a medieval prison tower. Off an anteroom opens George's Hall, built in 1911 for the visit of George V and Queen Mary – the last British monarchs to visit Dublin. Best of all is the blue, white and gold **St Patrick's Hall**, which once hosted ceremonies of the Knights of St Patrick (an order created in 1738) and is now used for presidential inaugurations and funerals. Ceiling paintings depict George III's coronation, Henry II receiving the surrender of the Irish chieftains, and St Patrick lighting the Paschal Fire on the Hill of Slane, watched by suspicious Druids.

The Lower Yard and Grounds

In the **Lower Yard**, the dramatic juxtaposition of the Record Tower and the Chapel Royal is marred by a hideous modern tax office. Beefed up with battlements in Victorian times, the **Record Tower**, a rough-hewn mass dating back to 1258, originally served as a prison. In 1592, Red Hugh O'Donnell made two celebrated escapes from here; first by climbing down a rope, and then via a privy. The adjoining **Chapel Royal** is a neo-Gothic gem by Francis Johnston. Mindful of the underground river that had undermined two earlier chapels, Johnston made it as light as possible by using plaster-coated brick rather than stone.

Tours currently finish at an **undercroft** exposing a wall and corner tower of the Norman castle and part of the original Viking ramparts. Only regular pumping stops it being submerged by the River Poddle, which originally flowed above ground into the "Dark Pool" (*Dubh Linn*) in the area of what is now the castle **garden**, around the back of the chapel, facing a side of the castle unexpectedly painted terracotta, grey and yellow. A small door at the rear of the Record Tower gives access to the **Garda Síochána Museum**, relating the history of Ireland's police force with a range of exhibits such as old police uniforms and a model of a 1930s police station.

Another attraction, due to open in 2001, is the **Chester Beatty Library and Gallery**, created on the bequest of Sir Alfred Chester Beatty, an Irish-American mining magnate who settled in Dublin in 1950 and later gave his entire collection of oriental art to the nation. Its superbly crafted *objets d'art* range from Japanese netsuke and Chinese rhino-horn cups (over two hundred of them – the largest collection in the world) to life-size Burmese Buddhas, while the books and manuscripts include the oldest surviving examples of Egyptian love poetry and illustrated miniatures of Persian and Moghul poetry. Opening hours will be as for the castle, with no extra charge.

DUBLIN'S VIKING ADVENTURE

Map 4, B5. Tues–Sat 10am–4.30pm, Nov–Feb closed 1–2pm; £4.75, students, under 18s and OAPs £3.95, under-12s £2.95, family £13.

North of the castle, on Essex Street West, is the site of ongoing excavations into Dublin's past. Though much was lost at Wood Quay (see p.73) and other sites, archeologists have been lucky to find a stratum of Viking dwellings from the tenth century, which may overlie the remains of an earlier Celtic settlement at the mouth of the Poddle. Unfortunately, though notices on the fence explain the basics of archeology, you're not told what's been found so far, and to the untrained eye there's little to see but a lot of people poking about in muddy pits.

Across the road from the excavations, **Dublin's Viking Adventure** offers an "experience" of Viking-age Dyflin that's short on facts but fun in its own way. You start by

The Vikings

The first **Vikings** to turn their attention to Ireland were Norwegian, in the eighth century. Having overrun the Picts in the Hebrides, their first recorded raid on Ireland was in 795 and in 837 sixty longships sailed up the Liffey to attack inland; four years later the fortified port that was to become the town of **Dyflin**, an important trading post, was created. Though the settlement was plundered by Danish Vikings, and the Norsemen were forced out by the king of Leinster in 902, they returned fifteen years later, this time reinforcing their position by building defences at the base of the high ground around the "Dark Pool" and houses on the hillside above the quays.

Intermarriage with the Irish (the name Doyle, for example, derives from *Dubh Gaill*, meaning "dark-haired foreigners") encouraged the growth of a **Hiberno-Norse culture**, consolidated by the Norse king Sitric IV's conversion to Christianity (Brian Ború, king of Munster, despite being credited with "driving out the Danes" at the battle of Clontarf in 1014, valued the Norse trading links and let Sitric remain in Dyflin). Meanwhile, Danish Vikings were forging the Duchy of Normandy into a formidable power. Having conquered England in 1066, the **Normans** were invited by the Gaelic chieftain Diarmuid Mac Murchada to invade Ireland and restore him to the throne of Leinster, in return for making it subject to the king of England. The offer proved irresistible, and by 1170 they had routed the Hiberno-Norsemen from Dyflin, obliging those that remained to live in Oxmantown, across the river, where they gradually lost their ethnic identity and merged into the general population.

boarding a "boat" that sails through a cinematic storm to reach Dyflin, to be greeted by actors in wigs and homespun wit with the best joke of the tour: "It's been a long journey; does anyone want to use the cesspit?" The pole-and-wattle houses, ponds and ramshackle fences are quite convincing (apart from the lack of foul smells), and catwalks zigzag up past a cross-section of the Wood Quay site, showing the layers of homes and graves that accumulated there over a thousand years. You end up in the hall used for Viking feasts, containing a life-size model of a longship whose "sail" is the screen for another film, full of stormy seas and majestic Scandinavian landscapes, which imparts a few facts about the Vikings' voyages.

To partake of the "Viking Feast" it's essential to book ahead, as the event is popular with coach parties (nightly, except Tues & Wed). Since Viking food seems gross to modern tastes, the menu is a mixture of Irish and Olde Medieval dishes, served at long tables. Nobody knows what Viking music sounded like, so the entertainment is based around the development of music and dance from traditional Irish to *Riverdance*. It'll set you back £31.50 (£20 per child), and that doesn't cover the drinks bill.

WOOD QUAY AND FISHAMBLE STREET

The most populous part of Viking Dyflin covered the hillside by **Wood Quay** – a site now occupied by the gigantic **Civic Offices** of the Dublin Corporation, a much-loathed lump known as "the bunkers". As layers of medieval timber structures were being destroyed by mechanical diggers, archeologists won an injunction allowing them to conduct an excavation of the site before remains of tenth-century houses and quay walls, as well as the finds currently on show in the National Museum, were lost forever. As a token apology, the bunkers are surrounded by ornamental references to the Vikings, with a wooden longship and brass images of axe-heads and other artefacts embedded on Wood Quay, and the outlines of a

Viking house picked out on the slope behind Christ Church.

Twisting uphill towards the cathedral, **Fishamble Street** has followed the same route for a millennium. A fish market for much of that time, it was the birthplace of Archbishop Ussher (of Trinity fame) and Henry Grattan, the founder of the Irish Parliament. A plaque outside the derelict Kennan's engineering works marks the site of the Musick Hall where the combined choirs of Christ Church and St Patrick's first performed Handel's *Messiah* in 1742. Ladies were asked not to wear hoops in their crinolines so that more people could attend, since proceeds went to charity. Swift's verdict was, "Oh, a German, a genius, a prodigy". Excerpts from the *Messiah* are performed here on the anniversary of the event (April 13, throughout the day).

DUBLINIA

Map 4, A6. Oct–March Mon–Fri 10am–7pm, Sat 11am–4pm, Sun 10am–4.30pm; £3.95, students/children £2.90, family £10. A visit to Christ Church Cathedral is included in the price.

As "a bridge to the medieval past", **Dublinia** falls short of virtual reality but conveys lots of impressions and facts with a light touch. The exhibition occupies the ex-**Synod Hall** of the Church of Ireland, which is connected to Christ Church Cathedral by an elegant bridge. Though both were created in Victorian times, the Hall incorporates a medieval tower and stands on the site of the palace of the last Viking ruler, Hasculf, who was chased out by the Normans in 1170.

Dublinia opens with a panoramic **model** of Dublin c. 1500, by which time its wooden suburbs had been burned and its population decimated by the Black Death, leaving the walled Norman city amid tracts of open land, with just one bridge across the Liffey. Wall-maps trace Dublin's subsequent evolution well into Georgian times, and humble **medieval artefacts** found at Wood Quay are displayed in two rooms offside.

Equipped with a guide-tape, you move on through life-size **tableaux** of events such as the crowning of Lambert Simnel and the rebellion of Silken Thomas. A timber-framed merchant's house and a quayside give a sanitized view of medieval life, which the captions admit was anything but salubrious.

The tour then moves upstairs to the **Civic Room**, a small room with panels explaining the history of the state sword, though its most impressive feature are the stained-glass windows, depicting the links between the Celts and the Normans. Between the Civic Room and the Great Hall is a reconstruction of a medieval fair with lots of interactive possibilities, such as wearing a chainmail costume, juggling or brass rubbing. The tour moves into the **Great Hall** where the Church of Ireland bishops once convened and voted on certain issues by standing under doors with "Aye" or "No" above the frames. It's worth finishing the tour by climbing **St Michael's Tower**, a lofty relic of the fifteenth-century Church of St Michael and All Angels, for a great view of Dublin and the Wicklow Mountains on fine days. Finally, the coffee shop in the **Malton Room** was named after the English artist James Malton (c. 1760–1803), whose watercolours (see p.54) were the basis for "A Picturesque and Descriptive View of the City of Dublin" – a set of 25 prints depicting buildings and streetlife during its Georgian heyday.

CHRIST CHURCH CATHEDRAL

Map 4, A6. Daily 10am–5pm; £1, students and children 50p; free with combined ticket for Dublinia.

In medieval times, Church of Ireland **Christ Church Cathedral** would have soared above the city's wooden houses from its commanding site on the brow of Dublin Hill. Today, the view is generally obscured by buildings till you get nearby, and the cathedral has been isolated from its surroundings by the traffic system.

A small Celtic church, Cill Céle Christ, may have stood on this site as early as 600 – long before the coming of the Vikings, who probably pillaged it. In 1028 their ruler Sitric IV ("Silkenbeard") converted to Christianity and requested that Bishop Dúnán found a cathedral on these grounds. Judging by Viking churches in Norway, Sitric's Christ Church was made of wood and probably decorated with pagan as well as Christian symbols, since both faiths co-existed for decades. When the Normans ousted the Vikings, their leader, Richard de Clare "Strongbow", made an agreement with Archbishop Laurence O'Toole to demolish the old cathedral and replace it with one symbol-

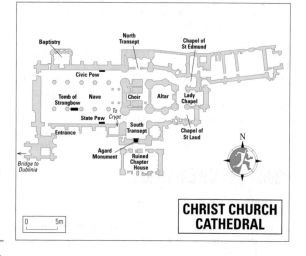

CHRIST CHURCH CATHEDRAL

izing their joint glory. Work began in 1172 but was not completed until 1240. Unfortunately, the structure had been built on a bog, and in 1562 the south wall collapsed, pulling down half the cathedral. The rest continued as a church (and a tavern and market) but steadily deteriorated until the distiller Henry Roe donated £230,000 (worth £23 million today) to finance its restoration in the 1870s. Architect George Street then refaced the exterior and transformed the cathedral's outward appearance by adding flying buttresses.

The interior was also renovated, but it preserves more of its original character: the choir and transepts belong to Strongbow's cathedral, to which the nave was added in 1234.

Close to the entrance lies the curious **tomb of Strongbow**. The original was destroyed by the collapse of the south wall, but was substituted with an effigy of an earl so that Dublin landlords could resume their practice of collecting rents around it. Depending on which version you want to believe, the smaller figure alongside is a fragment of the original tomb which may contain Strongbow's bowels – or an effigy of one of his sons, whom he cut in two for cowardice on the battlefield.

In Norman and Tudor times Christ Church was used for swearing in the viceroy, until the building of the Chapel Royal in Dublin Castle usurped its role. In 1487, the cathedral witnessed the pseudo-coronation of ten-year-old Lambert Simnel as "Edward VI"; within a month the revolt of which he was the figurehead was crushed by Henry VII, who amused himself by sparing Simnel's life to employ him as a kitchen-scullion. At one side of the nave the **Civic Pew** for Dublin's Lord Mayor has brass supports for his Great Sword and Mace (rarely used today), and on the other side the **State Pew**, used by the Irish president, still bears the royal arms of the Stuarts.

The area behind the **choir** contains oak stalls for the canons and choristers, and the archbishop's throne. Turning back to face the nave, you'll be startled by the "**leaning wall of Dublin**" – ever since the south wall collapsed, the north wall has leaned half a metre outwards.

....

Christ Church's excellent choir may be heard at Choral Evensong (Thurs 6pm, Sat 5pm, Sun 3.30pm).

....

In the north transept, notice the Romanesque carvings on the capitals of the archways: a troupe of musicians as you go in, and two human faces being absorbed by griffins (symbolizing wealth) at the exit into the aisle of the choir. The south transept is notable for its tiered **tomb** of the nineteenth earl of Kildare. There are also two medieval effigies of women, one of whom is reputed to be the wife or sister of Strongbow.

Of the three chapels extending off the choir, the right-hand one is the Chapel of St Laud, named after the fifth-century bishop of Coutances in Normandy. On the wall of Laud's chapel is a heart-shaped iron casket containing the **heart of Archbishop O'Toole**, the patron saint of Dublin, canonized after his death in Normandy. The original medieval floor tiles in the chapel were copied by the Victorians throughout the cathedral. The centre chapel is dedicated to the Blessed Virgin Mary, the centrepiece of which is the bronze *Virgin and Child* by contemporary artist Imogen Stuart, while the left chapel is the Chapel of St Edmund, dedicated to him by Strongbow and his knights.

Finally, visit the **crypt**, the purest remnant of the twelfth-century cathedral (you can still see parts of the timber frame used during construction), now a repository for effigies and curios. The grumpy-looking Charles I and II statues came from the city hall that stood opposite the cathedral until 1806, and the punishment-stocks remained in use in Christchurch Yard till 1870. One vault displays a tabernacle and a pair of candlesticks used by James II in 1689 (when, for three months only, Latin Mass was again used at Christ Church), and a mummified cat and rat known to generations of Dublin kids – the cat chased the rat into an organ pipe, where both perished.

ST WERBURGH'S AND ST AUDOEN'S

There are various reminders of past religious and political upheavals along the meandering route from Christ Church to St Patrick's Cathedral, via St Werburgh's, St Audoen's and the city walls.

Across Christchurch Place, on Werburgh Street, **St Werburgh's** has been lacking its spire since it was removed after Emmet's rising of 1803, for fear that future rebels would use it as a sniper's nest. Founded by the Normans in 1178, it was named after the daughter of the king of Mercia, the Abbess Werburgh. One of the leaders of the 1798 Rebellion, Lord Edward Fitzgerald, who was betrayed by spies and died of wounds sustained during his arrest, lies in the Fitzgerald vault. His captor, Major Henry Sirr, is buried in the yard. "Mrs Molly Malone, fishmonger" is listed in the parish records as having died in 1734. Rebuilt in 1715 and again in 1750, the church has an elegant Georgian interior that comes as a surprise after the dour exterior should you manage to gain entry (Sun 11am–noon for services).

....

If you're hungry after all that walking, Leo Burdock's, just across the road, serves the best fish and chips in town (see p.225).

....

To the west of Christ Church, on the corner of High Street and Bridge Street, stand two churches dedicated to St Audoen (the Norman saint, Ouen of Rouen). The Protestant **St Audoen's**, built around 1190, has been reduced to a nave that can only be entered on Sunday mornings; for centuries, its bells were tolled during storms to remind citizens to pray for those at sea. After the Catholics were displaced by the Reformation, they used a chapel on Bridge Street until the Emancipation enabled them to build their own St Audoen's on the adjacent hilltop in 1846. As Maurice Craig wrote, "It looks like some impregnable fortress of the faith, its rugged calp masonry battened like a medieval castle to its base, pierced only by windows at the very top and crowned with the cross which breaks up the silhouette against the sky." The door is flanked by two giant turtle shells from the South Pacific, given by a sea captain to his brother, the parish priest. Catholic St Audoen's celebrates Latin Mass at 11am on Sundays.

Behind the Protestant church, mossy steps descend to **St Audoen's Arch**, the only remaining gate in the **Norman city walls** – a dramatic remnant stretching for 200m along Cook Street, 7m high and tipped with battlements.

To reach St Patrick's Cathedral, cross the road at the Murphy's Pram Shop between the two St Audoen's church-es and walk down Back Lane, passing Mother Redcaps Market. This street meets up with Nicholas Street, where you'll find the excellent *Bite of Life* café, a favourite with the students of nearby Liberty College. The slums in this area were considered among the worst in Europe prior to their demolition in the 1890s, when they were replaced by the **Iveagh Buildings**, a model housing estate built by the Guinness family. Its decorative main block faces **St Patrick's Park**, once the cathedral green, where Cromwell's troops planted cabbages and thereby introduced them to Ireland.

ST PATRICK'S CATHEDRAL

Map 4, A8. April–Oct Mon–Fri 9am–6pm, Sat 9am–5pm;
Nov–March Mon–Fri 9am–4pm, Sun 10–11am & 12.45–3pm; £2.30,
concessions £1.60, family £5.50.

Like Christ Church, **St Patrick's** was restored by the
Victorians, though it seems closer to its origins than Christ
Church and is altogether quirkier, thanks to its array of odd
memorials. The cathedral stands on one of Dublin's earliest
Christian sites, where St Patrick is said to have baptized
converts in a well (c. 450). Bishop John Comyn founded St
Patrick's in 1191 in order to create his own diocese beyond
the city walls. However, it was Archbishop Henry de
Londres who raised it to cathedral status and entirely rebuilt
it (1220–70) at the same time as completing Christ Church.
In 1544 the vaulting of the nave collapsed, and in 1649 it
was used as a stable by Cromwell's cavalry, hastening St
Patrick's decline into separate chapels serving different
communities. Eventually, in the 1860s, Sir Benjamin
Guinness commissioned Thomas Drew to reconstruct the
cathedral, setting a precedent for the restoration of Christ
Church.

The sombre exterior is dominated by the fourteenth-
century **Minot tower**. Oddly misaligned with the rest of
the cathedral, the tower seems to have been built for
defence, a precaution necessitated by St Patrick's exposed
location outside the city walls.

This is the longest medieval church in Ireland and its
interior is majestically proportioned, the nave and transepts
scrutinized by enigmatic **figures** carved on the pillars of
the aisles. (Don't miss the Veiled Lady in the south transept
or the bestiary of monsters in the nave.) Most visitors make
a beeline for the **graves of Jonathan Swift and Stella**,
Swift's long-term partner, beneath brass tablets in the nave.
On the wall of the south aisle are a bust of Swift and two

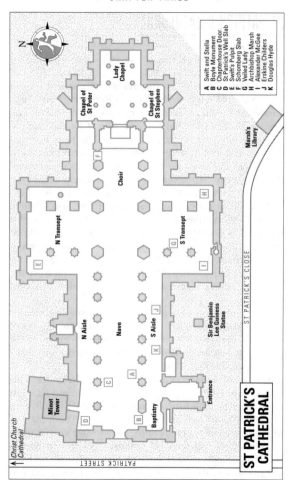

ST PATRICK'S CATHEDRAL

A Swift and Stella
B Boyle Monument
C Chapterhouse Door
D St Patrick's Well Slab
E Swift's Pulpit
F Schomberg Slab
G Veiled Lady
H Archbishop Marsh
I Alexander McGee
J Erskine Childers
K Douglas Hyde

Lady Chapel

Chapel of St Peter

Chapel of St Stephen

Choir

N Transept

S Transept

Marsh's Library

N Aisle

Nave

S Aisle

Minot Tower

Sir Benjamin Lee Guinness Statue

Baptistry

Entrance

ST PATRICK'S CLOSE

← Christ Church Cathedral

PATRICK STREET

plaques bearing their epitaphs, penned by him. His is in Latin but a translation reads:

> *Here is laid the body of*
> *Jonathan Swift, Doctor of Divinity,*
> *Dean of this Cathedral Church,*
> *Where fierce indignation can no longer*
> *Rend the heart.*
> *Go, traveller, and imitate, if you can*
> *This earnest and dedicated*
> *Champion of liberty.*

She is merely "Mrs Esther Johnson, better known to the world as Stella, under which she is celebrated in the writings of Dr Jonathan Swift, Dean of this cathedral." To add injury to insult, her body was exhumed by Victorian phrenologists, studying the skulls of the famous. There is also a tribute to Swift by his friend Alexander Pope, with whom he planned to share a home in retirement.

The gigantic **Boyle monument** teems with painted figures of the fifteen children borne by Catherine Fenton, the "dearest, dear wife" of Richard Boyle, earl of Cork. Erected in 1632, it originally stood near the altar but was moved after the viceroy objected to churchgoers being forced to pray "crouching to an Earl of Cork and his lady . . . or to those sea nymphs his daughters, with coronets upon their heads, their hair dishevelled, down upon their shoulders". The earl got his revenge by engineering Viceroy Wentworth's execution, years later.

His heir, Robert Boyle, is given a niche of his own on the monument. Boyle is famous above all for formulating Boyle's Law on the relationship between the pressure, volume and temperature of gases. He is less well-known for leaving a legacy to fund eight sermons a year, refuting "Atheists, Theists, Pagans, Jews and Mohammedans".

Jonathan Swift

Born at Hoey's Court near Dublin Castle in 1667, **Jonathan Swift** could read by the age of three, and at fifteen was accepted as a student at Trinity College. On graduating, he worked for the diplomat Sir William Temple and subsequently for the Church of England, hoping to secure "a fat deanery or a lean bishopric". This ambition clashed with his activities as a political pamphleteer, from 1704 onwards; as his pen had been deployed on behalf of the Tories, the incoming Whig administration of 1714 bore a grudge against Swift, who felt it wise to return to Dublin and take up the post of Dean of St Patrick's, which he had accepted the previous year.

Back home his commitment to Ireland and his social conscience grew, as expressed in a series of anonymous **tracts** during the 1720s. An early advocate of economic independence, Swift's *Proposal for the Universal Use of Irish Manufactures* argued that the Irish should burn all English imports, except coal. *The Drapier's Letters* exposed shady business deals, and *A Modest Proposal* bitterly suggested that the Irish poor could solve their problems by selling their babies to the rich, as food. He is now chiefly known for *Gulliver's Travels*, a dazzlingly diverse satire now too often misperceived as a children's story.

Besides his increasingly vitriolic writings, Swift was famous for his eccentricities and his mysterious relationship with **Esther Johnson**, known as "Stella". The daughter of Sir William Temple's housekeeper was variously rumoured to have been Swift's niece or sister, his secret bride or his platonic companion. Whatever the truth, Swift was heartbroken by her death, finishing his *Journal to Stella* in the darkened cathedral on the nights following her burial.

His final years were overshadowed by a malady causing giddiness, which Swift mistook for symptoms of insanity.

Eventually he *did* go mad, hailing the viceroy as "you fellow with the Blue String" and assaulting two clergymen in a carriage. As soon as Swift's death became public, admirers burst into the Deanery and cut off all his hair, carrying the locks away as souvenirs. In his will, he left money to build a mental hospital, which was one of the first in Europe when it opened in 1749.

Given Swift's reputation as a Dubliner and a patriot, he was astonishingly rude about both, calling Dublin "the most disagreeable place in Europe, at least to any but those who have been accustomed to it from their youth", in which case "a jail might be preferable"; and averring that "no man is thoroughly miserable unless he be condemned to live in Ireland".

Another curiosity is the **wooden door** leaning against a pier, once belonging to the cathedral's chapterhouse. In 1492, so the story goes, a quarrel arose between soldiers of the earls of Kildare and Ormond. Ormond barricaded himself in the chapter house, whereupon Kildare, eager to end hostilities, cut a hole in the door and stuck his arm through, inviting Ormond to shake hands. Peace was restored, and so the expression "chancing your arm" entered the English language.

In the northwest corner of the nave lies a stone **slab** with a Celtic cross that once marked the site of St Patrick's well. Marble statues and plaques commemorating such luminaries as the Marquis of Buckingham (the first Grand Master of the Knights of St Patrick) and the harpist Turlough Carolan, the "last of the Irish bards", are ranged along the north aisle.

The **north transept** is hung with flags of the Irish Regiments of the British army; 49,400 Irishmen died in World War I alone. In one corner are Swift's pulpit, chair and table.

ST PATRICK'S CATHEDRAL

Until 1869 the **choir** was used for investitures of the Knights of St Patrick – hence the helmets, swords and banners above the pews, scathingly described by Thackeray as "tawdry old rags and gimcracks" representing a "humbug of chivalry". A plain slab in the north aisle of the choir honours Duke Frederick Schomberg, slain at the Battle of the Boyne. As the tablet above relates, his heirs didn't care to erect a memorial, so his admirers had to make amends; in Swift's words, "The renown of his valour had greater power among strangers than had ties of blood among his kith and kin." Peering through the grille into the **Chapel of St Stephen**, you'll see the armchair used by William III at the thanksgiving service after his victory at Boyne. Also note the statue of Sir Benjamin Guinness's daughter, beneath a window inscribed "I was thirsty and ye gave me a drink."

The **south transept** (once the chapter house where Kildare chanced his arm) contains a magnificent stained-glass **window** and various opulent funerary monuments – that of Archbishop Marsh (see opposite) is the finest surviving carving by Grinling Gibbons in Ireland. In one corner is a small tablet dedicated by Swift to his manservant, Alexander McGee, "in memory of his discretion, fidelity and diligence in that humble station". McGee's discretion in the libel case arising from *The Drapier's Letters* (purportedly written by a humble tailor) saved Swift from financial ruin.

Plaques in the **south aisle** commemorate eminent Irish Protestants of the twentieth century, starting with Erskine Childers (Irish president 1973–74), whose father was executed by the Free State during the Civil War. The inscription relates how Childers never spoke of the war because his father made him promise on the eve of his execution not to do anything that might promote bitterness among the Irish people. The plaque in Irish honours Douglas Hyde, the founder of the Gaelic League, who became

Ireland's first president. At his funeral service in 1949, former government colleagues waited outside St Patrick's in their cars, adhering to a ruling which forbade them to enter a Protestant cathedral.

MARSH'S LIBRARY

Map 4, A8. Mon & Wed–Fri 10am–12.45pm & 2–5pm, Sat 10.30am–12.45pm; £1.

Almost right beside St Patrick's Cathedral, a crenellated wall with an arched gateway surrounds a Georgian edifice half faced in stone to match the cathedral. This is **Marsh's Library**, the oldest public library in Ireland, opened to "All Graduates and Gentlemen" in 1707. Its founder, Archbishop Narcissus Marsh, was a scholar and scientist who translated the Old Testament into Irish and first used the word "microphone" in his own works on acoustics. The core of the library is the collection of Edward Stillingfleet, archbishop of Worcester, whose entire collection of 10,000 books Marsh bought for £2500; donations by other clerics and bibliophiles have boosted the tally to 25,000 books.

Built by Sir William Robertson (the architect of Dublin Castle), it's a charming example of an eighteenth-century scholar's library, consisting of two L-shaped rooms whose oak bookcases have carved and lettered gables crowned by a bishop's mitre, and three alcoves or "cages" where readers were locked in with rare books. The middle one contains a cast of Stella's skull, and a case displays books owned by Swift, including a *History of the Great Rebellion*, with pencilled notations disparaging the Scots. The bindery for the conservation and repair of antique books (featured in *Ulysses*) has had the odd task of treating bullet-marks, as Marsh's Library was peppered by shots aimed at Jacob's Biscuit Factory in 1916 (see overleaf).

MARSH'S LIBRARY

AUNGIER STREET AND SOUTH GREAT GEORGE'S STREET

Between Marsh's Library and St Stephen's Green is an area of run-down flats bisected by **Aungier Street**, the seedier continuation of **South Great George's Street** at the Temple Bar end. Aungier Street is named after Francis Aungier, who developed this area on land seized from the Whitefriars Priory in 1537. An anonymous pamphlet of 1725 (possibly written by Swift) describes a throng of "Bawds with band-boxes, borrowed smocks, and scoured manteaus", apothecaries carrying "purges and potions" and "lap-dogs cleaning and dressing to go to church with their ladies". Today the street is renowned locally for its massage parlours, gentlemen's clubs and gay saunas.

There are, however, a number of places worth visiting as you follow the route up to Temple Bar. Easter Rising buffs may be curious about **Jacobs' Biscuit Factory**, a fortress-like complex where 150 rebels blocked a British advance from the Portobello Barracks for five days, as its walls proved impervious to rifle-fire and the narrow streets made it hard to use artillery. A crumbling wall bearing the Jacobs name shields remnants of the factory that are now incorporated into the Dublin Institute of Technology and the National Archives on Bishop Street, to the west of Aungier Street.

Raised in 1827 on the site of the bygone Carmelite priory slightly further up Aungier Street, **Whitefriar Street Carmelite Church** (Mon–Fri 8am–3.15pm, Sun 8am–7pm, bank holidays 10am–1pm) was blessed eight years later by Pope Gregory XVI's gift, that was said to be of the heart of St Valentine, patron saint of lovers. **Our Lady of Dublin**, a life-size, sixteenth-century Flemish oak statue of the Virgin and Child standing near the altar, is the only such image to have survived the sack of Ireland's monasteries. Hollowed-out and used as a cattle trough, it was rescued by a priest from a junk shop near St Mary's Abbey, whence it probably came.

Crossing over St Stephen's Street you hit South Great George's Street, lined with restaurants, pubs and the red-brick Gothic facade of the **Market Arcade** (Mon–Sat 10am–6pm), a Victorian market hall that sells jewellery, secondhand books, records and clothes – always worth a browse.

Exchequer Street, running parallel to the arcade and surrounded on both sides by elegant, red-brick Victorian buildings is one of the prettiest small streets in Dublin. Its name recalls the Exchequer that stood here in Tudor times; the word itself derives from a chequered tablecloth that was used to make and demonstrate tax calculations to illiterates.

AUNGIER STREET AND SOUTH GREAT GEORGE'S STREET

The Liberties and Kilmainham

To the west of St Patrick's Cathedral lies the sprawling district of the **Liberties**, so called after the patchwork of parishes with charters giving its residents "freedom from toll, passage, portage, lestage, pavage, quayage and carriage". Originally the area was known as Meath's Liberty, after the earl of Meath who invited Huguenot refugees from France to settle in the quarter known as the Coombe in 1650. Over the following sixty years the 10,000 Huguenots who settled here had a profound effect on the small and undeveloped city, introducing poplin- and silk-weaving, founding a horticultural society and encouraging the wine trade. However, in the 1770s industry in the Liberties was hit by competition from imported fabrics, unemployment soared and the area became a slum. As an American doctor wrote sarcastically: "Winds and rain have *liberty* to enter freely through the windows of half the houses – the pigs have *liberty* to ramble about – the landlord has *liberty* to take possession of most of his tenements – the silk-weaver has *liberty* to starve or beg."

The Liberty and the Ormond boys

Until the early nineteenth century, rivalry between the Liberty Boys (tailor- and weaver-apprentices of the Coombe) and the Ormond Boys (butchers from Ormond Market on the quays) frequently erupted into pitched battles of up to a thousand men. Captives were sometimes hamstrung and impaled on the hooks of their own butchers' stalls.

The harshness of working-class life was partly to blame for this sort of brutality. In the late eighteenth century landlords charged one to two shillings a week for a single room, so two or even four families would cohabitate to lighten the rent. At the same time, over 19,000 weavers faced unemployment due to the import of Indian muslin and French silks. To protect their jobs they formed gangs who went around cutting "every foreign dress worn by man or woman, no matter of what rank", and kidnapping haberdashers, dragging them through the mud to Weaver's Square, where they were tarred and feathered.

Although the Liberties have maintained their traditional self-sufficiency and many families are able to trace their local roots back for generations, there is little in the way of "sights" to attract tourists beyond the **markets** and **antique shops** on Back Lane and Francis Street.

Conversely, the area further west – Kilmainham – has less atmosphere but several bona fide attractions. The **Guinness Hop Store** on Crane Street reveals all you might wish to know about the famous stout produced at the nearby Guinness Brewery. Further out, the former Royal Hospital Kilmainham houses the **Irish Museum of Modern Art**, a venue for temporary exhibitions of contemporary work. Nearby is **Kilmainham Jail**, a prison indelibly associated with the struggle for Irish freedom and now a fascinating museum of penal and revolutionary history.

Wolfe Tone, the United Irishmen and the Rebellion of 1798

The French Revolution of 1789 had a profound effect on Ireland, where the credo *Liberté, Egalité, Fraternité* inspired a Protestant barrister, **Theobald Wolfe Tone**, to issue *An Argument on Behalf of the Catholics in Ireland* (1791), urging all denominations to unite in the cause of Irish freedom. Within months of its publication, societies of **United Irishmen** were formed in Dublin and Belfast, aiming to achieve the emancipation of Catholics and Dissenters. Though their "Back Lane Parliament" avowed change by constitutional means, the movement turned towards revolution after Wolfe Tone, exiled in 1794, travelled to the new republics of the USA and France trying to win support for an insurrection.

The **Rebellion of 1798** was the first major rising against British rule since the seventeenth century, and set a precedent for future attempts. Plans for the revolt were dealt a severe blow when, in March of that year, most of the leaders of the National Directory of the United Irishmen were arrested in Dublin on the word of spies who had infiltrated their movement. The leader, Lord Edward Fitzgerald, a radical aristocrat, evaded arrest but his freedom was shortlived as two months later he was captured and mortally wounded. Martial law was imposed and local uprisings took place in County Dublin, County Mayo and particularly County Wexford, where rebels made progress towards Dublin before being defeated in the town of Arklow. These local rebellions were virtually over when an 1100-strong French invasion force landed near Killala in County Sligo in August. After some success, the Franco-Irish army was defeated in County Longford on

September 8. More than 11,000 Irish fell in battle and 2000 were hanged or deported; the British lost 1600 men. In November a second French force, with Wolfe Tone on board, was intercepted off Donegal. Sentenced to death and denied the honour of a firing squad, Wolfe Tone cut his throat with a penknife to avoid being hanged, drawn and quartered as a traitor.

Henceforth revered as the founder of Irish **Republicanism**, Wolfe Tone was buried at Bodenstown in County Kildare – a place of pilgrimage for many Nationalists. On the anniversary of his birth (June 20, 1763), members of the Fianna Fáil party travel here to pay their respects.

In contrast, a few critics of Wolfe Tone argue that his actions destroyed any chance of the Anglo-Irish ruling class conceding reforms, for in response to the 1798 Rebellion Britain engineered the Act of Union, which dissolved the Irish Parliament and fettered Ireland to Britain more strongly than ever.

WEST FROM TAILORS' HALL

On Back Lane, near Christchurch Place, stands Dublin's last surviving guildhall, **Tailors' Hall**, a modest brick structure that was rescued from demolition when An Taisce (Ireland's National Trust) bought the building and restored it as their headquarters. Its assembly hall contains a plaque listing the masters of the tailors' guild from 1491 to 1841 and a gallery from which Wolfe Tone and Napper Tandy addressed the "Back Lane Parliament" in 1792 (see box opposite).

Directly opposite Tailors' Hall are **Mother Redcap's Market** (Fri–Sun 11am–5pm) and pub, both modern substitutes for their predecessors in an area that was bulldozed away in the 1960s. The market sells kitsch and household goods and the pub has live music at weekends.

Christ Church flea market is held outside Tailors' Hall at weekends, and Francis Street, to the west, is fast becoming the centre of Dublin's **antiques** trade, with numerous shops down the road from the **Iveagh Market Hall** (Tues–Sat 9am–5pm). As its name suggests, this was another bequest by Lord Iveagh of the Guinness family, who is said to have been used as the model for the winking face that's among the stone heads carved above the arches of the hall.

At the bottom of Francis Street you'll find the **Coombe**, an ancient route and one of the Liberties' main thoroughfares. Slum clearances have spared the **gateway** of the old Coombe Maternity Hospital, founded in 1826 as a result of the plight of two poor women and their newborn babies, who died in a blizzard while attempting to reach the Rotunda Hospital on the northside. Inscribed in concrete behind the gateway is an odd list of nicknames of well-known Dublin characters including Bang Bang, a shell-shocked veteran famous for "shooting" people with an imaginary gun, who died in 1981. Other intriguing names include Johnny Wet Bread, Nancy Needle Balls, Stab the Rasher and Harry Wank. **Meath Street**, across the road, is the site of an indoor market for cut-price clothes and tat – nothing to get excited about, but a good place to imbibe the atmosphere of the Liberties.

At the end of Meath Street you'll come to **Thomas Street West,** leading from High Street to the Guinness Brewery, on the middle section of which stands the **Church of SS Augustine and John**, possessor of Dublin's tallest spire; it was designed by Edward Pugin, whose father, Augustus, played a leading role in Britain's Gothic Revival. A discreet plaque about 200m away on *Laws Pub* commemorates the arrest of Lord Edward Fitzgerald, a leader of the 1798 Rebellion, who died of wounds received in the struggle.

Robert Emmet

The Thomas Street area is associated with a brief insurrection in 1803, led by 24-year-old Robert Emmet. The youngest son of a distinguished Dublin doctor and brother of Thomas Emmet, a leading United Irishman, Robert was too young to take part in the 1798 Rebellion, but in that year he followed in his brother's footsteps by becoming the leader of the United Irish movement at Trinity College. In protest at a clampdown on United Irish activities at the college, Emmet took his name off the college register and began to formulate plans for his own uprising. He sought help from the French and in an effort to secure weapons sailed to France in 1802, only to be frustrated by the French leadership's lack of commitment to his cause.

He returned to Ireland in October of the same year and set about executing a plan for rebellions in Dublin and Ulster. Having abandoned the idea of staging an insurrection to coincide with a French invasion of Britain, on July 23, 1803, Emmett put into action a plan to take Dublin Castle, which held the British forces' arsenal. The consequent killing of popular Chief Justice Lord Kilwarden and his nephew lost Emmet a lot of support, and the rebellion soon degenerated into a drunken fiasco, with Emmet's forces failing even to reach the Castle. Emmet was forced to flee, but rather than leave the country he returned to see his lover Sarah Curran, and was captured in a house near Harold's Cross in Dublin. Sentenced to death, Emmet assured his immortality with an eloquent oration which ended: "when my nation takes her place among the nations of the earth, then, and not till then, let my epitaph be written." Emmet was hanged and decapitated outside St Catherine's Church on Meath Street on September 20, aged 25.

THE GUINNESS BREWERY AND HOP STORE

Thomas Street becomes James's Street as it passes the **Guinness Brewery**, whose chimneys, tanks and wonderful aroma dominate the neighbourhood. The St James's Gate Brewery covers 64 acres on both sides of the road, making it one of the largest in the world. However, when 34-year-old Arthur Guinness leased the derelict brewery in 1759, the industry in Dublin was at a low ebb; ale was notoriously bad, and whiskey, gin or poteen were preferred throughout rural Ireland. Although he began by brewing ale, Guinness soon switched to producing a new black brew called "porter" (because of its popularity with the porters at London's Covent Garden and Billingsgate markets). His new formula proved so successful that it was being exported to England within a decade; by the nineteenth century brewing had become such a major industry that brewers were elevated to the House of Lords. An old joke has an outraged peer of ancient lineage asking, "Who is this fellow Moyne, anyway?" the reply being "Moyne's a Guinness". Today, the Guinness Brewery produces about sixty percent of all the beer consumed in Ireland (2,500,000 pints a day) and is the world's largest exporter of beer, exporting some 300 million pints a year.

Sadly the brewery is not open to the public, but you can learn all about the company and its products at the **Guinness Hop Store** (Map 5, C8), a four-storey building on Crane Street, just off Thomas Street West, which has been converted into a shrine to the dark stuff.

The Guinness Hop Store is open April–Sept Mon–Sat 9.30am–5pm, Sun 10.30am–4pm; Oct–March Mon–Sat 9.30am–4pm, Sun noon–4pm; £5, students £4, children £1. Bus #68A or #78A from Aston Quay.

You'll find a replica brewery here, plus a pub, a restaurant, a gift shop and various exhibition rooms. The best of these is the array of Guinness's award-winning advertisements, from the work of John Gilroy, whose animal cartoons and painful puns are still used to this day, to modern masterpieces such as the surfing ad (which led the songwriter Christy Moore to ponder "how yer man stayed up on that surfboard after thirteen pints of stout"). The other floors are something of a disappointment, especially the low-budget video tracing the history of Guinness brewing in the city, which, without a hint of irony, celebrates Brendan Behan's and Patrick Kavanagh's "healthy relationship" with Arthur Guinness' "eldest son". You'll end the tour by tasting what is arguably the best Guinness in Dublin – arguably because the honours traditionally went to *Mulligan's* pub in Poolbeg Street, which still has its supporters (see p.250).

To the west of the Hop Store rises the fifty-metre-high **St Patrick's Tower**, the tallest smock windmill (ie with a revolving top) in the British Isles. Originally used to facilitate work at Roe's Distillery on the other side of Watling Street from the Guinness Brewery, it's topped with a St Patrick's weathervane, but no longer has any sails.

ST PATRICK'S AND ST JAMES'S HOSPITALS

Further along Thomas Street the road forks at an obelisk that's optimistically equipped with four sundials. The road to the right, Bow Lane West, leads off to **St Patrick's Hospital**, known as "**Swift's Hospital**", having been founded for the care of the mentally ill by Jonathan Swift in 1749 (see p.85), whose bequest included a witty explanation: "He gave the little wealth he had, to build a house for fools and mad: And shew'd by one satiric touch, No nation wanted it so much." The larger **St James's Hospital**, off nearby James's Street, incorporates part of the old South Dublin Union, a nineteenth-century workhouse that was a rebel stronghold during the Easter Rising. Before becoming a workhouse it had been a foundling's hospital, where conditions were so wretched that over forty thousand babies died in thirty years.

IRISH MUSEUM OF MODERN ART

Map 3, B5. Tues–Sat 10am–5pm, Sun noon–5.30pm; free. Bus #79 or #90 from Aston Quay.

To get to the **Irish Museum of Modern Art** (IMMA), it's best to follow Bow Lane West until *Murray's* pub, taking the road opposite, Irwin Street, which leads to the back entrance of the museum. Much criticized when it opened in 1991, the museum is now acknowledged to have proven its worth. The project was backed by the government of Charles Haughey but many felt that the £20 million spent on converting a derelict hospital into a gallery could have been better used for buying artworks, and the end result was reviled as a blank space which denied the character of the building. Criticism has faded as IMMA has increased its holdings through bequests and loans and asserted its stature with bold exhibitions. There is no permanent display, only temporary shows, often two or three at a time.

You can usually expect to find one exhibition of stuff on loan, and another selected from IMMA's holdings. Items on long loan from other galleries include works by Picasso, Miró and Modigliani, and contemporary artists such as Gilbert and George, Damien Hirst, Richard Long, Julian Schnabel and Rachel Whiteread. The Madden-Arnholtz Collection, on display until 2001, includes works by Dürer, Goya, Hogarth and Rembrandt. There's a good bookshop by the lobby and a fine café in the basement of the north wing.

IMMA occupies the former **Royal Hospital Kilmainham**. Built by Sir William Robinson (who restored Dublin Castle) in 1680–87, this was one of the first classical-style public buildings in Ireland. Austerely elegant in shades of grey, it was modelled on Les Invalides in Paris and served as a home for retired veterans. Its rules decreed that if any inmate "presumed to marry, he be immediately turned out of the house and the hospital clothes taken from him". Group tours (Tues & Fri 10am, 11.45am, 2.30pm & 4pm; free; places must be booked in advance on ✆612 9900) are available of the north wing, whose lofty chapel has a magnificent Baroque ceiling and woodcarvings by the Huguenot master James Tarbery. You'll also see the panelled Great Hall, hung with portraits of monarchs and viceroys, and the Master's Residence.

When leaving the IMMA, depart by the arch in the west wing and aim for the **Kilmainham Gate** at the end of a tree-lined avenue. Formerly the Richmond Tower and sited at Watling Street Bridge near the Guinness Brewery, it was moved here in 1846 to improve access to Heuston Station. The avenue passes by **Bully's Acre**, one of Dublin's oldest cemeteries, and brings you out across the main road from Kilmainham Jail – the greatest attraction in this part of town.

KILMAINHAM JAIL

Map 3, A6. April–Sept daily 9.30am–4.45pm; Oct–March Mon–Fri 9.30am–4pm, Sun 10am–4.45pm; £3, students/children £1.25, family £7.50. Bus #51, #51B, #78A or #79 from the city centre.

A forbidding hulk on Inchicore Road, **Kilmainham Jail** is enshrined in Irish history as a symbol of political martyrdom and oppression.

Opened in 1796, Kilmainham replaced an earlier prison that epitomized the evils criticized by the English penal reformer John Howard, whose remedies were first applied in Ireland. Howard advocated the separation of prisoners to prevent criminal associations and encourage individuals to repent in solitude. In accordance with his stress on hygiene, the new jail was sited on a hill to ensure good ventilation. Unfortunately, it was built from a limestone that weeps in wet weather, so perennial damp and cold took a heavy toll on prisoners' health. Over the 128 years of Kilmainham's existence, some 100,000 men and women passed through its gates. Between 1845 and 1847, at the height of the Great Famine, it was swamped with destitute folk jailed for stealing food or begging, resulting in wretched conditions that made a mockery of Howard's intentions. Only after the Famine had abated did reformers build a new East Wing. Turned into a military detention barracks in 1911, Kilmainham later held insurgents from the 1916 Easter Rising. Even the end of British rule brought no respite, for 150 Republican women were interned here during the Civil War, including the daughter and the widow of two of the martyrs of 1916. The last prisoner to be released by the Free State in 1924 was Éamon de Valera – subsequently elected prime minister, then president, of Ireland.

Shut down after the Civil War, Kilmainham was left to rot till 1960, when volunteers (many of them ex-inmates) began to restore it as a memorial. Now one of Dublin's best museums, it can be visited only on **guided tours** (every 45min, until 1hr 15min before closing).

While waiting to start the tour, visit the **exhibition** on conditions at Kilmainham and the development of hanging. It was a Dublin surgeon, Samuel Haughton, who devised the "long drop" method, which the Victorians saw as an improvement on the old "short drop" technique which slowly asphyxiated victims. Altogether, over 140 hangings took place at Kilmainham, 24 of them involving political prisoners. Upstairs covers the struggle for independence,

KILMAINHAM JAIL

with numerous items relating to the Fenians, the Easter Rising and the IRA, including Countess Markievicz's dispatch-bag and Michael Collins's walking stick.

The tour begins in the **East Wing**, a lofty hall flanked by tiers of cells and walkways. Like many Victorian prisons it was based on philosopher Jeremy Bentham's "Panopticon", a layout that maximized light (thought to be morally uplifting) and enabled constant surveillance of prisoners. Its architect, John McCurdy, had previously refurbished the *Shelbourne Hotel*.

In the Catholic **chapel** you'll hear the moving story of Joseph Plunkett and Grace Gifford, who were married here on the eve of Plunkett's execution. British soldiers stood by with fixed bayonets as the vows were read. Immediately afterwards the newlyweds were separated; later they were granted ten minutes together – timed by a stopwatch – before Plunkett was taken out and shot. A short, emotive **film** on the history of Kilmainham and the struggle for independence leaves you in no doubt as to who the heroes and villains were, gliding over the moral and political ambiguities of the Civil War.

In the crumbling **West Wing** a chill seeps into your bones as the guide describes conditions at the prison: there was no glass in the windows nor any heating (there still isn't); an hour of candlelight each evening was the sole concession to comfort. Occasionally, certain prisoners were accorded privileges – when Parnell was jailed for sedition, he had a room with a fireplace and armchairs and was allowed to give interviews. Most, however, were obliged to do hard labour, oakum-picking or stone-beaking; the practice of "shot-drill" – passing cannonballs from one man to another – ceased after a prisoner threw one at the governor. Among those held here were Robert Emmet, the "Invincibles", and fourteen leaders of the Easter Rising on the night before their executions.

KILMAINHAM JAIL

You will also see the **yacht** *Asgard*, used by Erskine Childers and his sister Molly to run guns into Ireland in 1914. Despite being half-English, Childers was a devoted Republican; in 1923 he was executed at Beggar's Bush Barracks (see p.152) for the possession of a revolver given to him by Collins, when the two were still allies.

The inner northside

Much of the **inner northside** was developed in the eighteenth century by Luke Gardiner, a banker who married into the Mountjoys and Blessingtons and bought land – which had once belonged to St Mary's Abbey – from families who had fallen on hard times. Profits from commercial premises near the quays were used to finance **Henrietta Street**, a luxury development on Constitution Hill (then open country), followed by Gardiners Mall (now **O'Connell Street**). With the establishment of the Wide Streets Commission in 1757, Gardiner's schemes became the blueprint for a whole new city of elegant terraces and squares for society's elite. Soon, however, rival developments on the southside began to entice them away, and the Act of Union sunk the property market after Gardiner's grandson had invested heavily in Mountjoy Square. This proved to be the swansong of the dynasty, and of the northside too.

Although the present-day northside has many inner city problems, it also displays a vitality often missing in the more sedate southside. Certainly not as well preserved as its counterpart across the river, the northside's significance lies more in its associations with events and movements central to Dublin and Ireland's history – the **GPO**, which played a seminal role in the history of independent Ireland, is probably its most important landmark. And as home to the **Abbey Theatre**, **Dublin Writers' Museum**, **Municipal Gallery of Modern Art** and **Croke Park GAA Museum** it offers plenty of cultural interest too.

O'CONNELL STREET AND AROUND

The commercial hub of the northside and Dublin's main axis, **O'Connell Street**. was laid out by Luke Gardiner in the 1740s. Originally envisaged as an exclusive residential square, it became a public highway following the completion of Gandon's Carlisle Bridge (1794), causing Dublin's centre of gravity to shift eastwards from the old axis of Capel Street. Renamed Sackville Street after the British viceroy, the avenue was 45m wide (one of the widest in Europe) and lined with grand edifices that anticipated the Parisian boulevards of Haussmann by a century. Today the street's facades are marred by neon and plastic (leading one wag to describe its architectural style as "neon classical"), particularly near the Liffey, where buildings were destroyed in the Easter Rising of 1916.

At the southern end of the street near O'Connell Bridge stands the imposing statue of "The Liberator", **Daniel O'Connell**. Smack in the centre of the street and staring proudly towards the river, O'Connell is flanked at ground level by winged figures symbolizing his patriotism, courage, eloquence and fidelity (closer inspection of "courage" reveals a bullet hole gained during the War of Independence). Born in 1775 in County Kerry,

O'Connell was elected MP for Clare in 1828 and barred from entering parliament on the grounds of his Catholicism. He was re-elected in 1830 after Emancipation and became the first Catholic Lord Mayor of Dublin in 1841. Having secured the backing of Dublin for the repeal of the Union in 1843, he then organized mass rallies to put pressure on Westminster. These scared the British so much that they jailed him for sedition. Though he was released after a few months, O'Connell's health was failing; the Famine decimated his rural following, and in 1847 he died. His statue (financed by subscription) was unveiled in 1882, and his name was bestowed upon the new, wider bridge that replaced the Carlisle. Soon, Dubliners began to call Sackville Street "O'Connell Street", though its name was not officially changed until 1924. Directly below the O'Connell statue you can see one of the city's first public examples of nationalist iconography in the female figure of Erin, unshackled and pointing towards her liberator.

Further north, where the street is crossed by Abbey Street, the central strip is graced by smaller statues of two lesser nineteenth-century figures: William Smith O'Brien, leader of the Young Ireland Party, and Sir John Gray, the publisher of the influential *Freeman's Journal*. More arresting is the statue of **Jim Larkin**, the trade unionist who led Dublin's workers during the lock-out strike of 1913 (see p.316). It shows Larkin haranguing a crowd, as he did from a window of the *Imperial Hotel* across the road (now **Clery's** department store – see p.286), shortly before mounted police charged the demonstrators, killing two and injuring hundreds. The figure's huge hands, outstretched in a classic oratorical pose, give a sense of Larkin's imposing physicality; a larger-than-life demagogue, he made a formidable opponent, as Dublin's employers found out. At the foot of the statue is a poetic inscription in Gaelic, which, roughly

O'CONNELL STREET AND AROUND

translated, means "the great appear great because we are on our knees; let us rise".

The Hot Press Museum

Map 4, D3. Daily 10am–6pm; £6, students £4, family prices £12–16.

At this point you can make a couple of interesting diversions. Turning left down Abbey Street Middle, you'll come to the **Hot Press Museum**, a state-of-the-art multimedia exhibition which traces the history of Irish music.

After entering the centre via a replica stage door (an attempt to reproduce the sensation of a band walking onstage), you come to a display exploring the roots of Irish traditional music, which leads to an exhibit on the uniquely Irish phenomenon of the "Showband" (the formative musical world of Van Morrison). If the audio accompaniment and high-tech visuals aren't enough to keep your attention, there's all manner of memorabilia, from a cup and saucer signed by Daniel O'Donnell to a postcard from the late Luke Kelly, written while touring with the Dubliners. As you move into the punk era, the tour concentrates on Dublin bands such as the Boomtown Rats (Bob Geldof's "unwashed" Live Aid T-shirt is one of the displays), while the north is represented by the formidable duo of Derry's Undertones and Belfast's Stiff Little Fingers. Other parts of the museum include a section given over to the meteoric rise of U2 (complete with the original spray-painted security hut that stood outside Windmill Lane Studios where the band first recorded) and a special feature on Irish women in music (which includes Sinéad O'Connor's family scrapbook). The tour ends with a short film where many of those featured in the exhibition reflect on the nature of Irish music and musicians. The centre also has a gift shop, concert venue and decent restaurant.

The Abbey Theatre

Map 4, E3.

In the opposite direction, on the other side of O'Connell Street on Abbey Street Lower, stands the **Abbey Theatre** – the present structure, a much-maligned piece of 1960s Modernism made slightly more distinguished by the addition of a portico in 1991, is a replacement for the original Abbey, which burned down in 1951. In effect Ireland's national theatre, the Abbey has its beginnings in the Irish Literary Society founded by **W.B. Yeats** and **Douglas Hyde**, which, in 1899, became the Irish Literary Theatre. The site on Abbey Street (formerly a morgue) was bought by the English tea heiress Lady Gregory, the patron of Yeats and a driving force behind the Irish cultural revival at the turn of the century, and the playhouse itself opened in 1904, with Yeats and Lady Gregory as its first directors. Their 1907 production of John Millington Synge's tragicomedy *The Playboy of the Western World* caused outrage – one critic called it "the outpouring of a morbid, unhealthy mind ever seeking on the dunghill of life for the nastiness that lies concealed there" – and nightly affrays needed up to five hundred policemen to prevent bloodshed. In 1926 there was an equally fierce reaction to Séan O'Casey's *The Plough and the Stars*, which took a cynical view of the Easter Rising and displayed the Free State flag in a pub frequented by prostitutes – as the audience booed on opening night, Yeats rebuked them, "You have disgraced yourselves again. Is this to be an ever-recurring celebration of the arrival of an Irish genius?"

For more on the Abbey Theatre, see p.265.

As time went on, a general uneasiness about one theatre receiving the lion's share of state subsidies became widespread – a conviction that would lead to the establishment of the Gate Theatre (see p.116). The Abbey still produces dazzling drama, with two auditoriums and companies on the premises: the Abbey, devoted to the Irish classics and contemporary dramatists like Brian Friel and Frank McGuinness; and the **Peacock Theatre** (see p.267), which shows new experimental drama.

The GPO

Map 4, D3.

Back on O'Connell Street, beyond Larkin's statue, looms the **General Post Office** (**GPO**) designed by Francis Johnston, whose huge Ionic portico is still scarred by gunfire from the Easter Rising (see box, p.110), when the building was used as the insurgents' headquarters. From its porch, Pádraig Pearse read the Proclamation of the Irish Republic to onlookers bemused by the sight of his men smashing windows and sandbagging them with mailbags. For six days they held out against British attacks, until the GPO was set ablaze and survivors retreated to nearby Moore Street, where Pearse and Connolly agreed to surrender (see p.112). Their subsequent martyrdom conferred iconic status on the Rising and the GPO itself, which is still a focal point for political protests.

In the foyer, the building's historical significance is reinforced by a sequence of paintings by contemporary Irish artist Norman Teeling, depicting scenes from 1916. Near the foyer's main window stands the city's finest public sculpture, a bronze statue entitled *The Death of Cúchulainn*. Exquisitely wrought, the statue was created by Oliver Sheppard in 1935 and depicts the death of the mythical warrior Cúchulainn. Legend has it that Cúchulainn tied himself to a tree so that he could fight even when dying – his enemies were so afraid to approach him they only did so when a raven rested on his shoulder, proving beyond doubt that he was actually dead. The statue also features in a hilarious episode in Samuel Beckett's *Murphy*, where one character attacks Cúchulainn's buttocks (though in reality it is only the top half of the warrior's body that is revealed).

O'Connell Street Upper

North of the GPO, after the intersection of Henry Street and Earl Street North, is **O'Connell Street Upper**. At one time this section of O'Connell Street was dominated by **Nelson's Pillar**, located at the crossroads themselves and execrated by W.B. Yeats as "that monstrosity that destroys the view of the finest street in Europe". Erected 32 years before Nelson's Column in London's Trafalgar Square, this symbol of British imperialism survived several attempts to destroy it, until a bomb on the fiftieth anniversary of the Rising left it so damaged that it had to be demolished. Nelson's head now lies in the Civic Museum (see p.24). The monument's demise put paid to an old joke that O'Connell Street had statues honouring three notorious adulterers: O'Connell, Nelson and Parnell (see p.114). The site of the pillar will soon be occupied by a huge, illuminated stainless-steel spike, designed by London architect Ian Ritchie. It's intended to represent Dublin's hopes for the new millennium, but many commentators have argued that a city with a chronic heroin problem doesn't need a steel needle as its focal point. Local wags have already dubbed it "the stiletto in the ghetto", continuing a tradition for caustic rhyming couplets. (The Molly Malone statue near Grafton Street is "the tart with the cart", that of Kavanagh on the Grand Canal is "the crank on the bank", and Oscar Wilde in Merrion Square is "the fag on the crag".)

The Easter Rising

The heroic **Easter Rising** of April 1916 was one of the key events leading to Irish self-government. At the time however, most Dubliners saw it as a calamity; many Nationalists regarded it as a botched and futile attempt, while Loyalists reckoned it high treason, fermented by Imperial Germany.

The Rising was conceived by the **Irish Republican Brotherhood** (IRB) or "Fenians", a revolutionary organization dating back to 1858, led by a new generation of activists including **Pádraig Pearse** and **Joseph Plunkett.** For manpower and arms they relied on support from two legal militias: the **Citizen Army** under **James Connolly**, who helped in drawing up the battle plan and was given operational command; and the **Irish Volunteers** headed by Éoin MacNeill, who only agreed to commit his forces after Pearse showed him a forged document from Dublin Castle, ordering the suppression of the Volunteers. The final element was a shipment of arms from Germany, whose delivery was to be arranged by **Sir Roger Casement**, an ex-British diplomat turned Irish rebel.

Things started to go wrong quickly. The ship arrived prematurely and left without delivering its cargo, and Casement was caught by the British. MacNeill, on learning that he had been duped, revoked the mobilization order by placing notices in the Sunday papers, which resulted in only a minority of the 10,000 Volunteers turning up the next day. Though both mishaps foredoomed the Rising, its strategy was already flawed by Connolly's belief that "a capitalist government would never use artillery against private property". While the exact number of insurgents is uncertain (somewhere between 700 and 1750), the British ultimately committed over 20,000 troops to crush them.

The first shots were fired at noon on **Easter Monday**. A group of insurgents assaulted the castle, other units seized the

GPO, the Four Courts and sites such as Jacob's Biscuit Factory and Jameson's Distillery, which overlooked the routes from British barracks into the centre. As Pearse emerged from the GPO to read the Proclamation of the Irish Republic, his comrades were fortifying their positions against a British response. Initial attacks were beaten back, but the tide turned once reinforcements arrived from England with artillery. After six days of bitter fighting, which destroyed Sackville Street and other areas, the insurgents surrendered and were led away through jeering crowds.

This reaction was perhaps to be expected, since the Rising left 1351 people dead or gravely wounded, 179 buildings smouldering, and much of Dublin's population needing aid. The hostility towards the rebels was exacerbated by the fact that the Rising occurred on the first anniversary of the battle of Gallipoli, when many Dublin families were in mourning for the menfolk who had perished there.

In the 1980s the Corporation commissioned two other monuments along more whimsical lines. With its rakishly tilted hat and carefree air, the **James Joyce statue** outside *Café Kylemore* on the corner of Earl Street North captures the style of a writer who was always dapper despite his indigence. Further up O'Connell Street Upper is the recumbent **Anna Livia Fountain,** representing Joyce's personification of the River Liffey in *Finnegans Wake* – nicknamed "the floozie in the jacuzzi" or "the whore in the sewer" (which rhymes in a Dublin accent), she's treated as a rubbish bin.

On the central strip stands a **statue of Father Matthew** (1790–1856), the "Apostle of Temperance", whose Pioneer Total Abstinence Movement, founded in 1838, persuaded five million Irish (out of eight million) to take a pledge of teetotalism, and reduced the production of whiskey by half;

its influence is still widespread in a country that, despite the stereotypical image, has a higher percentage of non-drinkers than any other in Europe.

Many bus tours start at the offices of Bus Éireann and Dublin Bus, opposite the Father Matthew statue at no. 59 (see pp.10 & 12).

On the corner of O'Connell Street Upper and Cathal Brugha Street, the **Gresham Hotel** (see p.204) is Dublin's finest after the *Shelbourne* and surpasses it for nostalgia. This was where Michael Collins often met his agents during the War of Independence. After the Nationalists split over the Anglo-Irish Treaty, the anti-Treaty "Irregulars" led by Cathal Brugha and de Valera made it their headquarters during the insurrection of July 1922. Following a week of fighting that left central Dublin in ruins for the second time in six years, Brugha ordered his men to surrender but refused to do so himself and was mortally wounded outside the hotel.

O'Connell Street ends at a crossroads, where the **Parnell Monument** proclaims in gold letters: "No man has a right to fix the boundary to the march of a nation. No man has a right to say to his country, Thus far shalt thou go and no further. . . "

Moore Street

Turn left at the GPO and you're into Henry Street, an earthier version of Grafton Street, where black-market cigarettes are openly touted in front of department stores. To the right lies Moore Street, which from Monday to Saturday is more or less taken over by **Moore Street Market** (see p.283), where the loquacious vendors revel in their reputation as "true" Dubliners. The street also has historical significance; at no. 16 there's a small plaque commemorating the site where survivors from the GPO laid up in the back of a fish-and-chip shop – they decided against a fighting retreat through Henry Street and Ormond market to avoid further civilian casualties and gave themselves up to British soldiers. This shop is now a butchers, aptly called Plunkett's. Apropos of names, Henry Street, Moore Street and Earl Street are all named after **Henry Moore, earl of Drogheda**, who even managed to squeeze in a lane called "Of Lane" leading into Drogheda Street, so that his name and title would be blazoned across maps of Dublin.

St Mary's Pro-Cathedral

On the other side of O'Connell Street, and running parallel to it, Marlborough Street is home to **St Mary's Pro-Cathedral** (daily 8am–7pm). In 1814, Dublin's Protestants were up in arms about the plan to build a Catholic cathedral on O'Connell Street (where the GPO now stands), so the Castle decreed that St Mary's Pro-Cathedral be tucked away down a side road, with its facade, based on the Temple of Theseus in Athens, facing away from O'Connell Street. It was here in 1847 that funeral rites were performed over the body of Daniel O'Connell, brought back from Genoa for burial; crowds lined the streets all the way from the Custom House to the Marlborough Street Chapel (as it then was). St Mary's is Dublin's principal Catholic church and every Sunday at 11am you can hear Latin Mass sung by its famous **Palestrina Choir**, where the tenor John McCormack began his career in 1904.

PARNELL SQUARE

Map 4, C1.

At the end of O'Connell Street lies **Parnell Square**, one of the few on the northside which wasn't begun by Luke Gardiner. The credit goes to Sir Benjamin Mosse, the

Charles Stewart Parnell

"There is something vulgar in all success. The greatest men fail, or seem to have failed." So said Oscar Wilde of **Charles Stewart Parnell**, the "uncrowned king of Ireland".

Parnell was born into the Anglo-Irish Protestant hierarchy in Avondale, County Wicklow, in 1846. His family had originated in Cheshire and purchased an estate in Wicklow in the seventeenth century. His great-grandfather was Chancellor of the Irish Exchequer, and his mother the daughter of an American admiral, a connection that would subsequently bring financial rewards.

Parnell's nationalism came to the fore early with his devotion to the **Home Rule movement**, calling for the restoration of Irish self-government. This ensured his election to parliament in 1875, where his approach was one of obstruction – to delay and interfere with the passing of Bills – a policy much approved by the militant Fenians. The latter's support lost him favour in certain circles, but led to his commitment to the cause of land reform – Parnell recognizing that the move towards Ireland's autonomy would never prosper while the rights of tenant-farmers lay unprotected – and in 1879 he became president of the **Irish National Land League**. He sought financial backing in the USA, raising the colossal sum of £70,000 and the next year, on re-election, became the leader of the Irish Home Rule Party.

The **Phoenix Park Murders** in 1882 (see p.146) marked a major turning point for the affairs of the Home Rule movement. Parnell had already found himself imprisoned in Kilmainham jail that year on charges of sedition for his Land League activities (the League was later declared illegal after urging tenants to withhold payments of rent to absentee landlords, but revived in 1884) and attempts were made to implicate him in the murders. He denounced the crime in parliament and, in so doing, revived his own popularity at home, but Gladstone's Liberal government reacted by hurrying through a Prevention of Crimes Act, which, by temporarily abolishing trial by jury and increasing police powers, further diminished Ireland's administrative scope.

The Liberals' proposal to renew the Crimes Act in 1885 prompted Parnell to negotiate with the Tories, but the relationship didn't last long, and, with his support returned to the Liberals, he flung the Irish vote behind Gladstone, resulting in the fall of the short-lived first Salisbury administration. Returned to power, Gladstone was now committed to Home Rule but when the bill was put to parliament, his own party members defected and it was defeated. A consequent appeal to the country was overwhelmingly rejected and a new Tory government was elected in 1886 with a Unionist majority of more than a hundred. Parnell and the Irish Party no longer held the balance of power.

The affair that finally deposed Parnell, however, was personal rather than political. Named as co-respondent in a divorce case brought by Captain William O'Shea against his wife Katherine in 1890, his relationship with **Kitty O'Shea** became public knowledge. The decree was granted with costs against Parnell – public disgrace followed and he lost the chair of his party. Parnell now carried what was left of the fight back to Ireland but, with clerical condemnation there too, his credibility was destroyed. He died suddenly in 1891, five months after his marriage to Kitty, and, despite the notoriety of his latter years, 200,000 people jammed Dublin for his funeral.

surgeon who founded the **Rotunda Maternity Hospital**, which when it opened in 1748 was the first purpose-built maternity hospital in Europe. Designed by Cassels, the architect of Leinster House, it retains a gorgeous Baroque chapel which, with the tarnished glory of the west facade, suggests how fine it must have once looked. Mosse funded the project by laying out a pleasure garden and organizing fancy dress balls and concerts to be held there, including the premiere of Handel's *Messiah*. The gardens fell out of fashion as the northside declined, but the Rotunda on the corner remained a concert hall until it became the Ambassador cinema. (It had also previously witnessed the birth of Sinn Féin, founded by Arthur Griffiths at a public meeting there in 1905.)

For more on the Gate, see p.266.

Since 1930 the Assembly Rooms, to the East of the Square, have been home to the **Gate Theatre**, founded in 1928 by Hilton Edwards and Micheál MacLiammóir. Lifelong partners, Edwards and MacLiammóir were in fact English; the latter (real name Alfred Wilmore) started his career as a precocious young actor on the London stage before becoming enamoured with Ireland and its literary heritage (he also founded Taibhdhearc na Gaillimhe, a theatre dedicated to Irish language drama). Aside from setting up the theatre, MacLiammóir is also known for his portrayal of Wilde in one of the most famous productions to be staged at the Gate – the one-man show *The Importance of Being Oscar*, which ran from 1960 to 1975, with MacLiammóir performing the role 1384 times. Having been established as a showcase for European drama (it opened with *Peer Gynt*), the Gate quickly became a great rival to the Abbey (see p.107), which featured predominantly Irish repertoire – the two theatres were nicknamed "Sodom and Begorrah" in some quarters, in reference to the Abbey's fondness for kitchen sink Irish drama and the sexuality of the founders of the Gate.

Turning left at the Ambassador cinema and heading towards the west of the square you'll find **Conway's Pub;**

established in 1745, it's the oldest on the northside and has been a haven for nervous fathers-to-be since the hospital opened. Originally named *Doyle's*, it was another of Collins' local haunts – having survived the Easter Rising, he surrendered to the British on the corner right outside the pub. This area has traditionally been a focal point for republicans, as evinced by the Sinn Féin Bookshop (Mon–Sat 11am–4pm) at 44 Parnell Square West; the basement at no. 46 next door was once used by Collins to brief his hit-team, "The Apostles". On the other side of the road stands the part of the Rotunda that still functions as a Maternity Hospital; in January 1922 the hospital briefly became the "Irish Soviet Republic" when it was seized by a band of dockers and the writer Liam O'Flaherty, protesting against unemployment. Their republic fell in three days without a shot being fired.

On the eastern side the square slopes up to the **Garden of Remembrance**, dedicated to those who died for Irish freedom. The garden was created in 1966, the fiftieth anniversary of the Easter Rising, and carries its ideology very heavily. Celtic and Christian symbols are employed around the railings, while the pond in the middle is in the shape of a crucifix. The redeeming factor is the *Children of Lir* statue that adorns the western end of the garden. Hoping to create a new kind of nationalist iconography when he was given the commission for this statue, Oisín Kelly chose the myth of Lir, lord of the sea, whose four children by his first wife were turned into swans by her jealous sister Aoife, his second wife; the statue depicts the point at which they are transformed. Kelly felt that the swan, as an ideal of isolation and perfection, was a suitable symbol for contemporary Ireland.

During the 1760s and 1770s, Parnell Square North was Dublin's poshest address, nicknamed "Palace Row" and inhabited by the earls of Ormond and Charlemont. The

PARNELL SQUARE

needle-spired **Abbey Presbyterian Church** on the corner is known as "Findlater's Church" after the grocer and brewer Alex Findlater, who financed its construction in 1864.

Hugh Lane Municipal Art Gallery

Map 5, G3. Tues–Thurs 9.30am–6pm, Fri & Sat 9.30am–5pm, Sun 11am–5pm; free. Buses #10, #11, #13, #16 and #22.

Former residence to the earl of Charlemont, the **Hugh Lane Municipal Art Gallery** occupies a grey-stone town house on the other side of Parnell Square North, designed by the Scottish architect Sir William Chambers. The gallery was founded in 1908 by Sir Hugh Lane (a nephew of Lady Gregory), who had intended to bequeath his entire collection, but – piqued by the Corporation's refusal to build a special gallery – added a codicil leaving just 39 works to "the nation", before dying aboard the SS *Lusitania* when it was sunk by a German U-boat in 1915. With Ireland's independence, the question of exactly *which* nation arose, and an unseemly wrangle began that wasn't resolved till the 1980s, when the Irish and British governments agreed that half of Lane's bequest should remain in Dublin.

Though the mansion works well as a gallery, its modest size means that well-known pictures often disappear to make room for temporary exhibitions. The first room you come to on the left after entering the gallery showcases the art of stained glass, with panels by Evie Hone, Wilhelmina Geddes, James Scanlon and in particular, Harry Clarke. Dubliner Clarke was born into the craft of stained-glass-making and the two pieces on show here, *The Eve of St Agnes* and *The Unhappy Judas*, display his mastery of the art, especially the former piece, radiating with the rich blues that are a hallmark of Clarke's work.

PARNELL SQUARE

> The Hugh Lane Gallery also hosts free classical music
> concerts at noon on Sundays during the winter, and
> offers lectures throughout the year.

Room 1 begins with some contemporary Irish pieces,
most notably an uncompromising multimedia installation
by Patrick O'Reilly entitled *Shame*, which evokes the horrors of bullfighting, and a sculpture by F.E.M. McWilliams
entitled *Women of Belfast*, the artist's response to the bomb-
ing of the Abercorn Tearooms in Belfast in the 1970s. The
room ends with work from French masters including
Monet and Manet.

Rooms 2 and 3 house works by Irish painters including
John Yeats (father of poet W.B. and artist Jack), John Lavery,
Maurice McGonigle, Louis Le Broque and Jack B. Yeats
himself, whose exuberant *There is no Night* is the highlight
of the gallery. Room 4 shows modern Irish work, while
Room 5 is devoted to Roderic O'Connor, whose oeuvre
runs the gamut from Seurat to Gaugin; his most interesting
pieces are his paintings of Breton children. Rooms 7 and 8,
which you can reach via Room 2, contain the work of
Antonio Mancini, Corot and contemporary mixed media
Irish art.

Dublin Writers Museum

Map 5, H3. Mon–Sat 10am–5pm, Sun & bank holidays
11am–5pm, July & Aug Mon–Fri until 6pm; £3, students £2.40,
children £1.40, family £8.25.

Two doors along from the gallery, 18 Parnell Square houses
the **Dublin Writers Museum**, a combination of tourist
crowd-puller and serious literary venue, in a lovely
Georgian mansion. The ground-floor rooms constitute a
whistle-stop tour of Irish literature from the first Gaelic

Brendan Behan

Born in 1923 and raised in Dublin's slums, **Brendan Behan** came from a family of learning and talent. While his mother had a full repertoire of rebel songs, his father read extensively, introducing his children to literature from an early age. Brendan's grandmother gave him a taste for alcohol before he was ten, and the Gaelic clubs around Parnell Square fuelled his passionate political ideals. Republican-inspired acts of violence landed him with hefty prison sentences throughout his early adult years and while "inside" he learned Irish and gathered material for his writing.

Success came with the 1956 London production of *The Quare Fellow*, a play depicting events in a prison the night before an execution. Behan's drunken tie-in interview with the BBC's Malcolm Muggeridge made him internationally notorious, and in both England and America he became a media star – the big, burly Irish wit, drunk and rebellious and outrageously entertaining. This same personality comes through in *The Hostage* and in the autobiographical *Borstal Boy*, both written in 1958. Ultimately, however, his image was to overshadow him, and Behan collapsed into alcoholism, his creative output dwindling along with his health. At his death in 1964 obituaries lamented the tragic loss of talent, but Dublin has always remembered him and numerous bars around the city sport photographs of the man as he was in his heyday.

rendition of the Old Testament (1645) to twentieth-century greats such as Shaw, Joyce and Beckett. Though the exhibits are fairly dull (a typewriter belonging to Brendan Behan – see box, above – which he once threw through a pub window in a fit of rage, is as good as it gets), an accompanying guide tape canters through literary fashions and the lives of the writers in a light-hearted way.

> **If you're planning to visit other literary shrines in Dublin, it's worth buying a combined ticket (£4.50, students £3.80) for the Writers Museum and the Shaw Birthplace (see p.153) or the Joyce Tower at Sandycove (see p.163).**

Upstairs, the house itself is the main attraction. A staircase with stained-glass windows of the Muses and allegories of art, science, literature and music leads to a resplendent white and gold salon, called the **Gallery of Writers**. The ceiling is by Michael Stapleton, Dublin's finest stuccoist, who learnt his art from the Swiss-Italian Francini brothers. On the door panels are figures representing the months of the year and the quarters of the day, accompanied by aphorisms such as "Work is the great reality, Beauty is the great aim." Another room contains the **Gorham Library** of books by writers featured in the museum, and downstairs there's a well-stocked bookshop and a pleasant café. In the summer there's also a Zen garden, and *Chapter One* in the basement (see p.229) is one of the northside's best restaurants.

Next door is the Living Writers Centre, with an on-going programme of lectures and seminars.

THE JAMES JOYCE CENTRE

Map 5, H3. Mon–Sat 9.30am–5pm, Sun 12.30–5pm, closed Dec 24–26; £2.75, students £2, children £0.70, family £6.

From the Dublin Writers Museum walk along Great Denmark Street and turn in to North Great George's Street where, at number 35, the **James Joyce Centre** taps deeper into the life of Dublin's most celebrated author, whose formative years were spent on the northside. His life and genius are the subject of guided tours of this beautifully restored Georgian townhouse – which has a regular

A Joycean walk on the northside

Having been reared by governesses and sent to an exclusive Jesuit boarding school when he was six, Joyce was unprepared for the misfortunes that struck him at the age of eleven. Shortly after he was withdrawn from school with his fees unpaid, the family quit their last fashionable address in Blackrock, and two caravans transported all their possessions across the "gloomy foggy city" to the impoverished northside. As an adult, Joyce occupied several flats in the neighbourhood before leaving Ireland for good in 1912.

The James Joyce Centre is only a few doors downhill from no. 38, the last residence of the Trinity Provost John Pentland Mahaffy, who loathed Joyce, describing him as "a living argument in favour of my contention that it was a mistake to establish a separate university for the aborigines of this island – for the corner-boys who spit into the Liffey."

Were it not for the intervention of a Jesuit priest, Joyce might not have gone to university at all. Initially, he and his brother Stanislaus attended a local Christian Brothers school, before his old teacher, Father Conmee, arranged for them to study for free at **Belvedere College** – one of the most prestigious schools in Ireland. The college is on Great Denmark Street, at the top of North Great George's Street.

The Joyce family occupied a series of properties, moving on as they fell behind with the rent. One of the first was a boarding-house at **no. 29 Hardwicke Street**, recalled as "a kip" run by Mrs Mooney, who connived to pimp her daughter in *Dubliners*. At the end of the street, **St George's Church** (now deconsecrated) is a frequent landmark in Joyce's stories.

On nearby Eccles Street Joyce confided to his friend J.F. Byrne about his fears that Nora had been unfaithful. Byrne assured him that it was untrue, and in gratitude Joyce honoured her fidelity by making no. 7 Eccles St the fictional abode of Leopold and Molly Bloom. *Ulysses* fans must be satisfied with a plaque, as the house was demolished in 1982 to build an annexe to the Mater Hospital.

Following Lower Dorset Street downhill turn right into Upper Gardiner Street and you'll pass the **Jesuit House** where Stephen Dedalus "wondered vaguely which window would be his if he joined the order"; it's beside the Church of St Francis Xavier, where Father Conmee was a priest.

Finally, turn off the northeast corner of Mountjoy Square to find **14 Fitzgibbon Street**, the "bare cheerless house" that was the Joyces' first home on the northside in 1894. There is nothing to mark their stay, for the house lay derelict until 1997, but it is now being renovated and may eventually sport a plaque.

programme of films and lectures, runs walking tours of Joyce's haunts, and organizes the Bloomsday celebrations (see pp.290–291). One of the directors, Ken Monaghan, is a nephew of Joyce and gives talks on their family life by arrangement.

Copies of Joyce's cherished **family portraits** are on display (the ones in the centre are copies, the originals are at Buffalo university), while on the top floor is a **Ulysses portrait gallery** featuring some of the three hundred characters who appear in the novel. In the tea room at the back of the house you can see the front door of 7 Eccles Street, home of Leopold Bloom. The **Guinness Library** of Joycean literature is available to visitors, along with audio-readings of his works, so aficionados can really get stuck in.

The **house** itself, with its superlative stucco mouldings by Stapleton, was restored following a campaign led by the Joyce scholar Senator David Norris to save it from demolition in the 1980s. The house was built for the earl of

THE JAMES JOYCE CENTRE

Kenmare's annual visits to Dublin to attend parliament, but promptly sold after the Act of Union. At the turn of this century, the ground floor was leased by Denis Maginni, a well-known dancing teacher (really named Maginnis; he dropped the "s" to sound sophisticated) who makes six appearances in *Ulysses*. After his departure it continued as a ballroom run by Dickie Graham (whose grandson is a director of the Centre), a popular place with British officers, who never suspected that the basement was an arms dump for a Nationalist group that secretly met upstairs. It's said that de Valera was once smuggled into the house disguised as a woman.

THE WAX MUSEUM AND THE BLACK CHURCH

Map 5, G3.

To the northwest of Parnell Square, on the corner of Granby Row and Dorset Street, Dublin's **Wax Museum** (Mon–Sat 10am–5.30pm, Sun noon–5.30pm; £3.50, students £2.50, children £2, family £10) is a good way to while away a wet afternoon if you have children to entertain. There are over 300 exhibits, from Irish writers and rock stars to Power Rangers and the Flintstones. Young children will enjoy the tunnels to crawl through and the hall of mirrors, while older kids will get a kick out of the chamber of horrors. There are tableaux of historic events and a roomful of Irish presidents plus the Popemobile used by John Paul II on his visit to Ireland in 1979. They have yet to add Gerry Adams to the Northern Ireland duo of John Hume and Ian Paisley.

Across Dorset Street, the spiky finials of the **Black Church** brood over St Mary's Place on the brow of the hill. Built of black Dublin calp, the former St Mary's Chapel of Ease is associated with two legends. One holds that it was designed to be turned into a redoubt should the Catholics rise up (as the Protestants feared in the 1820s); the other is that you can summon up the Devil by walking three times around the outside of the church. It has now been deconsecrated and serves as an office.

TO KING'S INNS AND BEYOND

Head downhill into Bolton Street and everything speaks of deprivation: rubbish blowing in the gutters, broken glass, barred shop windows. The Corporation estates which replaced the worst of the old tenements in the 1960s and 1970s have themselves become a blighted area, where **Henrietta Street**, dowdy as it is, comes as a pleasant respite. Laid out by Gardiner between 1730 and 1740, it was the first street in Dublin to contain aristocratic mansions, and it remained a most fashionable address until the 1800s. Its residents included three earls, the primate of Ireland and the Speaker of the House of Commons; Gardiner himself lived at no. 10. In 1908, many houses were stripped and turned into tenements by Alderman Meade, who managed to squeeze seventy tenants into the huge four-bay house at no. 7 alone. As Joyce recalled in *Dubliners*, a "horde of grimy children . . . stood or ran in the roadway, or crawled up the steps before the gaping doors, or squatted like mice upon the thresholds".

The street ends at the rear gate of **King's Inns** (map 5, F4), crowned by the British lion and unicorn. The third of James Gandon's great edifices, it was designed in 1795 but work on it was delayed for seven years due to residents' objections that it would spoil their view; when completed in 1817 it was unanimously praised. The Inns are the home of Irish Bar, where Ireland's barristers are trained. During daylight hours you can walk through the courtyard to see the allegorical reliefs out front and the view of Dublin from **Constitution Hill**. It was at Glasmanogue (as the hill was

Mountjoy Prison

Built in 1847 as a holding centre for transportees to the Australian penal colonies, **Mountjoy Prison** off the North Circular road is the oldest working jail in Dublin, and the most notorious. Early this century its notoriety was due to the political prisoners held here, first by the British (1916–21) and then by the Free State (1922–23). It was here that the IRB leader Thomas Ashe died after forced-feeding during a hunger-strike in 1917 – one of the first instances of what would become a favoured method of protest by imprisoned Republicans. In 1939, Mountjoy also saw the first strike by IRA men demanding to be recognized as political prisoners, a status that the Free State refused to concede as the British would later refuse in Northern Ireland. After the IRA sprung three prisoners by landing a hijacked helicopter in the yard in 1973, most Republican inmates were moved to the high-security jail at Portlaoise. Nowadays, Mountjoy is Dublin's main jail for remand prisoners and convicted felons, and such is the scale of drug-related crime that you don't have to spend long on the northside to meet people who've served time or have friends or relatives in "The Joy". Its most famous inmate was Brendan Behan (see box on p.120), who was sentenced to fourteen years for the attempted shooting of a policeman but amnestied after five years in 1946. His play *The Quare Fellow* is set here.

anciently called) that St Patrick is said to have stopped on his way north after converting Dubliners to Christianity and, looking back on the settlement, prophesied, "Although it's small and miserable now, there'll be a big town here in time to come. It will be spoken of far and near and will keep increasing until it becomes the chief town of the kingdom."

Having come this far, there are two routes back to the river and the centre of town, with a few sights along the way. The easiest and most obvious route to take is down Church Street past St Michan's Church to the Four Courts – for details of both, see Chapter 6. Alternatively, you could take a more easterly route via King Street North and Halston Street, past **Black Dog Debtors Prison** (map 4, A3). Built in 1760, it had a window on the pavement where prisoners could beg for alms, and stood right beside the Green Street Court where Robert Emmet, the Young Irelanders and the "Invincibles" were later tried. This street leads on to Little Britain Street, which has a lively fruit market early in the morning, and on the corner stands the most recent incarnation of *Barney Kiernan's* pub, the setting for the "Cyclops" chapter of *Ulysses*.

CROKE PARK GAA MUSEUM

Map 3, H1. May–Sept daily 9.30am–5pm; Oct–April Tues–Sat 10am–5pm, Sun noon–5pm; open to ticket-holders only on match days. £3, students £2, children £1.50, family £6. Bus #3, #11, #11A, #16 or #16A from O'Connell Street to the bottom of Clonliffe Road, bus #51A from Lower Abbey Street down Clonliffe Ave.

The **Croke Park GAA Museum**, located on what is effectively the inner northside's boundary, is part of Dublin's famous Gaelic sports ground, but offers much more than cabinets full of trophies and well-worn kits. The history of the GAA (Gaelic Athletic Association) is inextricably linked with that of Irish nationalism (it was banned by the British Government in 1918 and still prohibits "foreign" matches from taking place on its grounds), and its importance in the political arena is highlighted in several displays, most notably the audio-visual presentation "National Awakening" which relates the details of one of the great tragedies of Irish history, Bloody Sunday. On November

CROKE PARK GAA MUSEUM

11, 1920, the notorious Black and Tans opened fire on the crowd and players at a match being played in Croke Park, in reprisal for the killing of members of the so-called Cairo gang – British Secret Service agents – by Michael Collins' men. Twelve people were killed, including Tipperary hurling captain Michael Hogan, after whom one of the stands in the stadium is named.

Of course the museum also has a wealth of exhibits relating to the tradition of Gaelic sports, ranging from a cast of a tenth-century High Cross panel depicting David slaying the lion (featured for its inclusion of a hurling ball and stick), to interactive stands testing one's mastery of the fundamental skills of hurling and football. The tour ends with a high-tempo fifteen-minute film entitled "A Day in September", which captures all the excitement, colour and energy both on and off the field on finals day in Croke Park.

The Quays:
the Custom House
to Phoenix Park

Temple Bar isn't the only area in Dublin to reflect the changing economic face of the city; **the quays** on the Liffey's north bank too give a very visible indication of the amount of money currently being invested in urban renewal, with traditional working-class areas the focus of intense property speculation and development. Right the way from the Sheriff Street area in the east to Smithfield and Stoneybatter in the west, you can see the awkward coexistence of old and new, with beggars and barristers, Georgian piles and Corporation sink-estates standing cheek-by-jowl. Nevertheless, this stretch along the river has much to recommend it, not least the fact it boasts two of the city's architectural masterpieces, the **Custom House** and the **Four Courts**, remnants of the city's former Georgian heyday. A walk along the north bank quays can also be a very pleasant experience (endless stream of noisy

The Liffey and its bridges

The distance from the source of the **Liffey** in the Wicklow Mountains to its outlet in Dublin Bay is just 20km as the crow flies, but the river itself meanders for over 128km, a feature of the countryside for the majority of its course. Over the thousand years of Dublin's history, the Liffey has become narrower and deeper as channels have been dredged and land reclaimed and the harbour has moved eastwards. The River Poddle, which once joined the Liffey at the "Dark Pool" which gave Dublin its name (Dyflin), now runs underground for 5km, to trickle from a grating on the south bank, downstream from the Grattan Bridge.

Dublin's early settlements grew around the river and from it the city derives its Gaelic name Báile Áth Cliath ("Ford of the Hurdles"). The oldest **bridge** still standing dates from 1764; formerly Queen's Bridge, it is now known as Mellowes Bridge, named after the IRA "Irregular" Liam Mellowes (other Nationalists so honoured are Sean Heuston, Rory O'Moore and O'Donovan Rossa). While each bridge had localized effects, the Carlisle (now O'Connell) Bridge changed Dublin's axis from east–west to north–south, which had profound consequences for the city's development. Today fourteen bridges of varying shapes and sizes cross the Liffey, from the universally loved Ha'penny Bridge (1816) – which derives its name from the halfpenny toll that was levied on pedestrians wishing to cross until early this century – to the ugly railway Loop Line Bridge that ruins the view of Gandon's Custom House.

trucks aside), and offers plenty of interesting detours: **St Michan's Church** for its ghoulish "mummies", **Smithfield** for its monthly horse sales, and, for anyone who enjoys a tipple, the **Jameson Distillery**.

Exploration further west by catching a bus (#25, #67 or #67A from Middle Abbey Street) along the quays will take you to Dublin's latest museum space, the **Collins Barracks**, home to the decorative arts collection of the National Museum of Ireland. Further out lies the huge expanse of **Phoenix Park**, one of Europe's largest urban parks and home to the Irish president, Ashtown Castle and Dublin Zoo.

THE CUSTOM HOUSE

Map 4, F3. Visitors centre: mid-March to Nov Mon–Fri 10am–5pm, Sat & Sun 2–5pm; Dec to mid-March Wed–Fri 10am–5pm, Sun 2–5pm; £1.

The majestic **Custom House**, just beyond Eden Quay, has surveyed Dublin's waterfront for the past two hundred years. James Gandon, an English architect of Huguenot extraction, was considering going to work in St Petersburg when he received the commission for the building in 1781. Gandon went on to create the Four Courts and the Carlisle Bridge, and spent the rest of his life in Ireland, dying at his home in Lucan at the age of eighty.

Plans for the Custom House were opposed by dockers and merchants, who resented moving from the old customs point near Crane Lane, and by the genteel residents of Lower Gardiner Street, who feared contagion by a "low and vulgar crowd with the manners of Billingsgate". When petitions failed, objectors resorted to violence (Gandon wore a sword to work) and took heart that the proposed site was on a submerged mudflat where it seemed impossible to lay foundations. Gandon, however, confounded everyone by building atop a layer of four-inch-thick pine planks. The Custom House took ten years to build and cost the unheard-of sum of £500,000; nine years later the Act of Union made it redundant by transferring customs and

Monto

The fears of residents of Lower Gardiner Street proved justified after the docks moved east and the area west of where Connolly Station now stands declined into "one of the most dreadful dens of immorality in Europe". Known as **Monto**, after Montgomery (now Foley) Street, its seedy terraces were once inhabited by 1600 prostitutes, who were tolerated by the police, provided they kept within the quarter. Among the "flash houses" on Railway Street were Mrs Arnott's, Mrs Meehan's and Mrs Cohen's – all of which feature in the "Nighttown" section of *Ulysses*.

Although the departure of British troops in 1922 hit trade badly, Monto was dealt its fatal blow during Lent in 1925, when Catholic vigilantes and the Garda raided the area, resulting in 120 arrests (including a member of the Dáil). The following morning the Legion of Mary arrrived on the scene, pinning holy pictures on brothel doors and offering succour to penitent prostitutes.

During the 1930s much of the area was swept away and replaced by Corporation flats, now among the most run-down in Dublin. Bloomsday tours skip "Nighttown", and you'd be wise to do the same.

excise to London. In 1921 the building was set alight by Sinn Féiners and totally gutted; since its restoration it has housed government offices.

The building displays some of the most elaborate architectural detailing in the city: its embankment facade, 114 metres long, is flanked by arcades culminating in pavilions crowned with the arms of Ireland; around the building are fourteen heads representing Ireland's rivers (only the Liffey is a goddess, above the main door), and cattle heads symbolizing the beef trade; the Four Continents (Africa, America, Asia and Europe) decorate the rear portico; and the 38-metre-high dome is topped by a figure of Commerce.

The visitors centre occupies the only part of the interior to survive the fire, on the first floor. The displays on transport and revenue collection in Ireland are pretty insipid, but it is worth paying the entrance fee to enjoy the beauty of the Gandon's original decor.

Around the Custom House

After viewing the Custom House you can make a loop around it by walking up Beresford Place, the first road upriver. Downstream, the tall edifice of **Liberty Hall** rises above the city's skyline; built in the 1960s, it's home to the country's largest trade union, SIPTU (the Services, Industrial, Professional and Technical Union). Facing Liberty Hall, near the Custom House railings, you'll see a statue to the father of Irish trade unionism, James Connolly, with the flag of the Irish Citizen Army ("the Plough and the Stars") in the background, proclaiming that "the cause of labour is the cause of Ireland: the cause of Ireland is the cause of labour". A little further along, where the road meets with Lower Abbey Street, stands the *Chariot of Life* sculpture by Oisín Kelly – the struggle between the charioteer and his horses is Kelly's interpretation of the fight between reason and passion. Continuing round, **Busáras**, Dublin's central bus station, comes into view; in 1953 it was the city's first unashamedly Modernist building, but it has since been overshadowed by a younger contender, the Financial Services Centre. Designed in 1987, this monument to Ireland's economic success provides the backdrop to a group of figures commemorating the country's greatest economic and human catastrophe, the Great Famine.

THE CUSTOM HOUSE

At the end of the loop is the Talbot Memorial bridge, on the other side of which you'll find the **City Arts Centre**; its gallery (daily 11am–5pm) features socially related exhibits by amateur and professional artists, while the centre's venue hosts a mix of music, theatre and dance. To the left of the bridge is a statue of Matt Talbot (see box, below), after whom the bridge is named.

Matt Talbot

Born in 1856, Matt Talbot grew up in Dublin's "Monto" district and started work at the age of twelve at a wine merchant's, where he began to steal ale – by the time he was sixteen he was working at the Custom House docks and drinking whiskey. Alcoholism was rife in Dublin, and Talbot spent much of his early life alternating between work and drink, funding his habit by pawning possessions and stealing.

One day in 1884, having forgone his usual visit to the pub he returned home sober, and so commenced a period of abstinence that would last the rest of his life. He took the oath of Temperance (see p.111), attended Mass daily (partly to avoid his drinking friends) and started donating to charity. Self-denial became a defining feature of Talbot's fervent piety: he fasted, remained on his knees for long periods, and slept on a plank, with a wooden block for a pillow. He would often be found, trance-like, with arms spread in the shape of a Cross, but the extent of his devotions came to light when, having been ill for some time, he collapsed and died outside his church in June 1925. The coroner, on removing his clothing, found large chains wrapped around his body – Talbot's sign of his "slavery" to God. For many, the discovery confirmed Talbot as a truly holy man. In 1931, his cause for canonization was brought before the pope, and is still under consideration today. Matt Talbot's tomb is in Our Church of the Lady of Lourdes.

FROM O'CONNELL BRIDGE TO THE FOUR COURTS

O'Connell Bridge marks the point to the west of which the quays really come alive: cars and pedestrians jostle for position here, while red-headed children try to make a few pounds by posing for tourists' photographs and street vendors try to do the same by selling posters of Irish Republican heroes.

Bachelors Walk was laid out in 1678 as an extension of the Ormond Quay, ending at Bagino Slip, where a ferry used to cross the Liffey. It's chiefly associated with a violent clash in 1914, when British troops fired on a crowd, killing four of them and wounding thirty-eight. Near the corner of Liffey Street are The Winding Stair Bookshop (with a laid-back café where you can sit and gaze over the Ha'penny Bridge; see p.227) and a pair of life-size statues of two housewives taking a rest from shopping, irreverently known as the "Hags with the Bags".

Ormond Quay bears the name of one of the few viceroys who actually liked Dublin and is well remembered here. James Butler, the duke of Ormond, served two terms (1662–69 and 1677–85) and did much to restore Dublin's pride after a century of intermittent war. Exiled in France when Cromwell was in power, Ormond was inspired by continental city planning and longed to tear down the old city and build anew. He then took advantage of the new Essex Bridge and laid out three quays along the north bank, which were to form the east–west axis of the city. This development spurred the growth of an extensive **market quarter** behind the quays. The infamous Ormond Boys (see box, p.91) used to meet in the lanes backing onto Chancery Street (near the Four Courts).

Between Ormond's terms of office, the job was held by Arthur Capel, earl of Essex, after whom a new bridge was named in 1676. Further downstream than the others,

Capel Street Bridge (now Grattan Bridge) became the main crossing point over the Liffey and was to remain the marker for Dublin's north–south axis until the Carlisle Bridge was built, its role then being usurped by Sackville (now O'Connell) Street. The well-to-do left the area, which soon assumed a more proletarian character owing to the nearby Ormond market. It still caters for tradesmen, and in and amongst the development blocks you'll spot dozens of tool shops, builders' merchants and greasy spoon cafés in the neighbourhood.

Two blocks inland, the former **St Mary's Church**, built in 1702 on Mary Street, is now home to a decorating centre. However the church's history is littered with various Dublin personalities; here, Richard Brinsley Sheridan and Seán O'Casey were baptized, Arthur Guinness got married, John Wesley preached his first sermon in Ireland and Lord Norbury, the Hanging Judge of 1798, was buried. Wolfe Tone, the leader of the 1798 Rebellion, was born opposite the church, where the Guardian Life Assurance building now stands. It's also strange to imagine that Joyce opened Ireland's first cinema at 45 Mary Street in 1909 – the Volta's diet of continental films was not to Dubliners' tastes, however, and his Italian backers sold out after a few months.

Just west of Capel Street, a tiny cul-de-sac, Meetinghouse Lane, harbours what's left of **St Mary's Abbey** (mid-June to mid-Sept Wed 10am–5pm; £1). All that remains is the vaulted chamber of its chapter house, with a model of how the complex once looked. Founded by the Benedictines in 1139 and transferred to the Cistercians eight years later, St Mary's was one of the most important monasteries in the country until the Réformation, when meetings of the Council of Ireland were held here. It was during such a meeting in 1534 that Silken Thomas Fitzgerald renounced his allegiance to Henry VIII and stormed out to raise a rebellion, only to be captured and executed the following year. The monastery was dissolved in 1539 and turned into a quarry in the seventeenth century, when its stones were used to build the Essex Bridge.

Returning to the quays you'll find the *Ormond Hotel* (see p.205), which has recently undergone a much-needed facelift and whose bar and restaurant retains the name *Sirens*, since its erstwhile barmaids were likened to the alluring creatures by Joyce in his *Ulysses*.

The Four Courts

Map 5, E6.

Continuing up Inns Quay, you come to the second of Gandon's masterpieces on the northside, the **Four Courts**, which would be a perfect foil to the Custom House were it not for a slight bend in the river making it impossible to view both buildings together from O'Connell Bridge. Built between 1786 and 1802 at a cost of £200,000, the courts provoked criticism of lawyers' "contemptible vanity" for having "the grandest building in Europe, in the world, to plead in". This failed to stop Gandon from undertaking another commission for the legal profession, King's Inns (see p.125). The courts and inns were originally located south of the river, but the latter moved to the site of the present-day Four Courts after Henry VIII gave the legal society land stolen from a Dominican convent; the courts moved north in the seventeenth century, whereupon the society of lawyers got their own premises on nearby Constitution Hill.

> **If you're curious to observe a trial, the courts are open to the public (Mon–Fri 11am–1pm & 2–4pm).**

Like the GPO, the building is virtually synonymous with a specific event that was to have momentous consequences for

Ireland – not the Easter Rising (when it fell to the insurgents without a shot being fired), but the seizure of the Four Courts by anti-Treaty Republicans in July 1921, an event that marked the onset of hostilities that led to the Civil War. Michael Collins saw it as a direct challenge to the Free State and shelled the rebels into submission. Before surrendering, they blew up the Public Records Office with two lorry-loads of gelignite, sending scraps of historic documents floating above Dublin. In an unwelcome message of congratulation to Collins, Churchill wrote: "The archives of the Four Courts may be scattered, but the title deeds of Ireland are safe."

ST MICHAN'S CHURCH

Map 5, E6. Mon–Fri 10am–1pm & 2–5pm, Sat 10am–1pm; £1.50.
Bus #34 from Middle Abbey Street.

St Michan's Church stands on Church Street, the first street upriver from the Four Courts. Built by the Danes and named after one of their saints, it dates from 1095 – the oldest surviving building on the northside. For five hundred years it was also the only church north of the river, ensuring it the largest parish in Dublin and sufficient funds for a complete rebuild in 1685. Since then its fortunes have declined and its roof has long required costly repairs – hence the exploitation of the "mummies" in its vaults.

Strictly speaking, the dozen **bodies** have not been mummified – they've been preserved by the constant temperature, the limestone masonry that absorbs moisture from the air, and methane gas secreted by rotting vegetation beneath the church. The "best" ones are 300–700 years old – a man thought to have been a Crusader, a woman who may have been a nun, and a man missing a hand, possibly a thief-turned-monk. Later burials are better accounted for, with the brass-studded coffins of a hated family of landlords in one vault, and the Sheares brothers, who were executed for their part in the 1798 Rebellion, in another. It's said that Robert Emmet, the leader of the 1803 rising, is buried in an unmarked grave at the back of the cemetery; a priest from St Michan's attended him on the scaffold.

Outwardly dour, the church is dominated by the one element that was not part of the seventeenth-century revamp – a grim tower from medieval times. Its much-remodelled interior contains an early eighteenth-century **organ** which was played by Handel; the organ gallery is dominated by a superb carving of seventeen musical instruments cut from a single piece of wood, made by an unknown apprentice as his examination piece. Flanking the organ are the eighteenth-century pulpit and the font in which Edmund Burke was baptized – he was born nearby at 12 Arran Quay. At present a carpet covers the skull on the floor near the altar that's said to symbolize Cromwell's crimes against Ireland, while in the corner you'll notice a pew known as the **Penitent's Pew** (facing out toward the congregation) because at one time erring parishioners knelt at this and confessed their sins publicly. Although the stained-glass windows of the church were shattered during the shelling of the Four Courts, they have been tastefully replaced; one that catches the eye in particular is the middle window, inspired by the *Book of Kells*, which was installed in 1958.

SMITHFIELD VILLAGE

The area just to the west of St Michan's Church, **Smithfield village**, formerly only famous for its horse sales, is fast being redeveloped as the city's latest cultural centre. The mixture of old and new is very apparent here, with exhibitions such as the Jameson Distillery and the high-tech Ceol, whose emphasis is firmly on Irish traditions, interspersed with modern Temple-Bar-like establishments such as *Chief O'Neill's* hotel (see p.203).

The village is centred on the cobbled expanse of **Smithfield** itself, just west of Bow Street, which has been earmarked as the city's largest civic space. For the time being, however, the first Sunday of every month still sees the renowned Smithfield **horse sales**. At this time the area is completely transformed, with horse-boxes arriving in a continuous stream from 9am, so that by midday the market is buzzing, staying busy until around 4pm. Though there's nothing glamorous about the event, there's plenty to watch; blacksmiths shoeing horses at mobile forges, kids riding bareback on ponies, and weather-beaten farmers spitting into their palms and clapping their hands together to seal agreements. After the sales you'll see ragged ponies being ridden away towards the northern suburbs, where impromptu races are held. How long this will remain the case, however, is another matter; the passing of the Control of Horses Act has limited the ownership of horses in an urban setting, making the issue of "urban ponies" a contentious one, and the plans for the square's future do not seem to include the horse fair.

Jameson Distillery

Map 5, E6. Tours daily 10am–5.30pm (every 30min); £3, students £2.50, children £1.50.

Though it's a blatant plug for Ireland's distillers, you'd have to be a vehement teetotaller not to enjoy the museum in the old **Jameson Distillery** on Bow Street. Taking its name from the Irish *uisce beatha* (water of life), Irish whiskey is almost as integral to Dublin's pub culture as Guinness, and quite distinct from Scotch whisky in that it's distilled three times rather than only twice. The oriental art of distillation was probably brought to Ireland by Phoenician traders or missionary monks in the sixth century; the exhibits on the tour explain the modern-day malting, fermenting, distilling and maturing processes, how proof value is assessed and mature whiskeys are blended ("nosed" and left to "marry", as they say in the trade). An audio-visual show fills you in on the pioneering whiskey families – the Jamesons and the Powers in Dublin, the Murphys of Midleton and the Bushmills in the North – now amalgamated as the Irish Distillers Group, which produces all the well-known brands at its ultramodern Midleton distillery.

Tours finish with a ritual **tasting** of five types of whiskey, Scotch and bourbon, poured out by the *Shelbourne*'s former head barman, and the presentation of a "taster's certificate". Tots are watered down, as the Irish believe that this brings out the flavour, but neat refills are available on request and connoisseurs are rewarded with a dram or two of vintage stuff. To sober up, read the rules of the lodging house for distillery workers; their minutely detailed laundry allowance ends, "and once every fortnight, one night-shirt". The complex also has a fine souvenir shop and popular restaurant.

Ceol

Map 5, E6. Mon–Sat 9.30am–6pm, Sun 10.30am–6pm; £3.95, students £3, family £12.

In complete contrast to the easy relation of setting and subject matter in the Jameson Distillery, **Ceol** (Gaelic for "music") approaches its topic from a very different angle, with an ambitious attempt to explore traditional Irish music using cutting-edge technology and visually progressive design. The exhibition is set up as a series of rooms, each with a specific artistic "theme" that's explicated by a visual accompaniment to an excellent soundtrack.

The first room in the exhibition, the Coat Room, displays great originality in its reconstruction of the musicians' pre-session cloakroom; the circular room is decorated with

SMITHFIELD VILLAGE

casts of coats on which video footage of leading musicians is projected. The main room contains a series of touch-screen consoles that give a history of traditional music, though the archive it draws upon seems to be somewhat limited. For something a bit more interactive the children's room (popular with adults too) has floor-panel sensors which allow you to walk out a tune to the sound of an uileann pipe or accordian. The final room is the most visually daring, in which musicians are represented by metal figures with TV screens for heads, showing a house music session in full swing. The tour ends in a souvenir shop that stocks an impressive collection of traditional music.

THE COLLINS BARRACKS AND CROPPIES ACRE

Map 5, B6.

Further along the quays towards Phoenix Park, the imposing grey-stone **Collins Barracks** are an annexe of the National Museum (Tues–Sat 10am–5pm, Sun 2–5pm; free). The Barracks themselves date from 1701 and until being decommissioned in 1997 claimed to be the oldest continuously inhabited barracks in the world, with the largest drill square in Europe – it could hold six regiments.

The museum itself houses artefacts, both Irish and otherwise, ranging from glassware and china to textiles and musical instruments. If time is limited the best thing is to head straight for the superb "**Curator's Choice**" room on the first floor, where museum curators from all over Ireland have chosen items of particular interest. While every one of the 25 objects on display is fascinating, two that stand out for their superlative craftmanship and historical significance are the seventeenth-century Fleetwood cabinet given by Oliver Cromwell to his daughter on her wedding day, and the William Smith O'Brien Gold Cup, named after an Irish patriot who took part in the abortive Young Ireland rebellion of 1848 and was exiled to Australia. The cup was given to him on release from jail in Australia in 1854.

The adjacent room, entitled "Out of Storage", contains a huge diversity of artefacts, from Samurai suits of armour to early Edison phonographs; putting this eclectic mix into context is made easy by the excellent interactive touch-screen computers, which offer information on every item. The Irish Silver Room is also recommended, which houses examples of early Irish silverware – such as the 1494 de Burgo Chalice – as well as various exuberant nineteenth-century pieces. The south block of the Barracks houses less interesting displays of furniture. At the time of writing there are also plans to open an exhibition on Irish costume, jewellery and accessories.

Between the barracks and the river lies a railed-in plot of grass called **Croppies Acre**, with a monument on the spot where the executed rebels of 1798 were buried. During the Great Famine, Ireland's largest soup-kitchen was set up on the esplanade, where policemen supervised mass feedings from a three-hundred-gallon pot. The quay is now named Wolfe Tone Quay, after the Rebellion's leader (see pp.92–93). The prostitution racket centred on Heuston Station, just across the river, leaves a tidemark of condoms on the sheltered side of Croppies Acre.

PHOENIX PARK

Map 3, A3. Bus #25, #25A, #66, #66A, #66B or #67A from Middle Abbey Street.

Phoenix Park, a rolling landscape over twice the size of London's Hampstead Heath or New York's Central Park, is a pleasure to visit at any time of year – but be sure to leave before dusk, as it's unsafe after dark. Since the attractions are scattered over seven hundred hectares, it's also wise to conserve your energy by getting there by bus – though if

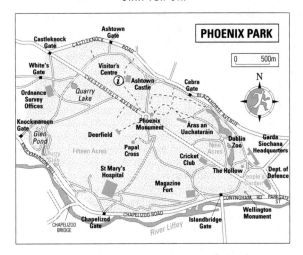

PHOENIX PARK

0   500m

N

Castleknock Gate, *Ashtown Gate*, *White's Gate*, *CASTLEKNOCK ROAD*, *Visitor's Centre*, *Ashtown Castle*, *Cabra Gate*, *BLACKHORSE AVENUE*, *Ordnance Survey Offices*, *CHESTERFIELD AVENUE*, *Quarry Lake*, *Knockmaroon Gate*, *Glen Pond*, *Furry Glen*, *Deerfield*, *Phoenix Monument*, *Áras an Uachtaráin*, *Dublin Zoo*, *Garda Siochana Headquarters*, *KNOCKMAROON HILL*, *Fifteen Acres*, *Papal Cross*, *Nine Acres*, *Cricket Club*, *The Hollow*, *People's Garden*, *Dept. of Defence*, *St Mary's Hospital*, *Magazine Fort*, *CONYNGHAM RD*, *PARKGATE ST*, *CHAPELIZOD BRIDGE*, *CHAPELIZOD ROAD*, *Chapelizod Gate*, *Islandbridge Gate*, *Wellington Monument*, *River Liffey*

you've already walked as far as the Collins Barracks, it's only another ten minutes to the main entrance off Parkgate Street.

> **Ryan's pub at no. 28 Parkgate Street is the ideal place to take a break for refreshments; see p.252.**

Landscaped in the English fashion, the park harbours three hundred **deer** which bask on the Fifteen Acres or roam the woods nearby. Frequented by joggers and dog-walkers on a daily basis, and families at the weekends, it's also a venue for **cricket**, **football** and **hurling** matches in season, and occasional pop concerts over summer.

The name "Phoenix" is a corruption of the Irish *fionn uisce* ("clear water"), from the days when this land belonged to St John's Priory in Kilmainham, before the Reformation.

PHOENIX PARK

After the Restoration of Charles II, the duke of Ormond supervised the construction of a viceregal lodge which remained a private preserve until 1747, when it was opened to the public by Lord Chesterfield.

For decades, Head Ranger Nathanial Clements ensured that "every impropriety was vigorously expelled", but after his death in 1777 the "gates were opened wide to Tag, Rag and Bobtail" and the Sabbath was profaned by hurling matches "productive of blasphemous speaking, riot, drunkenness, broken heads and bones". Eventually, up to three hundred tents were pitched on the Fifteen Acres for gambling and drinking on Sundays – a fitting spot for a Temperance rally in 1875. A tradition of political meetings going back to 1792 reached its zenith with the Land League demonstration of 1880, whose 30,000-strong crowd set a record only surpassed by religious events, with 500,000 at the Eucharistic Congress of 1932, and over twice that number attending Papal Mass in 1979.

On entering the park you'll find the 1980s **Peoples Garden**, the only part with formal flowerbeds and hedges, which merges into the hillocks and ponds landscaped in the 1830s by Decius Bruton, who also laid out **Chesterfield Avenue**. Near the Parkgate Street entrance also stands **the Wellington Monument**, a 61-metre-high granite obelisk which bears reliefs cast from cannons captured at Waterloo, depicting the triumphs of the "Iron Duke".

Off the avenue to the right, **Dublin Zoo** (May–Sept Mon–Sat 9.30am–6pm, Sun 10.30am–6pm; Oct–April Mon–Fri 9.30am–4pm, Sat 9am–5pm, Sun 9.30am–5pm; £5.50, children £3, family £15) dates back to 1830 – the second oldest in Europe. In recent years the zoo's decline led to a public campaign for its closure, but it has been granted £15 million to modernize and extend its premises into something fit for the next millennium. Where the zoo once boasted of having bred the MGM lion, it now lays

The Phoenix Park Murders

The Phoenix Park Murders of 1882 shocked society on both sides of the Irish Sea. One Saturday evening in May, the viceregal Chief Secretary and Under-Secretary were strolling home along Chesterfield Avenue when four men jumped out of a hansom cab, stabbed them to death and escaped towards Chapelizod. The killings struck fear into every official in Ireland, where cold-blooded assassination had never been encountered before. The *Illustrated London News* blamed a "foul conspiracy of the enemies of civilized society – Nihilists or Anarchists, or Fenians, or by whatever name they may be called", aiming "to subvert all regular Government, for the purpose of Communistic plunder". Most Irish nationalists were equally appalled, as Parnell had just been released from jail after making a pact with Gladstone, and the murdered Chief Secretary was Gladstone's nephew. Parnell offered to resign, to forestall any imputation of support for the murders, but was dissuaded by Gladstone. It was discovered that the assassins belonged to a Fenian splinter group, the Invincibles, when one of their comrades turned state's evidence. (He was later killed by Fenians aboard a boat bound for South Africa, where he hoped to start a new life.) A plaque on the roadside of the Polo Grounds marks the spot where the murders took place; the four Invincibles were executed at Kilmainham and are now remembered by a monument in Glasnevin cemetery.

stress on breeding endangered species for subsequent release into the wild.

Heading up the avenue past the Army and Garda athletic grounds and Nine Acres polo fields, you'll see the Palladian **Áras an Uachtaráin** (Presidential Residence), which was built in 1751 as the viceregal lodge. Queen Victoria stayed here during her first visit to Ireland in 1849, and appeared not to notice the Famine at all, while the young Winston Churchill spent three years at the nearby "Little Lodge" when his father was secretary to his own father, the duke of Marlborough. The lodge which became the home of the Irish president in 1937, proudly flies the Harp from its flag-post and, since the presidency of Mary Robinson, keeps a candle burning in its window for "the Irish Diaspora". The latest occupant, Mary MacAleese, has had a much lower profile than her predecessor since taking office in November 1997.

A spur road across the way leads to a 27-metre-high stainless steel **Papal Cross**, on the spot where John Paul II celebrated Mass on September 29, 1979. Further along, at a crossroads, Lord Chesterfield's **Phoenix Monument** resembles an eagle more than a mythical bird and obfuscates the origin of the park's name. One road leads towards Deerfield, the US Ambassador's residence; the other to a **Visitors Centre** (daily 9am–5pm; £2, children/students £1, family £5) featuring a reconstruction of the Knockmaree cist grave found on the Fifteen Acres in 1838, which is older (c. 3500–3000 BC) than the famous Neolithic passage tomb at Newgrange (see p.188).

The ticket for the centre includes a tour of **Ashtown Castle**, a slender seventeenth-century tower house built to safeguard the family and assets of a distant ancestor of Daniel O'Connell. The tower has such defensive features as a "murder hole" by the door and a spiral staircase with a "trip step" on the threshold of the living quarters.

For more seclusion, head off past the Ordnance Survey Offices to the **Glen Pond** and **Furry Glen** on the edge of the Fifteen Acres, a huge meadow once used for military manoeuvres.

Beyond St Mary's Hospital (formerly the Hibernian Military School) a path continues to the derelict **Magazine**

Fort, dug into a hilltop in 1734. "Lo, here's proof of Irish sense / Here Irish wit is seen / Where nothing's left worth defence / They build a magazine", quipped Swift. After the British left, the fort became the main arms depot of the Irish Army until a daring raid by the IRA in 1939 got away with over one million rounds of ammunition, since when its bunkers have been impregnably secured against interlopers and abandoned to the elements.

The Grand Canal and around

Although it hasn't been used commercially for over twenty years, parts of the **Grand Canal** are still very pleasant for a stroll – the stretch between Lower Mount Street and Lower Leeson Street is especially attractive, with some good places to stop for a drink around Portobello Bridge. There are a few low-key tourist attractions along the way too: the **Waterways Visitor Centre** and the **National Print Museum** towards its eastern extreme and **Shaw's birthplace** and the **Irish Jewish Museum** off Portobello Road.

To the south of the Grand Canal lies leafy middle-class Ballsbridge and its adjacent suburbs. The Royal Dublin Society (see p.294) and Lansdowne Road (see p.297) are in this part of town, but unless you're going to a sporting event at one of these venues, or are staying in accommodation hereabouts, it's not a district you're likely to explore. To the south of Ballsbridge, however, you'll find a couple of minor sights that merit a brief excursion: the **Pearse Museum** and **Rathfarnham Castle**; to the south west of the city lies the miniature medieval tower house of **Drimnagh Castle**.

The Grand and Royal canals

True Dubliners, it's said, are born within the confines of the city's two canals: the Grand Canal, which makes a six-kilometre loop around south Dublin, and the Royal Canal, which performs a similar loop through the northside.

The **Grand Canal**, which was intended to link Dublin to a vast area of central Ireland, had two branches: one joined the River Barrow to extend navigation to Waterford, the other met up with the great natural waterway of the River Shannon. Work began in 1756 but proceeded so slowly that only 20km had been dug by 1763, when the Dublin Corporation took over the project to speed things up, handing it back to private investors in 1772. Nine years later the first cargo barges began operating between Dublin and Sallins, and passenger services started the following year. Boats terminated at the St James's Street Harbour near the Guinness brewery until the Circular Line opened, encircling the southside to meet the Liffey at Ringsend. The inauguration of the Grand Canal Basin locks in 1796 marked the completion of the longest canal system in Ireland and Britain, extending for 550km (of which the Shannon and Barrow account for about 250km).

While much of its revenue came from shipping turf (Dublin's fireplaces burnt 40,000 tonnes a year), the Grand Canal Company had horse-drawn barges that could carry up to eighty people, and ran five hotels along the route to accommodate them. By 1852 however, passenger services had been killed off by the railways, though cargo was transported by barge for a further century – the last haulage company went bust in 1950. A decade later Guinness stopped transporting its stout by barge from St James's Street Harbour, which was filled in in 1974.

The **Royal Canal** was a later rival venture by John Binns, a director of the Grand Canal who quit after taking offence to a jest, and vowed to wreck its business. The Grand Canal Company claimed breach of charter but failed to stop it, though they did win a stipulation that it maintain a distance of 6km from their own canal once it had advanced 22km from Dublin. Unfortunately, the duke of Leinster, a major backer, also put restrictions on the canal's route, insisting it run past his mansion near Maynooth. As a result, construction was longer and costlier than anticipated, and it never made a profit; in 1840 it was bought by a railway company as a route (their line still runs alongside the canal today), and in 1961 it was closed for navigation, as so much of it had dried up. Since realizing its tourist potential, the stretch between Dublin and Mullingar has been restored, and work on the next section is in progress.

WATERWAYS VISITORS CENTRE

Map 3, J5. June–Sept daily 9.30am–6.30pm; Oct–May Wed–Sun 12.30–5pm; £2, students/children £1, family £5.

Raised on stilts above the water of the canal, in the manner of an ancient bogland settlement, the **Waterways Visitors Centre** is a purpose-built tourist attraction that strives to convey the beauty of Ireland's waterways from a Dublin backwater. It's no substitute for a holiday on the Shannon, but if you're considering such a trip it's worth a visit, as it provides a good overview of Ireland's extensive inland waterways (a video monitor upstairs runs through the scenic highlights) – and sells navigation charts, books and towpath trails. There's plenty to absorb enthusiasts of canal engineering, including a working model of a barge going through lock gates, along with pictorial displays covering history and ecology. Having

WATERWAYS VISITORS CENTRE

151

fallen into disuse in the 1950s, the canal system has revived since the 1970s thanks to tourism, so it's unfortunate that the romantic image of the waterways conjured up by the centre is weakened by the grimy vista of the Grand Canal Basin and its downstream locks from the rooftop viewing platform.

NATIONAL PRINT MUSEUM

Map 3, J7. May–Sept Mon–Fri 10am–12.30pm & 2.30–5pm, Sat, Sun and bank holidays noon–5pm; Oct–April Tues, Thurs, Sat & Sun 2–5pm; £2.50, students/children £1.50, family £5.

It's possible to walk from the Waterways Centre to the leafier stretches of the Grand Canal in about ten minutes, or to take a detour to the **National Print Museum** in the former chapel of the Beggars Bush Barracks on Haddington Road. The collection traces the development of printing presses from an eighteenth-century "handcaster" through the nineteenth-century keyboard-operated "Linotype", revolutionary in its day, down to the earliest Apple word-processors, most of which are still in working order. There's material too on bookbinding and on changes in design and typefaces.

Built by the British in 1830, the barracks were constructed in an effort to control a lawless area on the edge of Dublin – **Beggars Bush** – and were the first barracks to be handed over to the Free State in 1922. It was here that Erskine Childers was executed for possessing a revolver during the Civil War – an ironic end for someone who became a Nationalist hero for smuggling 900 rifles into Ireland in 1914. The barracks now house the Irish Labour Court.

MOUNT STREET TO PORTOBELLO BRIDGE

There's a verdant stretch of canal between Mount Street and Portobello Bridge that isn't far from the centre of town and has a choice of approaches. One is from Merrion Square along **Mount Street Upper**, past the pepperpot church of St Stephen's; another is by **Baggot Street Lower**.

The stretch of **canal** by Baggot Street Lower is 3–6m wide at this point, with swans on the cleaner parts, shaded by trees that once provided cover for prostitutes and their clients (it was here that Joyce lost his virginity). In the 1950s and 1960s, *Parson's Bookshop* by Baggot Street Bridge (now a café) was a meeting place for writers like Brendan Behan and the poet Patrick Kavanagh, who lived nearby and produced a short-lived "journal of literature and politics" called *Kavanagh's Weekly*, written largely by himself (with contributions from Behan and Flann O'Brien). After Kavanagh's death in 1967, his home on Pembroke Road was found to contain little more than a bed, and his friends erected a plain memorial **seat** on the Mespil Road side of Baggot Street Bridge in accordance with his wish: "O commemorate me with no hero-courageous/Tomb – just a canal-bank seat for the passer-by". A life-size **statue of Kavanagh** muses on a bronze bench on the other side of the canal.

Just under a mile past Kavanagh's statue you'll reach a trio of **pubs** as the canal dwindles to a ditch near the Portobello Bridge: *The Barge Inn*, on Charlemont Street, *The Portobello*, just by Portobello Bridge, and *The Lower Deck*, around the block from **Portobello House**. Originally a hotel for passengers at the terminus of the Grand Canal, this was Jack B. Yeats's last residence, and now serves as a college.

THE SHAW BIRTHPLACE

Map 3, F7. May–Oct Mon–Sat 10am–1pm & 2–5pm, Sun & bank holidays 11am–1pm & 2–5pm; £2.60, students £2.10, children £1.30.

There are two places of interest in the side streets beyond Portobello Bridge, whose houses are minor versions of the

Georgian houses of Dublin's centre. The first is at no. 33 Synge Street, the **birthplace of George Bernard Shaw**, the interior of which has been painstakingly restored to provide a picture of Victorian domestic life. Shaw lived here until he was ten and recalled that "neither our hearts nor our imaginations were in it". This "loveless" atmosphere arose from his parents' failing marriage and the strain of keeping up appearances when the family was sinking into debt – a mood conveyed by the claustrophobic rooms and a terse inscription acknowledging that "Bernard Shaw, author of many plays", lived here.

THE IRISH JEWISH MUSEUM

Map 3, F8. May–Sept Sun, Tues & Thurs 11am–3pm; Oct–April Sun only 10.30am–2.30pm; closed on Jewish holy days; free.

Further along the widening canal, you can turn into Kingsland Parade and take the second turning on the left to find the other place of interest, the **Irish Jewish Museum** at 3 Walworth Road. Opened in 1985 by President Chaim Herzog of Israel, who was born in Belfast and educated in Dublin, the museum relates the history of the Jewish community in Ireland (the first were Portuguese and Spanish Jews, fleeing the Inquisition), who established a synagogue off Dame Street in the 1720s. The house itself functioned as a synagogue from 1915 until the mid-1970s, when its congregation moved to the suburbs. Upstairs you can see a wedding canopy, circumciser's instruments and other artefacts of Judaic culture.

RATHFARNHAM CASTLE

Map 2, F6. June–Sept daily 10am–6pm; May & Oct daily 10am–5pm; mid- to end April Sun 10am–5pm; Easter Sat–Mon 10am–5pm; closed Nov to mid-April; guided tour £1.50, students/children £0.60. Bus #16 or #16A from O'Connell Street.

George Bernard Shaw

Born in Dublin in 1856, **George Bernard Shaw** was technically a member of the privileged Ascendancy, but his father's failed attempt, after leaving the civil service, to make money meant that Shaw grew up in an atmosphere of genteel poverty and, by the age of sixteen, was earning his living in a land agency. When his mother left his father for a singing teacher and took her two daughters with her to London, Shaw soon joined them and set about educating himself. Subsidized by his mother's meagre income, he spent his afternoons in the British Museum's reading room and his evenings writing novels.

Shaw's novels were unsuccessful, but his plays were a different matter entirely and he was acclaimed the most important British playwright since the eighteenth century. However, Shaw recognized his foreignness as being a big part of his success: "the position of foreigner with complete command of the same language has great advantages. I can take an objective view of England, which no Englishman can." In the 1890s, influenced by the drama of Ibsen, he began to write plays hinged on moral and social questions rather than romantic or personal interests – *Man and Superman*, *Caesar and Cleopatra*, *Major Barbara*, *St Joan*, and, of course, *Pygmalion*, from which the musical *My Fair Lady* was adapted. As well as a dramatist he was an active pamphleteer, critic, journalist and essayist, on subjects ranging from politics and economics to music. Shaw was awarded the Nobel Prize for literature – which he refused. He died in Hertfordshire, England, in 1950.

Rathfarnham Castle has been undergoing restoration since 1987, and work is far from finished, but if you're interested in historic monuments and their conservation, the **guided tour** is worthwhile. Built around 1583 by Sir Adam

Loftus, it appears today as an impressive semi-fortified mansion. Loftus was a Yorkshireman who came to Ireland as the Lord Deputy's chaplain and went on to become both Archbishop of Dublin and the first Provost of Trinity College – clearly a man of considerable wealth. The Dublin Hearth Money Roll of 1664 found only twenty establishments in the county with over eight hearths, and Rathfarnham was the largest of these with eighteen. In the 1720s the battlements were removed and, while the overall exterior retains its sixteenth-century appearance, the interior is that of a stately Georgian residence.

The castle passed through a number of hands in the seventeenth and eighteenth centuries, but in 1767 it was bought by Nicholas Loftus, second earl of Ely, a descendant of the archbishop and something of an eccentric, who erected a triumphal arch at the north entrance to the grounds. At one point he was nearly judged insane, but escaped committal thanks to his uncle, Henry Loftus, who defended him in court and inherited Rathfarnham after his death. It was Henry who made Rathfarnham a byword for luxury and refinement, hiring Sir William Chambers and James "Athenian" Stewart to remodel the rooms and installing aviaries and menageries in the grounds. In subsequent years the castle fell into decline, and in 1913 part of the land was sold off for a golf course – the castle itself was bought by the Jesuits.

Today the kitchen wing has been fully restored and although conservation work is still ongoing in the eighteenth-century apartments, they do give you some sense of the scale of Rathfarnham's former grandeur.

PEARSE MUSEUM

Map 2, G6. Daily: Feb–April & Sept–Oct 10am–1pm & 2–5pm; May–Aug 10am–1pm & 2–5.30pm; Nov–Jan 10am–1pm & 2–4pm; free. Bus #16 from O'Connell Street or Rathfarnham Castle.

If you're interested in the background to the 1916 Easter Rising, it's worth visiting the **Pearse Museum** in former St Enda's School in Rathfarnham village. The school was run by Pádraig Pearse from 1910 and set about promoting Gaelic culture by teaching its curriculum in Gaelic and encouraging students to take part in sports such as hurling, Gaelic football, camogie and handball. Sadly, the school attracted fewer pupils than Pearse had hoped for and in 1916, facing bankruptcy, it closed down. It was from here that Pearse and his brother Willie went out to fight on Easter Monday of that year. As a signatory to the Proclamation of the Irish Republic, Pearse was one of the first leaders to be executed at Kilmainham Jail (see p.99). His idealism and heroism are the leitmotif of a twenty-minute audio-visual show, entitled "This Man Kept a School".

The museum also has a nature study centre with a self-guiding trail around **St Enda's Park** (open until slightly later than the museum), which features riverside walks, a waterfall and a walled garden where outdoor concerts are held during the summer.

DRIMNAGH CASTLE

Map 2, E5. April–Oct Wed, Sat & Sun noon–5pm; Nov–March Sun 2–5pm; £1.50, students £1, children £0.50. Bus #56A from Eden Quay.

Drimnagh Castle is well worth the bus journey through the pebble-dashed suburb of Drimnagh, three miles south-west of the centre. Visible from Long Mile Road, behind a Christian Brothers School, the castle's rugged profile attests to eight hundred years of inhabitation and alterations.

The **tower house** was built in the thirteenth century by the Anglo-Norman Barnewall family, who occupied it for nearly four hundred years, but its defensive role declined as the lawless clans of the Wicklow Mountains were subdued. Sir Adam Loftus of Rathfarnham Castle leased Drimnagh in the seventeenth century, replacing some of the arrow-slit windows with mullioned ones, adding a rooftop fumerelle for smoke to escape, and a front staircase to supersede the low ground-floor entrance beneath a "murder hole", designed to force attackers to stoop as lime or boiling water was poured on their heads.

Inside, the **spiral staircase** unusually turns anticlockwise, as stairways were built to favour the defender's swordhand and Sir Hugh Barnewall was left-handed. At the top is a garderobe (toilet) sited conveniently near the **Great Hall**, which was an all-purpose living room and sleeping quarters. Its floor would originally have been strewn with rushes, but restorers have surfaced it with tiles bearing the coats of arms of the Barnewall, Loftus and Lansdowne families. Over the centuries there have been sightings of the **ghost of Eleanora**, Hugh de Barnewall's niece, who is said to have killed herself on hearing that she was destined to marry her cousin. The Jacobean-Tudor minstrels' gallery and the hammer-beamed roof of Roscommon oak are modern replicas. Some of the craftspeople involved in their creation were honoured by statues in medieval guise, carved on the beams. The chandeliers come from the film *Excalibur*, which was shot in Ireland at the Powerscourt Estate (see p.179).

Behind the house are a small seventeenth-century French-style **garden** with bay hedges and a **poultry-run** for diverse breeds of fowl. The aim is to restore the grounds to something of the self-sufficiency that prevailed in medieval times and persisted as late as 1954, when Drimnagh was vacated by the Hatch family, who lived and ran a dairy business here.

The outskirts

A huge arc of coastline has effectively become part of the greater Dublin metropolitan area, but even so, you'll feel like you're leaving the city behind as you head down the coast. You'll pass **Dún Laoghaire** with its great harbour overlooked by the Martello tower in **Sandycove**, immortalized in *Ulysses*, and the charming seaside towns of **Dalkey** and **Killiney**, with the Wicklow Mountains on the outskirts of **Bray**, further south.

All of these places are accessible from Dublin by frequent DART trains, making it easy to visit several in a day's outing. The DART isn't quite as useful for northerly outskirts, but a bus ride will take you to the exquisite Casino in **Marino**, or on to **Glasnevin**, home to the Botanic Gardens and Prospect Cemetery, or further east, towards the dunes and seabirds on **Dollymount Strand**, just offshore from Clontarf.

The headland of **Howth** is the scenic highlight of this part of Dublin, with a cliffside walk as fine as any on the south coast. Beyond Howth, **Malahide** deserves a visit for its delightful castle, while **Donabate** is home to the quirky Newbridge House and a traditional farm. Both are accessible by suburban trains or buses from Dublin.

SOUTH ALONG THE COAST

The DART line south follows the course of Ireland's first railway, opened in 1834, which ran from Dublin to Kingstown (as Dún Laoghaire was then called) where, at the townsfolk's insistence, it terminated on the outskirts. After their intolerance had abated, the railway was extended to Dalkey along the route of a quarry-railroad called "The Metals", and finally right down to Arklow – though the DART itself terminates at Bray.

Boarding a train in the centre, you'll catch a first glimpse of the sea on the horizon at Sandymount. Two stops later, the track starts to trail along beside Dublin Bay, past the UNESCO-designated bird sanctuary of Booterstown Marsh, whose wading birds are visible from the station platform. Glimpses of the sea alternate with views of the railway as you pass through Blackrock and Monkstown, till Dún Laoghaire harbour comes into view.

Dún Laoghaire

By DART, or bus #7, #7A or #45A from Trinity College. Night buses (Thurs–Sat) from College Street.

The seaside town of **Dún Laoghaire** (pronounced "Dunleary") is virtually a suburb of Dublin but there's still a residue of a resort atmosphere here. The harbour, now a port for ferries from Britain and the base for lightships and yacht clubs, was built to hold a great fleet within its two mile-long granite piers and was the largest artificial harbour in the world at the time of its construction (1817–42).

The **East Pier** has all the requisites for an edifying stroll: a bandstand, a lifeboat memorial, a compass pointer, and an anemometer for measuring windspeed (one of the first in the world when installed in 1852). Along the landward side are the crusty members-only Royal Irish Yacht Club (dating from 1850), Royal St George Yacht Club (1863) and National Yacht Club (1876) – with the non-elitist National Sailing School over on the **West Pier**.

Just inland from the Carlisle Pier, which is within the harbour, stands an odd **monument to George IV** (commemorating his state visit of 1821), which was described by Thackeray as "a hideous obelisk, stuck upon four fat balls, and surmounted by a crown on a cushion". The king had been expected to disembark here, but landed, visibly drunk, at Howth instead, though he tried to make amends by departing from Dún Laoghaire. One of the balls is newer than the others; the original was blown away by the IRA, who also put paid to a statue of Queen Victoria that stood nearby. A little way uphill is Andrew O'Connor's sculpture **Christ the King**, which the civic fathers purchased in 1949 but kept in storage till 1979 because Church authorities objected to it.

Further along the main street, past the shopping centre and the post office, stands the former Mariners' Church on Haigh Terrace, a fitting home for the **National Maritime Museum** (map 7, C3; April & Oct Sun 1–5pm; May–Sept Tues–Sun 1–5pm; £1.50, children £0.80, family £4). Its star exhibit is a giant clockwork-driven **Baily Optic** which was used in Howth lighthouse from 1902 to 1972. Vying for second place is a French ship's longboat captured at Bantry Bay in 1796 from Wolfe Tone's failed invasion, and sea charts and other items from the German U-boat that landed Sir Roger Casement in 1916. Ask to see the brass nail from *HMS Bounty* – one of the few that the mutineers didn't use to barter sexual favours from the Tahitians. Among the scale models is one of Brunel's early steamships, *The Great Eastern* (1858), which proved a commercial failure as a passenger ship but laid the first transatlantic cable between Ireland and North America.

To blow any cobwebs away, try the **Dublin Bay Sea Thrill** (£150 for ten people or £16 per person). You'll be togged up to withstand a deluge of spray on this forty-minute zoom about in a high-speed inflatable. Trips depart every hour from 9.30am in summer, but less regularly during other seasons; the ticket office (℗260 0949) is just outside the Arts Centre by the entrance to Carlisle Pier.

More sedate boat trips down to Sandycove, Dalkey Island and Killiney Bay can be arranged at short notice for £40 (the boat can carry twelve passengers) at Dún Laoghaire Boat Charter (℗282 3426) on the East Pier.

Sandycove

By DART, or bus #8 from Dún Laoghaire.

Not far down the coast from the East Pier, Dún Laoghaire merges into **Sandycove**, a quieter suburb whose most famous son was Roger Casement, the British diplomat turned Irish rebel. Casement made his name as a consul championing the rights of indigenous tribes in the Belgian Congo and the Peruvian Amazon, and retired with a knighthood, convinced that Irish freedom was his next cause. In 1914 he travelled to Berlin to enlist German support; he returned by U-boat shortly before the Easter Rising, but was soon captured. Charged with high treason, Casement was stripped of his honours and hanged at Pentonville prison in London.

Today, Sandycove is more widely associated with James Joyce, who for a brief period lived in the **Martello tower** – now a Joyce museum and the starting point of the Bloomsday pilgrimage. Originally it was just one of 21 such towers built against the threat of French invasion in 1804–06. Their walls are 2.4m thick and an armoured door 3.6m off the ground is the sole means of entry, making them almost impregnable – but they never fired a shot in anger. You'll see other Martello towers at Dalkey, Bray, Howth and Sandymount.

The Sandycove tower is called the **James Joyce Tower** (April–Oct Mon–Sat 10am–1pm & 2–5pm, Sun & bank holidays 2–6pm; £2.70, concessions £2.20, children £1.40), not so much for its association with his life – Joyce spent barely a week here in August 1904, four months before eloping with Nora Barnacle – but more because it features so prominently in the opening chapter of *Ulysses*. The characterization of "stately, plump Buck Mulligan" was Joyce's revenge on his host, Oliver St John Gogarty. On the sixth night of Joyce's stay, a fellow guest, Samuel Chenevix Trench, had a nightmare about a panther and fired some shots into the fireplace; Gogarty seized the gun and shot down a row of saucepans above Joyce's head, shouting, "Leave him to me!" Joyce took the hint and left promptly.

All of the items on show are donations to the museum, which was opened in 1962 by Sylvia Beach, who first published *Ulysses*. An edition illustrated by Matisse vies for attention with a plaintive letter from Joyce to Nora, accusing her of "treating me as if I were simply a casual comrade in lust", and such odd exhibits as a pandybat of the kind with which Joyce was beaten for "vulgar language" at school. In the first-floor guardroom, Gogarty's abode has been re-created complete with a life-size ceramic panther representing Trench's *bête noire*. The spiral staircase emerges on the rooftop gun-platform where Buck Mulligan does his ablutions at the start of the novel.

From there you can see right over the back yard of **Geragh**, a Constructivist seaside villa which the architect Michael Scott built for his family in the 1930s. Beyond it lies a knobbly brown headland with a famous bathing place known as the **Forty Foot Pool** (so called not for its size but because the 40th Regiment of Foot used to be stationed in a battery nearby). The pool was long reserved for male nude bathing: nowadays both sexes can use it but "Togs must be worn" – though nude bathers still get away with it before 9am. If you're tempted to join them, bear in mind the water temperature only varies by about 5°C throughout the year, so you'll find it pretty chilly.

Dalkey and Killiney

By DART or bus #8 from Dún Laoghaire or Sandycove.

Just down the coast from Sandycove is the charming seaside town of **Dalkey** (pronounced "Dawky"), immortalized in Flann O'Brien's satirical novel *The Dalkey Archive*. On sunny days its narrow streets and cliffside villas have an almost Mediterranean lushness that makes Dublin itself seem a little cold and grey. Historically, Dalkey has thrived on comparisons with the capital: for two hundred years, it was the only natural harbour on the east coast of Ireland. Goods unloaded here filled Dalkey's warehouses and swelled its coffers, until the dredging of the Liffey in the sixteenth century wiped out its business and Dalkey dwindled to a village. In time, though, Dalkey's beauty ensured that fresh comparisons were made, as well-to-do Dubliners built seaside homes and the advent of the railway brought day-trippers with it. Today, its nostalgic old quarter merges into a commuter-belt hinterland under the cover of forested slopes and azaleas.

From the DART station it's a short walk down Railway Road to Castle Street, distinguished by two fortified warehouses from the fifteenth century, when Dalkey was dubbed the "Port of the Seven Castles". **Goat Castle**, across the way from **Archibold's Castle**, serves as Dalkey's town hall, with a **Visitors Centre** (Mon–Sat 9am–5pm; £2.50) that features detailed exhibits on the town's history, set within the castle's impressive interior. Further north stands **Bulloch Castle**, built by the Cistercians in 1180 to protect the fishing harbour not far from Sandycove.

Dalkey's main attraction is the lovely walk down **Coliemore Road** past Georgian houses and Victorian villas, to the harbour facing Dalkey Island, from which you can then head south along the cliffside **Vico Road** to view the fabulous coastline.

From mid-April till the end of summer there are daily boat trips, weather permitting, from Coliemore Harbour (℡283 4298; £3 return) to **Dalkey Island**, 300m offshore, although it is advisable to phone in advance as even when the weather is fine the service can be a little erratic. First inhabited 8500 years ago (the dwelling sites are marked by thickets of nettles), the island was known in Gaelic as Deiliginish (from which Dalkey derives), a name which recalls a spiked wooden fort (*Deilig* means "thorn" or "spike") that once existed there. Here you'll find another Martello tower and the ruins of an early Irish church, St Begnet's, on the other side of the saddle-shaped island. **Fishing trips** can be arranged through the *Dalkey Island Hotel* (by the harbour; ℡285 0377); you can charter a boat for the day or hire a rowing boat for a few hours.

Dalkey Hill is definitely worth climbing; steps and a path ascend steeply from Vico Road, or there's an easier route from the park on Ardbrugh Road. Shavians can track down **Torca Cottage**, where George Bernard Shaw spent much of his boyhood; the house is privately-owned, but a plaque on the wall acknowledges Shaw with his words, "The men of Ireland are mortal and temporal but the hills are eternal." En route to the summit there's a fine view of Dalkey **quarry**, where the granite blocks that form the walls of Coliemore Harbour and the great piers of Dún Laoghaire were hewn. To give your lungs a workout, follow the ridge up to **Killiney Hill**, where a park has been laid out for visitors to enjoy the glorious **view** of Dublin Bay and the Wicklow Mountains.

Killiney, in the next bay, is the Irish equivalent of Beverly Hills, where stars like Mel Gibson, Tom Cruise, George Michael and Lisa Stansfield own property alongside such indigenous luminaries as Chris De Burgh, Bono and The Edge, writers Maeve Binchy and Hugh Leonard, and film director Neil Jordan. Celebrity-spotting aside, the real attraction is the wide grey beach running along the length of the bay.

Bray

Beyond Killiney the coast relapses into humdrum suburbia, but things pick up as you approach **Bray**, whose rugged headland contrasts with the softer flanks of the Wicklow Mountains. Its fine surroundings make amends for the resort, which is a poor relation to Dalkey and Dún Laoghaire. Though the amusement arcade and places to eat and drink are open all year round, Bray only really comes alive in the summer, especially during the **International Festival of Music and Dance** (see p.292) in August. The **Oscar Wilde Autumn School** (see p.292) in October marks the end of the festive calendar. Details of both events are available from the tourist office (daily 10am–5pm; ℂ286 6796) in the Old Court House on Main Road, which doubles as a heritage centre devoted to local history and the achievements of Sir William Dargan, the builder of the Dublin–Kingstown railway and founder of the National Gallery.

One interesting diversion here though, especially if you have children, is the **National Sea-Life Centre** on the seafront (Mon–Sat 10am–5pm; £5.50, students and OAPs £3.95, family £17), an aquarium specializing in Irish marine life that is both entertaining – the touch pool, full of crabs and starfish, is a particular favourite – and educational, with a strong emphasis on the need for conservation.

Bray Head is worth climbing for the view of the town and the hills enclosing the bay. The leeward side partakes of the softness of Wicklow, the "Garden of Ireland", where trees and plants from five continents flourish in gardens that throw open their gates during the **Wicklow Gardens Festival** (mid-May to late July, see p.288). A full list of the gardens and viewing days is available from the tourist office; the easiest to reach is the seventeenth-century French-style garden of **Killruddery House** (May, June & Sept daily 10am–5pm; £1.50), off the Southern Cross Route on the edge of Bray (bus #84 from Main Street or a twenty-minute walk from Strand Road). By paying £2.50 extra you can tour Killruddery House itself, the Tudor Revival seat of the earls of Meath, which was a famous hunting-lodge for generations.

NORTH TO HOWTH AND BEYOND

Heading northwards from the centre of Dublin, you won't catch sight of the sea from the DART until you're nearly at Sutton, and there isn't much time to enjoy the view before the line terminates at Howth, the rugged northern head-land of Dublin Bay. Aside from Howth, the bay's only real seaside spot is Dollymount Strand, a few miles from the centre. The other main attractions are in the suburbs of Marino and Glasnevin, and out beyond Howth in Malahide and Donabate. While **buses** are the only way to get to Marino, Glasnevin and Dollymount, Malahide and Donabate can also be reached by **train** from Connolly Station. You'll need to catch a suburban train bound for Drogheda, which can also be boarded at Howth Junction – an interchange between the DART and suburban lines (not to be confused with Howth, the DART terminus). Until 1959, Dubliners enjoyed riding the famous Hill of Howth trams, which crested the summit of the peninsula; bus #31B does the same today, sans romance – though the view is still pretty spectacular.

The Casino at Marino

Map 2, F4. May daily noon–4pm; June–Sept 9.30am–6.30pm; Oct daily 10am–5pm; Nov Sun & Wed only noon–4pm; £2, students/children £1, family £5. Bus #123 from O'Connell Street, or #20A, #20B, #27, #27A, #27B, #42, #42B or #42C from Beresford Place.

Marino, off Malahide Road 5km northeast of O'Connell Street, originally enjoyed a sweeping view of Dublin Bay that made it an ideal location for a stately home. It was here that the earl of Charlemont endeavoured to bring the civilization of ancient Rome and Renaissance Italy to Ireland by creating a splendid park and a mansion to display the antiquities he had collected during his nine-year Grand Tour of Europe. While nothing remains of Marino House you can still admire the elegant summer residence that was the *pièce de résistance* of his estate, the **Casino** (*casino* being the diminutive version of *casa*, the Italian word for "house"). Regarded as one of the finest Neoclassical buildings in Ireland, its construction preoccupied Charlemont from 1758 to the 1770s.

The Casino cost £20,000 (equivalent to about £3 million today) and was designed by Sir William Chambers – the architect of Charlemont's town house on Parnell Square (now the Hugh Lane Gallery – see p.118). Its most remarkable feature is the way Chambers plays with your perception of its scale, so that what outwardly seems to be a one-roomed pavilion actually contains two floors of rooms, each designed to appear larger than it is. To maintain the illusion, the "doorway" is a dummy with only one panel that opens, and the large windows are masked to hide the fact that they illuminate two levels, with curved panes of glass to reflect the outside world. With equal ingenuity, the downpipes that carry rainwater into underground cisterns are hidden in the columns, and the chimney pots are disguised as urns.

Among the curiosities on the top floor are a child's bed that could be extended as the infant grew, and the earl's own bedroom, with a huge "boat" bed modelled on one at Versailles. Charlemont married in late middle age after he fell out with his brother and decided to sire an heir so that his sibling would be disinherited. In public life, he was regarded as one of the most enlightened and cultivated men of his day; his belief in Irish self-government led him to become the first commander-in-chief of the Irish Volunteers and to leave his deathbed to vote against the Act of Union in the last session of the Grattan Parliament.

If you're catching a bus back into town, try to sit upstairs on the left for a view of **Marino Crescent**. This elegant row of Georgian houses was once nicknamed "Ffolliot's revenge" after the man who built the crescent out of spite, to block Charlemont's view of the sea. To further upset him, Ffolliot ensured that the side facing Marino House was an unsightly jumble of chimneys and sheds. No. 15 was the **birthplace of Bram Stoker**, the author of *Dracula*, and now hosts an annual summer school devoted to the author and his creation.

As bus #42 runs on to Malahide, it's easy to visit the Casino en route to (or back from) Malahide Castle (see p.173).

Glasnevin

Bus #13, #19 or #19A from Upper O'Connell St.

A village on the cattle-road from Meath, **Glasnevin** remained quite bucolic until the establishment of two civic amenities catalysed its evolution into a genteel suburb of pebble-dashed maisonettes and B&Bs. It now coexists uneasily alongside Finglas, a sprawl of new estates built to rehouse inner-city slum-tenants, which is rough enough for the Alsatian dogs to walk around in pairs (so locals joke).

NORTH TO HOWTH AND BEYOND

As you head off Botanic Road on to Glasnevin Hill you'll see the gates of the **National Botanic Gardens** (map2, F3; March–Oct Mon–Sat 9am–6pm, Sun 11am–6pm; Nov–Feb Mon–Sat 10am–4.30pm, Sun 11am–4.30pm; free), founded by an act of the Irish Parliament in 1795. Ireland's mild climate makes it an excellent place for growing exotic species, and its Botanic Gardens were the first in the world to raise orchids from seed and the first in Europe to grow pampas grass and the giant waterlily. Some 20,000 species and varieties flourish over nineteen hectares of rockeries and arboretums, and in cast-iron glasshouses that are early masterpieces of the genre. The **Curvilinear Range** was fabricated by Richard Turner, a Dublin ironmaster who built the Palm House at Kew Gardens in London; its newly restored ironwork is sublime. The **Palm House** is showing its age, but the new **Alpine House** is a worthy addition to Turner's legacy.

Alongside the Botanic Gardens lies the Glasnevin or **Prospect Cemetery** (daily 8.30am–4pm; free), a place ennobled by the remains of national heroes. Established as a burial place for Catholics by Daniel O'Connell in 1832, its jungle of Celtic crosses, shamrocks, harps and other patriotic iconography is elucidated by **guided tours** (late May–Sept Sun 11.30am; free). The 51-metre-high Round Tower is a monument to O'Connell, whose body was interred in its crypt in 1869, having been brought home from Genoa in 1847. Similar pomp attended the burial of Parnell, whose tomb is topped by a huge granite boulder; his beloved Kitty was buried with far less ceremony in Sussex. Other historical figures among the 11.5 million dead at Glasnevin include Roger Casement, Michael Collins, Arthur Griffith, Jim Larkin, Countess Markievicz and Éamon de Valera; from the arts, Gerard Manley Hopkins, Maud Gonne MacBride and Brendan Behan. The main entrance is on a small square at the end of Prospect Avenue, where *Kavanagh's*, one of the city's finest pubs, has consoled mourners since 1833; it's best reached by retracing your steps and taking the first small lane after the cemetery walls.

Dollymount Strand

Bus #32X from St Stephen's Green, or the Fairview/Clontarf Road near Marino.

In fine weather it's pleasant to stroll along **Dollymount Strand**, the popular name for **North Bull Island**, which was built in 1821 to prevent Dublin Harbour from silting up, at the suggestion of Captain Bligh of *HMS Bounty* fame. Besides holidaying Dubliners, the island accommodates over 40,000 birds, many of them Arctic migrants. Shelducks, curlews and oyster-catchers wade upon the mudflats and larks nest in the dunes (now designated a UNESCO Biosphere Reserve), which also sustain foxes, shrews, badgers, rabbits and many plant species. You can find out more at an interpretive centre at the end of the causeway road from the mainland, one mile's walk from the bus stop on James Larkin Road.

Howth

By DART or bus #31B from Lower Abbey Street or Howth Road (near Marino).

A rugged peninsula at the northernmost point of Dublin Bay, **Howth** derives its name from the Danish *hoved*, or "cape", and is pronounced to rhyme with "both". While the DART gives you a glimpse of the northern coast of the peninsula, the bus crosses the summit, with views right across Dublin Bay to the Wicklow Mountains, and even the Mountains of Mourne on fine days.

For the best places to stay in Howth see p.207;
for the nicest places to eat see p.242.

NORTH TO HOWTH AND BEYOND

Howth **village** is a sleepy place of steep streets and dramatic views. Poised above Harbour Road but accessible by Church Street, the Gothic shell of **St Mary's Abbey** dates from the fourteenth to the seventeenth centuries and traces its origin to the first church founded by the Norse king Sitric, in 1042. You can see a fair bit of the interior without going to the trouble of obtaining the keys from Mrs O'Rourke at no. 3 Church Street, but will need them to view the fifteenth-century double tomb of Lord and Lady Howth. St Mary's offers a fine view of Howth harbour and Ireland's Eye, and there's food and music to be enjoyed at *Ye Olde Abbey Tavern*, on the road below.

Howth Castle, built in 1564, is the oldest inhabited house in Ireland and is a weather-beaten and battlemented veteran of numerous restorations down to the present century. For many years the St Lawrence family kept open house at mealtimes, a custom said to have arisen from an incident in 1575, when Grace O'Malley, the "Uncrowned Queen of the West", was turned away because the family was at dinner, and reacted by kidnapping their eldest son and holding him until Lord Howth promised to keep his gates open at mealtimes in the future. Although the castle isn't open to the public, you can wander along to a barn that enthusiasts have turned into a **National Transport Museum** (June–Aug daily 10am–5pm; Sept–May Sat, Sun & bank holidays noon–5pm; £1.50, children £0.50, family £3), with vehicles from buses to fire engines and armoured cars, including a Hill of Howth tram. In spring, don't miss the **rhododendron glades** behind the Deer Park golf club, where four hundred species flourish in the peaty soil below Mud Rock. Just downhill is a prehistoric dolmen, its gigantic 91,000-kilo capstone balanced on a dozen smaller rocks.

On a fine day you can enjoy Howth's famous **Cliff Walk**, with imposing rockscapes and superb **views** south past the mouth of the Liffey to the Wicklow Mountains, and north

to the flatlands of the Boyne. The footpath runs right
around the peninsula, but the four-kilometre arc from the
Nose of Howth to the lighthouse is the most scenic. You
can get there by walking out along Balscadden – which
commits you to the whole distance – or conserve your
energy by taking a #31B bus to the summit, and cutting
down to the **Baily Lighthouse** on the southeast point.
Built in 1814 on the site of a Celtic fort (*baile*), it was, until
March 1997, the last manned lighthouse on Ireland's coastline. From the so-called summit, you can climb to the 171-
metre **Ben of Howth**.

Malahide

Map 1, E4. Castle April–Oct Mon–Sat 10am–5pm, Sun & holidays
11.30am–6pm; Nov–March Mon–Fri 10am–5pm, Sat, Sun &
holidays 2–5pm; £3.15, students/children £2.65, family £8.75.
Combined ticket for Castle and Newbridge House £4.95,
unemployed £3.90, children £2.55, family £12.50. Bus #42 from
Beresford Place (or Marino), or suburban train from Connolly
Station or Howth to Malahide Junction (no service on Sun).

A few miles up the coast from Howth, the old feudal estate
of **Malahide** lends its name to a commuter village of pretty
houses and quiet streets sloping gently down to a yachting
marina. Its chief attraction is **Malahide Castle**, a medieval
tower house that was modified and expanded over the eight
hundred years that it was owned by the Talbot family. The
Talbots were of Anglo-Norman origin but remained
Catholic until the eighteenth century; dispossessed while
Cromwell was in power, they regained Malahide after the
Restoration, and it stayed in the family until the death of
Lord Milo in 1975, when the estate was acquired by Dublin
County Council. Its charm lies in its disparate styles, as the
twelfth-century **tower house** evolved from a defensive to a
domestic building while retaining the look of a romantic

NORTH TO HOWTH AND BEYOND

173

castle. The first room, whose stone walls are hidden behind dark Jacobean panelling, was the principal one in the tower house. The Virgin carved over the fireplace was the family totem and is said to have disappeared during the years that Malahide was given to Cromwell's general, Myles Corbet, as a reward for his signature on the death warrant of Charles I.

You then pass on through the west wing to the **family bedrooms**, featuring a four-poster bed which is said to have belonged to the actor David Garrick. From there you descend to the Great Hall, whose oak hammer-beam ceiling and minstrels' gallery date from 1475. The low door in the corner is known as "Puck's Door", after the ghost of a servant who fell asleep on the night when invaders attacked, and hanged himself in shame. It's said to appear whenever there are changes Puck dislikes and made its last appearance in 1975, when the contents of the castle were auctioned. A picture of the Battle of the Boyne is flanked by portraits of "Fighting Dick" Talbot and thirteen other family males who breakfasted here on the morning of the battle, never to return. The tour ends in a small library with Flemish wall-hangings and an exquisite inlaid table. In 1928, many of the papers of James Boswell (the great-grandfather of Emily Boswell, who married the fifth Lord Talbot) were found here, including an unexpurgated draft of his *Life of Johnson*.

Having seen the castle, most visitors make a beeline for the **Fry Model Railway** (April–Sept Mon–Thurs 10am–6pm, Sat 11am–6pm, Sun & holidays 2–6pm, June–Aug also Fri 10am–6pm; Oct–March Sat, Sun & holidays 2–5pm; £2.90, students and OAPs £2.20, children £1.70, family £7.95) installed in the old Corn Store. The nation's largest model railway layout (covering 240 square metres), it represents Ireland's transport system in all its diversity, from canal barges to the DART and ferry services.

Another sight in the vicinity is the fifteenth-century **Church of St Sylvester**, wherein lies Maud Plunkett, the heroine of Gerald Griffin's ballad *The Bride of Malahide*, who was "maid, wife and widow" in one day, after her husband was killed in battle on their wedding day (she later married a Talbot). On the west gable is a *sheela-na-gig*, a relic of pagan times featured on many medieval Irish churches, depicting naked figures. Finally, there is the twenty-acre **Botanic Gardens** laid out by Lord Milo early this century, which contain 5000 species from Australia, New Zealand and Chile.

Newbridge House

Map 1, E3. April–Sept Tues–Sat 10am–1pm & 2–5pm, Sun & bank holidays 2–6pm; Oct–March Sat, Sun & bank holidays 2–5pm; £3, students £2.60, children £1.60, family £8.25. Bus #33B from Eden Quay, or suburban train from Connolly Station or Malahide (no service Sun).

Next stop along the Malahide line is **Donabate**, a trim commuter village that is graced by **Newbridge House**, a solid brownstone edifice built in 1737 for Charles Cobbe, archbishop of Dublin from 1742 to 1765. It remained in the Cobbe family until 1985, when the estate was sold to Dublin County Council.

The **Dining Room** has a lovely Rococo ceiling commissioned by Lady Betty Beresford, who married the archbishop's son. Off the adjacent library lies the family's **Museum of Curiosities**, containing all sorts of shells and artefacts from around the world, including an intricate Kashmiri sari box and a pair of tiny shoes from China, used to cover a woman's bound feet. The inner hall, beyond, leads to the upper floor via a stairway featuring a portrait of one of Swift's beloveds – either Stella or another woman called Vanessa (it is not known which) – and the magnificent **Red Drawing Room**, which was added to the house around 1760, and, though dominated by its crimson curtains, wallpaper and carpet, also has a fine hand-moulded plaster ceiling. Finally, you descend to the basement, where the laundry features a manually-operated washing machine and an early vacuum cleaner, while the **kitchen** is crammed with fascinating devices such as a duck-press for squeezing juice from poultry, and a mousetrap that drowned its victims. The house remained unelectrified until the 1960s, when it was wired up for the filming of *The Spy Who Came in from the Cold*.

Attached to the house is a traditional farm (£1, students/children £0.80, family £2), home to various breeds of sheep, fowl, pigs and cattle. In the coach house you can see the gilded ceremonial coach made for "Black Jack" Fitzgibbon, who was such an unpopular Lord Chancellor that someone once threw a rat through the window during a procession.

Day-trips from Dublin

I t's feasible to travel to most parts of the country in less than a day from Dublin, making the list of possible excursions endless. In this chapter we've concentrated on six places within a short range of the capital which represent a geographical and historical cross-section of what's on offer, covering an arc from the Wicklow Mountains to the Neolithic sites of the Boyne Valley.

To the south, the **Wicklow Mountains** are modest in height (the highest peak is under 1000m), but have remained very sparsely populated – for many centuries they were bandit country. From a tourist's point of view, three attractions stand out from the rest: the **Powerscourt Estate**, famous for its splendid gardens; the early monastic site of **Glendalough**; and **Russborough House**, renowned for its decoration and art collection. If you're travelling around by car, you may want to visit the award-winning **Larchill Arcadian Gardens**, one of Ireland's most fascinating artificial landscapes.

The landscape is less inspiring to the west, with small towns and villages fast becoming suburbs of Dublin. But if

Tours out of the city

There's a plethora of one-day and half-day tours available from Dublin and, given the limitations of public transport, they're well worth considering. Most need to be booked a day or two ahead in advance during high season – the Tourism Centre (see p.7) can do this for you in most instances. The price of the tour includes admission charges for the site.

Bus Éireann (℃836 6111) runs excursions to Glendalough and the Wicklow Mountains (mid-Jan to March & early Nov to mid-Dec Wed, Sat & Sun; April–Oct daily; £17), and Newgrange and the Boyne Valley (Feb–April & Oct–Nov Thurs & Sat; May–Sept Mon–Thurs, Sat & Sun; £17). Buses depart from the Busáras.

Cultúr Beo (℃459 9159; £10, groups at other times by arrangement). Leisurely guided walk, generally three to five miles (approx 2–3 hours), taking in myth and prehistory in the Glenasmole Valley, County Wicklow. Depart Wed 9.30am opposite Hazelbrook House, 85 Gardiner Street.

Dublin Bus (℃873 4222; see p.12) runs a "South Coast Tour" (daily, £12) which takes in fine coastal scenery, with a stop-off at Avoca handweavers, and views of the Sugarloaf mountain. Their "Coast and Castle Tour" (daily, £12) takes in Howth and Malahide Castle.

Fingal Traditional Sailing (daily, by advance arrangement and weather permitting; ℃843 0340; £230 half-day, £400 full day, prices for six people). Explore the coast and sail around Lambay's Island or Ireland's Eye in an exhilarating Galway Hooker – the traditional forty-foot vessel of Connemara. Starting point either Howth, Malahide or Skerries – the company can arrange pick-ups.

Gray Line (℃605 7705) runs half-day tours (£15.50) to Glendalough, Newgrange, Malahide Castle and Powerscourt Estate, and full-day tours (£27) taking in a combination of these. Gray Line operate at times of the year not covered by Bus Éireann, and coaches leave from the Tourism Centre on Suffolk Street.

The Wild Wicklow Tour (℃280 1899). Fun, sociable tour of the wilds of Wicklow, taking in Glendalough and stupendous scenery. (Sat & Sun, March–Nov also Wed–Fri; £22).

you're interested in stately homes and the lifestyle of the old Anglo-Irish Ascendancy, it's worth taking a suburban bus out to Celbridge to explore **Castletown House**, which was founded by William Connolly, one of the most influential figures of Dublin's golden age.

The Boyne Valley in County Meath, north of Dublin, has the distinction of being Ireland's richest pasture land. The area known as the **Brú na Bóinne** (Palace of the Boyne) is the site of three prehistoric passage graves – **Newgrange**, **Knowth** and **Dowth** – that are among the most remarkable archeological structures in Europe. We haven't covered Dowth in this chapter as it's currently closed to the public.

While most of these places can be reached by public **transport**, in some cases – especially Brú na Bóinne and Powerscourt – you may want to take an **organized tour** from Dublin, which makes for a smoother day out (see box opposite).

POWERSCOURT ESTATE

Map 1, E7. Gardens daily: March–Oct 9.30am–5.30pm; Nov–Feb 9.30am to dusk; £3.50, students £3, children £2. **House** daily: 9.30am–5.30pm, winter times may vary; £1.50, students £1.30, children £1. Combined ticket for gardens and house £5, students £4.50, child £3. **Waterfall** daily: summer 9.30am–7pm; winter 10.30am–dusk; £2, students £1.50, children £1. Bus #44 from Hawkins Street (off Burgh Quay) or #185 from Bray DART station to Enniskerry.

Nestled in the foothills of the Wicklow Mountains, the village of **Enniskerry** originally belonged to the **Powerscourt Estate**, which was owned by a dynasty founded by one of James I's generals, Richard Wingfield. The great house, 1km from Enniskerry, is one of the largest Palladian mansions in Ireland, but its real attraction is the magnificent gardens which are blended into the backdrop of the Great Sugarloaf and other Wicklow peaks.

The grey-stone **house** with its twin copper domes was designed by Richard Cassels for the first Viscount Powerscourt and took a decade to build (1731–41). From afar it still looks impressive, inside, however, only shadows of its former glory remain. Although gutted by fire in 1974 (on the eve of a party to celebrate the completion of extensive renovation) you can at least get some sense of its past grandeur from the smoky brickwork remains of the double-storey ballroom, based on Palladio's version of the "Egyptian Hall" designed by Vitruvius. Photographs of the room before the fire, with its classical columns and lavish gilt decoration, survive and are on display in the exhibition alongside an interesting audio-visual display on the history of Powerscourt.

The twenty-hectare **Garden** is entered through the gilded **Bamberg Gate**, which originally belonged to Bamberg Cathedral in Bavaria. The great stone terrace, with its angels of Fame and Victory, was designed in 1840 by Daniel Robertson, who used to be wheeled about in a barrow, clutching a bottle of sherry while working on the job. When his creative powers were exhausted and the bottle was empty, he'd call it a day. Fourteen years later, the seventh viscount began the terraced **Italian Gardens**, which accompany a grand staircase leading down to the circular **Triton Lake** with its central eponymous statue (based on Bernini's fountain in Rome).

At the far end of the terrace the land falls away sharply, enhancing the beauty of the North American conifers planted by Robertson. Behind the **Pepper Pot Tower** is the Killing Hollow, where the last of the O'Toole bandit clan was beheaded, and a little further down lies a very fragrant Edwardian **Japanese Garden** of Japanese maples, azaleas and Chinese Fortune Palms. Skirting the Triton Lake, you can carry on to the **Pet Cemetery**, where the graves of family dogs and horses are accompanied by that of a cow which produced seventeen calves and over 100,000 gallons of milk during her lifetime. Back at the house the **terrace café bar** and **restaurant** make an ideal spot from which to enjoy views over the gardens to the Wicklow Mountains.

The famous **Powerscourt waterfall** lies three miles from the house: turn right as you exit the main gate and follow the signs along the road. At 121m it's the highest in Ireland, leaping diagonally down the rockface into a valley where it joins the River Dargle.

Returning to Dublin from Powerscourt, you may want to pass through Glencullen, three miles from Enniskerry, to visit *Johnnie Fox's*, a popular pub which was once Daniel O'Connell's local.

GLENDALOUGH

Map 1, D8. Daily: mid-March to May & Sept to mid-Oct 9.30am–6pm; June–Aug 9am–6.30pm; mid-Oct to mid-March 9.30am–5pm; free. **Visitors Centre** same hours; £2, students/children £1, family £5. St Kevin's bus service from the Royal College of Surgeons, St Stephen's Green, Mon–Sat 11.30am & 6pm, Sun 11.30am & 7pm; £10 return.

Deeper into the Wicklow Mountains lies **Glendalough** (the "valley of the two lakes"), a magical setting for one of the best-preserved monastic sites in Ireland. Despite the car parks and the coach parties, there is a sense of peace and spirituality around here that makes it easy to imagine how hermits and monks once lived. The **Visitors Centre** features a film that sets Glendalough in the context of ancient monasteries elsewhere in Ireland and has a model of how it probably looked in those days.

The monastery's foundation is attributed to St Kevin, a scion of the royal house of Leinster who studied under three holy men before retreating to Glendalough to fast and pray in solitude. His piety attracted followers, and in 570 he became abbot of a monastic community. As a centre of the Celtic Church, the monastery became famous throughout Europe for its learning, and despite being sacked by the Vikings, Normans and English, it was restored each time, until being dissolved during the Reformation. However, as the pope decreed that seven visits to Glendalough would procure the same indulgence as one pilgrimage to Rome, pilgrimages continued until the mid-nineteenth century, when a local priest banned gatherings due to the licentious behaviour of the pilgrims following their devotions on St Kevin's day (June 3).

You enter the grounds through a double stone archway that was once surmounted by a tower. The nearest ruin is the **Cathedral**, dating from the early ninth century, whose roofless nave and chancel contain numerous grave slabs. Among the tombs outside stands **St Kevin's Cross**, a granite monolith that was left unfinished. Nearby is a small **Priest's House** from the twelfth century, above the door of which are carved three barely discernible figures, thought to represent Kevin and two abbots. Further downhill is a two-storey edifice with a steeply pitched roof and bell-turret, known as **St Kevin's Kitchen**, though it was probably

The Wicklow Way

If you prefer to explore the Wicklow Mountains on foot, there are plenty of opportunities for hiking, and the Wicklow Way provides access to some of the choicest spots, following a series of sheep tracks, forest firebreaks and bog roads, above 1600ft for most of the way. Running 82 miles from Marlay Park in the Dublin suburbs to Clonegal on the Wexford border, the whole route can be walked comfortably in ten to twelve days. If you want to do this, Marlay Park is accessible via the #47B bus from Hawkins Street. If you're short of time, the best part to walk is probably the three-day section between Knockree, three miles west of Enniskerry, and Glendalough; the path reaches its highest point at White Hill (2073ft), from which you can get a view of the mountains of North Wales on a fine day. Take the #44 bus from Hawkins Street to Enniskerry, and pick up St Kevin's bus service at Glendalough for the return journey. Alternatively, try one of the circular walks detailed in *Easy Walks Near Dublin* by Joss Lynam.

Low as they are, the Wicklow Mountains are notoriously treacherous, and even if you're planning on spending no more than a day walking, you should make sure you have the Ordnance Survey's map no. 56 (Wicklow/Dublin/Kildare; 1:50,000). If you begin your explorations at Glendalough, call in to the Wicklow Mountains National Park **information centre** for advice on routes and conditions. Bad weather can close in rapidly, and all the customary warnings about mountain walking apply; in addition to this you should avoid areas marked on the OS map marked as rifle ranges.

an oratory. The most impressive structure is the thirty-metre-high *Cloigtheach* or **Round Tower**, which served as a belfry, watchtower and place of refuge – the doorway high above the ground would have been reached by a ladder that could be pulled up in times of danger. (Such towers were a distinctive feature of Irish monasteries.) Further west, outside the enclosure, you'll see the remains of **St Mary's Church**, which is believed to have been the first building in the lower valley, and may mark the site of Kevin's grave.

Downhill from the Kitchen is a footbridge, on the far side of which is the hollowed-out **Deerstone**, so called after a legend claiming that tame deer squirted their milk into it to feed the motherless twins of one of Kevin's followers. By following the signposted "Green Road" skirting the Lower Lake, you'll come to the ruined **Reefert Church** and the start of a path to **St Kevin's Cell**, or rather the spot where he slept on a promontory overlooking the Upper Lake. He later moved into a cave halfway up the cliff – dubbed **St Kevin's Bed** – to avoid the advances of a maiden called Kathleen. She eventually found his hiding place and, awaking one morning to find her beside him, he reacted with the misogyny characteristic of the early church fathers by throwing her into the lake, where she drowned. (Kevin himself is said to have died in 617 or 618, at the age of 120.) The cave is only accessible by boat from the far shore of the lake in summer.

RUSSBOROUGH HOUSE

Map 1, B7. April & Oct Sun & bank holidays 10.30am–5.30pm; May & Sept Mon–Sat 10.30am–2.30pm, Sun & bank holidays 10.30am–5.30pm; June–Aug daily 10.30am–5.30pm; tours £4, students £3, children £2. Bus #65 from Eden Quay.

Five kilometres south of Blessington stands the classic Palladian structure of **Russborough House**, designed, like Powerscourt, by the German architect Richard Cassels (with the assistance of Francis Bindon). The house was constructed for Joseph Leeson, son of a rich Dublin brewer who became MP for Rathcormack then **Lord Russborough** in 1756.

Russborough epitomizes the great flowering of Anglo-Irish confidence before the Act of Union deprived Ireland of its parliament, much of its trade and its high society.

The **lake** in front of Russborough provides the house with an idiomatically eighteenth-century prospect – it is actually a thoroughly twentieth-century reservoir, created by damming the Liffey, which provides Dublin with twenty million gallons of water a day.

The chief reason why Russborough is so firmly on the tourist trail is its collection of **paintings**. The German entrepreneur Alfred Beit (1853–1906), co-founder with Cecil Rhodes of the De Beer Diamond Mining Company, poured the fortune he derived from that enterprise into amassing works of art. His nephew, Sir Alfred Beit, acquired Russborough in 1952, which explains why such an extraordinary collection of Dutch, Flemish and Spanish masterpieces are displayed both here and in the National Gallery (the pictures are frequently moved between the two).

Russborough has been burgled twice: first in 1974, when Bridget Rose Dugdale stole sixteen paintings to raise money for the IRA (her booty, worth £18 million, was recovered undamaged from a farmhouse in County Cork a week later); and again in May 1986. Some of the paintings taken in this second heist have since been retrieved in the Netherlands. Nowadays security is tight; the forty-five-minute guided tour limits study of the paintings in detail, but for all that it's still well worth a visit.

CASTLETOWN HOUSE

Map 1, B5. April & May Sun & bank holidays 1–6pm; June–Sept Mon–Fri 10am–6pm, Sat, Sun & bank holidays 1–6pm; Oct Mon–Fri 10am–5pm, Sun & bank holidays 1–5pm; Nov Sun 1–5pm; tours £2.50, students/children £1, family £6. Bus #67 or #67A from Middle Abbey Street to Celbridge.

Some 20km west of Dublin, on the upper reaches of the River Liffey, the village of **Celbridge** is the site of one of Ireland's great Palladian mansions, **Castletown House**, a building remarkable both for its size and ostentation.

Castletown was built for William Connolly, a publican's son from Donegal who made his fortune by dealing in forfeited estates after the Battle of the Boyne, as legal adviser to William III. Unanimously elected Speaker of the Irish House of Commons in 1715, he was acknowledged as the richest man in Ireland by the 1720s. He later joined the Hellfire Club (see p.64), holding sessions of debauchery at his hunting lodge outside Dublin. Castletown was begun in 1722, in a somewhat haphazard fashion, and the interior was still unfinished when he died seven years later. Work on the house didn't resume until his nephew, Tom Connolly, inherited it in 1758. The driving force was his wife, Lady Louisa, who was only fifteen years old when she assumed responsibility for the job, which carried on into the 1770s. Castletown was sold by the Connolly family in 1965, and would have been demolished to build houses if the property developers hadn't gone bust. Desmond Guinness stepped in to buy the house on behalf of the Irish Georgian Society, which used Castletown as its headquarters until 1994.

The **guided tour** starts in the Main Hall and takes in the pine-panelled Brown Study and the **Red Drawing Room**, which is covered in torn French damask. Its ceiling was designed by Sir William Chambers for Lady Louisa, as was the adjacent **Green Room**. The **Print Room**, next door, is the only surviving example in Ireland of the eighteenth-century fad for glueing prints onto walls. A splendid yellow-and-blue-silk canopied bed dominates the **State Bedroom**, beyond.

The grand cantilevered **staircase** has wonderful plasterwork by the Francini brothers on the walls and a painting of bears being savaged by hunting dogs. Upstairs the highlight is the **Long Gallery**, with its Pompeiian murals and gilded sconces bearing busts of poets and philosophers.

From the gallery's windows you can see the "**Connolly Folly**" two miles away. This bizarre structure appears to be a monument to chimney-sweeping, but was actually a memorial to William Connolly. His widow also commissioned the **Wonderful Barn**, a weird conical tower with an external stairway, which can be seen from the N4 motorway. Both projects were set up to provide relief work for estate labourers hit by the famine-ridden winter of 1739. Unfortunately, the land on which they stand no longer belongs to the estate, and both are too far from the house to reach on foot.

LARCHILL ARCADIAN GARDENS

Map 1, A4. May–Sept noon–6pm; £3.25.

If you're exploring this area by car, **Larchill Arcadian Gardens**, around eight miles from Castletown House, just north of Kilcock off the N4, is well worth a detour. Recently treated to a painstaking restoration, Larchill is the only surviving example in Ireland or England of a *ferme ornée*, a type of garden (literally an "ornamental farm") that represents a midway point between the true landscaped garden and the rigorously formal style of garden that preceded it. A one-kilometre circular walk links ten classical and Gothic follies, the most notable of which are the fortified island named "Gibraltar" and the curious "Fox's Earth". The latter was built on the instruction of a Mr Watson who, convinced he would be reincarnated as a fox, wanted to be sure of a bolt-hole from the hounds in his next life – it appears today as a grass-covered mound with tunnels for escape, topped by a cluster of rubble-rough columns. A new *ferme ornée*, containing rare breeds of farm animals, is currently being developed, and you'll find some interesting material on the conservation project at the pleasant tea-room.

BRÚ NA BÓINNE

Map 1, B1–C1. Access to the sites is via the Visitor Centre.
Visitor Centre and Newgrange daily: March, April & Oct
9.30am–5.30pm; May & mid- to end Sept 9am–6.30pm; June to
mid-Sept 9am–7pm; Nov–Feb 9.30am–5pm. **Knowth:** same times
but May–Oct only. **Visitors Centre** £2, students £1, family £5;
combined ticket with **Newgrange** £3, students £1.25, family
£7.50; combined ticket with **Knowth** £2, students £1, family £5;
all three £5, students £2.25, family £12.50. Suburban train from
Connolly Station to Drogheda, then a bus to the Visitor Centre.

Around forty-five kilometres north of Dublin, caught within
a curve of the River Boyne between Tullyallen and Slane, is
the area known as **Brú na Bóinne**, an extraordinary landscape which retains forty or so related prehistoric tombs,
vestiges of Neolithic settlements that sprang up here as a
result of the valley's rich soil. The three most important
sites, Dowth, Knowth and Newgrange, are passage graves –
high round mounds raised over stone burial chambers.
Access to Newgrange and Knowth is by guided tour from
the visitors centre only; Dowth is currently closed for excavation. As one of Ireland's most important prehistoric sites,
Brú na Bóinne attracts a huge number of visitors – in summer especially it makes sense to arrive as early in the day as
possible to be sure of viewing the burial chambers.

Newgrange

Newgrange, a **Neolithic tumulus** situated about 13km
west of Drogheda, is an artificial mound built between 3500
and 2700 BC, when stone was the only material available for
use as tools. The mind boggles at the effort required to

transport the building materials, which amounted to 450 giant boulders and over one million sackfuls of small stones – a task believed to have taken forty years. Though evidently important, its purpose remains unclear: a burial place, a cenotaph, a solar temple or a kind of astronomical chart have all been suggested as functions.

To confuse matters, the mound is surrounded by later additions, such as the **Great Circle** of massive standing stones, of which a dozen of the estimated 35 originals remain upright. There is also a series of concrete **slabs** and wooden **stakes**, the former representing the remains of a satellite passage grave which has largely been destroyed over the centuries, the latter marking the centre point of deep pits whose purpose remains unknown.

The mound itself covers about an acre. It has been so completely restored that at first sight it reminds you of a grounded flying saucer, but once you accept the incongruity, its sparklingly new appearance heightens the wonder. The white quartz **retaining wall** gives some hint of the power this stone must have had for the builders, since the nearest source is the Wicklow Mountains. The base is girdled by a ring of 97 granite **kerbstones** weighing between four and eight tonnes apiece. The stones were quarried in the Mourne Mountains of County Down – it's estimated that it would have taken eighty men four days to drag one from the quarry to the river, whence it was transported by boat to Newgrange.

The most important feature, and one which distinguishes Newgrange from Dowth and Knowth, is the **roof-box** above the entrance, containing a slit through which the light of the rising sun penetrates the tomb on the **winter solstice** (December 21). At 8.58am, the rays start edging their way slowly up the passage, to illuminate the chamber at the far end with an orange glow, which fades away fifteen minutes later. Guided tours feature a speeded-up "re-creation" of this phenomenon, using electric light; there's a nine-year waiting list to witness the real event, though the effect is almost as good a couple of days before or after the solstice.

The **passage** extends for 19m into the tumulus (about a quarter of its depth), sloping gently upwards so that the floor of the chamber at the end is the same height off the ground as the roof-box. The **chamber** is roughly cross-shaped with a corbelled roof of huge slabs that stands exactly as it did some five thousand years ago, without renovation or repair. When the chamber was excavated in 1967 the charred bones of four or five people were found, which some take as proof that only priests and rulers were buried here – others argue that is where bodies were merely laid out before being interred elsewhere (a theory given credence by the discovery of hundreds of cremated remains in other tumuli).

Knowth

Major excavations have been going on at **Knowth** since 1962, but recently about a third of the complex has been opened to the public. Though there's less to see for visitors, the discoveries here have already surpassed what was excavated at Newgrange. At Knowth alone, about 250 decorated stones have been found: over half of all known Irish passage grave art.

Several periods of occupation by different cultures have been identified, from the **Neolithic**, when the original passage tombs were built (around 3200 BC), through occupation by the Beaker people (2000–1800 BC) – so called because of a distinctive beaker left with each of their dead – and a late **Celtic** settlement in the early centuries AD. Early **Christian** occupation has been identified from the eighth to twelfth centuries, bringing a glut of souterrains (underground passages and chambers), followed by **Norman** usage during the twelfth and thirteenth centuries.

The main passage tomb is about twice the size of that at Newgrange – with a tunnel over 30m long leading to the central chamber – and even more richly decorated. At Knowth there is also a smaller second passage tomb within the main tumulus, and up to seventeen **satellite tumuli**. Structurally the main mound is similar to the one at Newgrange, with a cruciform chamber, high corbelled roof and richly decorated stones, but here there is also evidence of settlement around the mound.

BRÚ NA BÓINNE

LISTINGS

LISTINGS

LISTINGS

Accommodation

Despite the many new places that have sprung up around the city centre recently, the ever-rising demand for **accommodation** means that there's hardly a slack season any more. Unless you're willing to risk a frustrating search for a bed, it's necessary to make **reservations** if you're arriving at the weekend (Fri–Sun) any time of year; on weekdays over summer; or around Easter or major sporting events. How far in advance depends: one or two weeks should be OK in February or November, but one or two months is more appropriate for peak times. If you arrive without a reservation, it's possible to book on the spot at any of the Dublin Tourism offices (see p.7). With a credit card, this can also be done by phone (✆1800/668668 from within Ireland, ✆00800/6686 6866 from the UK or ✆353-669/792082 from outside Ireland and the UK), or by using the touch-interactive videos outside the offices. If you book directly at the tourist office the charge is £1; booking over the phone costs £3; and using the video is free. However all three services require you to pay a deposit of ten percent of your hotel or guesthouse bill – you pay the balance at the establishment. Alternatively, you can run through the listings here and phone around yourself.

The telephone code for the Dublin area is ©01.
Calling Dublin from abroad (or Northern Ireland),
dial ©00-353-1, followed by the subscriber's number.

The accommodation in this chapter is divided into the
following categories: **hotels and B&Bs** (bed and breakfasts), **hostels**, **student accommodation** and **camping**.
Our listings are divided geographically, starting in the centre and moving, first northwards and then southwards,
through the suburbs to the outskirts. Central Dublin is split
into the southside and Temple Bar, and the inner northside.
The **southside** has traditionally been the focus for top-
quality accommodation in Dublin and the best establishments around Fitzwilliam Square and St Stephen's Green
share the elegance and charm of the surrounding streets;
Temple Bar, by contrast, is home to some of the city's
newest hotels and hostels – the area is packed full of young
revellers so it can be exceedingly noisy. Accommodation on
the **inner northside** is concentrated around Gardiner
Street, which used to be a little dingy but has, in places,
improved of late. That said, take care with your bags here
and avoid walking back alone late at night.

**Our listings are divided into the following categories
and regions; hotels and B&Bs: the southside and
Temple Bar (p.198), the inner northside (p.203),
Clontarf, Drumcondra and Glasnevin (p.206), Howth
(p.207), Ballsbridge, Donnybrook and Sandymount
(p.208), Dún Laoghaire (p.209), Dalkey and Killiney
(p.211); hostels: the southside and Temple Bar (p.212),
the inner northside (p.214), Ballsbridge, Donnybrook
and Sandymount (p.216), Dún Laoghaire (p.216);
student accommodation (p.217); and camping (p.218).**

The suburbs to the north of the city, **Clontarf, Drumcondra and Glasnevin**, are quiet areas easily accessible from the airport and served by regular buses into the centre. To the south are **Ballsbridge, Donnybrook and Sandymount**. Ballsbridge and Donnybrook are affluent suburbs with plenty of decent accommodation – again all three are served by regular buses, and Sandymount, situated on the coast, is also accessible by DART (Sandymount or Sydney Parade station).

The seaside towns on the outskirts of Dublin, **Howth** in the north and **Dún Laoghaire, Dalkey and Killiney** in the south, are all attractive places to stay and served by DART, making a commute into the centre very easy.

Accommodation prices

Accommodation prices vary throughout the year, with the highest rates from June to September, during events like international rugby championships, and over Christmas, Easter and St Patrick's Day. Our listings for **hotels**, **guesthouses** and **B&Bs** feature a code (eg ③) signifying the minimum high-season rate, including breakfast (unless otherwise stated), for *one* person sharing a double room (reckon on 15–20 percent more for single occupancy), as follows:

① £10–15	④ £30–40	⑦ £60–80
② £15–20	⑤ £40–50	⑧ £80–100
③ £20–30	⑥ £50–60	⑨ Over £100

For **hostels** and **campsites**, the low- and high-season prices appear in £, again referring to what one person will pay; in the case of hostels this usually includes bed linen and a light breakfast.

CHAPTER TEN

HOTELS AND B&BS

Hotels in Dublin are generally quite expensive, especially those on the southside, though it is worth bearing in mind that many offer competitive weekend rates, particularly those geared towards the business market. B&Bs and guesthouses are in abundance, ranging from an extra room in a family home to luxurious houses that are hotels in all but name (and which charge similar prices) – again the pick are on the southside, although you'll find some good deals in the suburbs.

THE SOUTHSIDE AND TEMPLE BAR

Adams Trinity Hotel
Map 5, G7. 28 Dame Lane ©670 710, fax 7101.
Small, welcoming hotel with comfortable rooms furnished with Victorian reproduction furniture. Breakfast is served on a gallery overlooking the bar, there's no private lounge and street noise is inevitable, so not ideal if you want to unwind at the end of the day. Reductions available at weekends and on triple rooms. ⑦

Bewley's Hotel
Map 4, E5. 19–20 Fleet St ©670 8122, fax 8103.
Cosy, friendly three-star hotel on the edge of Temple Bar, with old-style decor in keeping with the famous café below. The pleasant lounge has something of a lived-in feel, and breakfast is served on a small gallery overlooking the café till 9.30am, after which it is available all day in the self-service section downstairs. Non-smoking rooms. Secure public parking nearby. ⑦

Buswell's Hotel
Map 4, F7. 23–27 Molesworth St ©614 6500, fax 676 2090.
This superb Georgian townhouse offers comfortable three-star accommodation in a prime, quiet location near Leinster House.

Decorative plasterwork, ornamental fireplaces and antique furniture in the lobby and brasserie ensure a sense of tradition; the homely bedrooms have been recently refurbished. No car park. ⑦

Central Hotel
Map 5, H8. 1–5 Exchequer St ℂ679 7302, fax 7303.
Refurbished nineteenth-century establishment on the corner of South Great George's Street, not far from Dublin Castle and Temple Bar. Pleasant, cheery rooms, although those overlooking the main road can be noisy. Comfortable Victorian bars and lounge enlivened by contemporary Irish paintings. No car park. ⑧

The Clarence Hotel
Map 6, B4. 6–8 Wellington Quay ℂ670 9000, fax 7800.
Ultra-stylish five-star Temple Bar hotel owned by U2, containing *The Kitchen* nightclub (see p.261) and the award-winning *Tea Rooms* restaurant (see p.239), as well as penthouse suites used by the likes of Tina Turner and Simon Le Bon. All rooms come with video, candles and Egyptian linen. Price doesn't include breakfast. ⑧

Fitzwilliam
Map 4, G9. 41 Upper Fitzwilliam St ℂ660 0448, fax 676 7488.
A plush southside guesthouse near Merrion Square, with a restaurant, bar and en-suite rooms with TV and phone. Parking. Child discount; babysitting. ⑤

Georgian House Hotel
Map 4, G9. 18 Lower Baggot St ℂ661 8832, fax 8834.
Five Georgian townhouses form this pleasant three-star hotel, a short walk from St Stephen's Green. Breakfast is served in the ancient cellar, while the modern bar sports the whackiest seats in the city. Extension work scheduled for completion by March 2000 includes a pool and leisure complex. Parking; child discount. ⑦

HOTELS AND B&BS: THE SOUTHSIDE AND TEMPLE BAR

The Grey Door
Map 4, F10. 23 Upper Pembroke St ℘676 3286, fax 3287.
A superior southside guesthouse, with seven spacious, comfortable rooms and two award-winning restaurants, one serving modern variations of Irish dishes and the other specializing in seafood. Non-smoking. ⑥

Harcourt Hotel
Map 4, D10. 60 Harcourt St ℘478 3677, fax 2013.
Pleasant three-star hotel not far from St Stephen's Green. George Bernard Shaw once had a flat in one of the houses, now knocked together. All rooms en suite, plus bar, noted for its traditional music sessions, restaurant and nightclub. Child discount. ⑦

Harding Hotel
Map 4, A6. Copper Alley, Fishamble St ℘679 6500, fax 6504.
Attractive two-star USIT hotel facing Christ Church Cathedral. Bright and cheerful rooms with en-suite facilities. The twin/triple rooms are good value for three people. Restaurant and Viking-theme bar with pool table; wheelchair accessible. ④

Jury's Christchurch Inn
Map 4, A6. Christchurch Place ℘454 0000, fax 0012.
A three-star eyesore opposite Christ Church. Comfortable, modern rooms accommodate up to three adults, or two adults and two children, so their flat room rate of £62 makes it good value. Bar and restaurant; price doesn't include breakfast. ④

The Leeson Inn
Map 4, F10. 24 Lower Leeson St ℘662 2002, fax 1567.
This elegant Georgian townhouse just off St Stephen's Green is a delightful southside option. Bedrooms are individually

designed around original Georgian sash windows with natural colours and contemporary furnishings. Breakfast is a continental-style buffet. Friendly staff. Attractive low-season rates available; parking. ⑦

Longfield's Hotel

Map 4, H9. 9–10 Fitzwilliam St Lower ℂ676 1367, fax 1542.
A haven of peace within walking distance of the National Gallery, *Longfield's* stands on one of Dublin's finest Georgian streets, and has a real air of gentility. Bedrooms vary in size, but all are comfortably furnished with lavish drapes and large firm beds, some four-posters. Renowned for its excellent gourmet restaurant. ⑦

The Merrion

Map 4, G8. Upper Merrion St ℂ603 0600, fax 0700.
This five-star hotel, housed in four restored eighteenth-century townhouses, offers every modern amenity including its own spa and pool, plus the exclusive *Patrick Guilbaud* restaurant (see p.237). ⑨

Mont Clare Hotel

Map 4, G7. Merrion Square ℂ607 3800, fax 661 5663.
Huge, smart three-star hotel near the National Gallery, with generously proportioned, well-furnished rooms. Popular with middle-aged tourists, but with none of the stuffiness associated with that market niche. Facilities include room service, valet parking and fitness centre. Good weekend discounts available. Bar and restaurant. ⑧

The Morgan

Map 6, H3. 10 Fleet St ℂ679 3939, fax 3946.
Small, style-conscious hotel, whose minimalist bedrooms come with just about everything covered in cream cotton, except the occasional abstract, plus TV, CD player and tape deck.

HOTELS AND B&BS: THE SOUTHSIDE AND TEMPLE BAR

Continental breakfast is served either in your room or the *House of Rock* diner next door – a bit of a shock after the tranquillity within. ⑦

Number 31, Leeson Close

Map 4, F10. Off Lower Leeson St ✆676 5011, fax 2929.
A stylishly converted stable block forms the sitting and breakfast areas of this fine secluded Georgian guesthouse – the sunken lounge, turf fires and ethnic rugs give it the air of a country retreat in the heart of the city. Comfortable rooms, excellent breakfasts and great hospitality. ⑥

The Shelbourne Méridien Hotel

Map 4, E8. St Stephen's Green North ✆676 6471, fax 661 6006.
Dublin's most prestigious hotel and a society watering-hole. Elegantly furnished period interiors and a buzzing social life (afternoon tea in the Lord Mayor's Lounge is a Dublin tradition), plus an excellent restaurant, bar (see p.248), and swimming pool. ⑨

Staunton's on the Green

Map 4, E8. 83 St Stephen's Green ✆478 2300, fax 2263.
One of the swankiest guesthouses on the southside: an elegant Georgian house overlooking the Green, with private garden. All rooms are en suite with phone and TV. Bar. Parking. Child discount; family-friendly. ⑥

The Temple Bar Hotel

Map 6, H3. 13–17 Fleet St ✆677 3333, fax 3088.
A spacious lobby of tasteful prints and generous sofas sets the tone for this superior three-star hotel. Breakfast is served in a light-filled, glass-roofed dining room; comfortable bedrooms each with TV, phone and en-suite bathroom. Front rooms can be noisy. Triples available; free for under-12s; reductions on weekend breaks. ⑦

The Westbury Hotel
Map 4, D7. Grafton St ℗679 1122, fax 7078.
Lavish five-star hotel. Facilities include underground parking,
fitness centre, restaurant, bistro and elegant lounge bar.
Luxurious throughout – you can even watch TV while having
a soak since bathrooms have TVs blended into their mirror-
lined walls. Reductions available at weekends. ⑨

THE INNER NORTHSIDE

Anchor Guest House
Map 4, F2. 49 Lower Gardiner St ℗878 6913, fax 8038.
A tastefully refurbished Georgian house. All rooms are en suite
with TV and phone. Limited parking available, but ring ahead,
as street-parking in this area is not recommended. Infants free;
child discount. ④

Celtic Lodge Guesthouse
Map 4, F2. 82 Talbot St ℗677 9955, fax 878 8698.
A new businesslike guesthouse overlooking the street.
Bedrooms are brightly decorated and comfortably furnished, all
en suite with TVs, and breakfast is served in an even brighter
canteen. No residents' lounge, but there is a bar. An unattrac-
tive location, although it's just a short walk into town. ④

Charleville Lodge
Map 3, D2. 268–272 North Circular Road, Phibsboro ℗838 6633,
fax 5854.
A fine guesthouse run by the friendly Stenson family, in a
Victorian terrace on the North Circular Road near Phoenix
Park. Price includes an excellent breakfast. Babysitting service;
parking available. ⑥

Chief O'Neill's Hotel
Map 5, D6. Smithfield, Smithfield Village ℗817 3838, fax 3839.

HOTELS AND B&BS: THE INNER NORTHSIDE

Ultramodern hotel deploying minimalist styles. Bedrooms combine bold contemporary design-pieces with cool light and lines, plus en-suite showers, TV, CD players and tea-making facilities. Similarly-styled lounge and bars occupy the lower floors. Centrally located, but take care coming back at night as this isn't the safest part of town. Special weekend rates; limited parking. ⑦

Clifden House

Map 5, H2. 32 Gardiner Place ℂ874 6364, fax 6122.

This guesthouse, on an old Georgian street just off Mountjoy Square, has nine pleasant en-suite rooms, each with TV. Extremely helpful owners. Child discount; babysitting service; private car parking. ④

The Gresham Hotel

Map 4, D2. 20–22 Upper O'Connell St ℂ874 6881, fax 878 7175.

Dublin's oldest hotel – and one of the classiest. The grandiose lobby, with its crystal chandeliers, decorative stucco work and potted palms, makes the perfect spot for afternoon tea. Recently refurbished, comfortable rooms, some with over-size beds, and a huge range of amenities including room service, valet parking and a well-equipped business centre. Family-friendly. ⑨

Marian Guesthouse

Map 5, H2. 21 Upper Gardiner St ℂ874 4129.

The best budget B&B option near to the city centre, with six rooms, shared bathrooms and a garden. Unlike other options in the centre, there are no price hikes at peak times so this is recommended for lone travellers on a budget who want a basic, clean, private room. ②

Morrison Hotel

Map 4, C4. Lower Ormond Quay ℂ878 2999, fax 3185.

A minimalist *tour de force*, and one of the most stylish new hotels around. Perfectly proportioned throughout, with dark ash browns and cream stone floors. Aside from offering aesthetic bliss, bedrooms have en-suite bathrooms plus mod cons including CD players and ISDN links. Very mellow bar and the restaurant serves Asian-fusion cuisine. ⑧

Ormond Quay Hotel

Map 4, A5. Upper Ormond Quay ✆872 1811, fax 1362.
Historic hotel (it features in *Ulysses*) on the north bank of the Liffey, offering bright and cheerful, recently refurbished rooms. The *Sirens* bar and restaurant is a popular spot; there's no separate sitting-room, but guests looking for a more relaxed evening can use the fairly spacious and comfortable lobby. No car parking. ⑥

Othello Guesthouse

Map 4, F2. 74 Lower Gardiner St ✆855 4271, fax 7460.
A dozen en-suite rooms in one of the area's longest-established guesthouses. All rooms have basic amenities, there are family rooms at good rates, and the Irish breakfast is very good. Parking available; child-friendly. ③

Talbot Guesthouse

Map 4, E2. 95–97 Talbot St ✆874 9202, fax 9672.
The newest, most centrally located northside guesthouse, close to O'Connell Street and the Liffey. All rooms en suite and non-smoking, with TV and phones. Child discount; cot available. ④

The Townhouse

Map 4, F2. 47–48 Lower Gardiner St ✆878 8808, fax 8787.
A snazzily refurbished Georgian house that once belonged to the playwrights Dion Boucicault and Lafcadio Hearn, and definitely the classiest guesthouse on the northside, with a hostel attached. All rooms en suite with TV, fridge and tea-maker. Fine healthy breakfast. Secure parking. Higher rates at weekends. ⑤

HOTELS AND B&BS: THE INNER NORTHSIDE

CLONTARF, DRUMCONDRA AND GLASNEVIN

Mrs Nuala Betson

Map 2, G4. The Villa, 150 Howth Rd, Clontarf ℂ & fax 833 2377.
Comfortable detached house near the DART and a bus stop
(#31, #31B, #32, #32A). Most rooms en suite with TV. Child
discount. ③

Mary Dunwoody

Map 2, G4. Eldar, 19 Copeland Ave, Clontarf ℂ833 9091.
A long-established, semi-detached house in the vicinity of the
Casino. Mrs Dunwoody's welcome is as warm as ever, and the
four rooms, two en suite, the others with showers, are basic,
but clean, and represent good value for money. Non-smoking.
Open April–Oct. ②

Egan's Guest House

Map 2, F3. 7–9 Iona Park, Glasnevin ℂ830 3611, fax 3312
Situated in a quiet road near the Botanic Gardens this friendly,
family-run guesthouse is an excellent option. Car parking is
available at the front of the house and there are child-minding
facilities, though the price doesn't include breakfast. ③

Hedigan's

Map 2, G4. 14 Hollybrook Park, Clontarf ℂ853 1663, fax 833 3337.
Fine detached Victorian house just off Howth Road next to
Clontarf Golf Club. *Hedigan's* is well furnished, with rooms
themed according to different countries, and offers secure
parking, child-minding facilities, a small playground and reductions for children and pensioners. ⑤

Kathleen Hurney

Map 2, F4. 69 Hollybank Rd, Drumcondra ℂ837 7907.
Four comfy rooms with TV, two of them en suite. Near the

bus stop for easy access to the centre. Child discount. Non-smoking. ②

Iona House

Map 2, F3. 5 Iona Park, Glasnevin ℂ830 6217, fax 6743.
One door away from *Egan's* in the pleasant Iona Park, *Iona House* is of an equally high standard, with no supplementary charges for single occupancy and a good breakfast. ④

The White House

Map 2, G4. 125 Clontarf Rd ℂ833 3196.
Very friendly house near to Dublin Bay that offers excellent value for money, including a substantial breakfast, and is on the bus route into the centre. Booking early is essential for the summer months. ②

HOWTH

Margaret Campbell

Map 8, H5. Highfield, Thormanby Rd ℂ832 3936.
Up towards The Summit this guesthouse has three rooms with TV, two of them en suite (the front rooms offer views of Malahide). Mrs Campbell is a fine host who makes families particularly welcome. Child discount; cot available. ③

Hazelwood

Map 8, D3. 2 Thormanby Woods, Thormanby Rd ℂ & fax 839 1391.
A large modern bungalow set in its own extensive grounds, one mile away from the seafront near Howth Golf Club. Non-smoking with fifty-percent child discounts and plenty of parking space. ③

Sutton Castle Hotel

Map 8, A4. Shielmartin Rd, Sutton ℂ832 2688, fax 4476.
A rambling Victorian pile makes up this seventeen-bed three-star hotel in a quiet location on the southwest side of the

HOTELS AND B&BS: HOWTH

peninsula, backed by woodlands and overlooking Dublin Bay. Bus #31B runs fairly close by, though the service is infrequent. Child discounts. ⑦

BALLSBRIDGE, DONNYBROOK AND SANDYMOUNT

Aaronmor

Map 2, G5. 1B/1C Sandymount Ave, Ballsbridge ☎668 7972.
This is an elegant red-brick house on the road leading from Ballsbridge to Sandymount. Large, comfortable en-suite rooms and excellent service, with breakfasts to match. ④

Aberdeen Lodge

Map 2, G5. 53–55 Park Ave, off Ailesbury Rd, Ballsbridge ☎283 8155, fax 7877.
Luxurious accommodation in an Edwardian house on Park Avenue, a quiet street running parallel to the coast. A cut above the average guesthouse, *Aberdeen Lodge* offers amongst other things, rooms with a private jacuzzi, a fine garden, child-minding services and a license to sell alcohol. ⑦

Anglesea Town House

Map 2, G5. 63 Anglesea Rd, Ballsbridge ☎668 3877.
First-rate accommodation in an elegant Edwardian family house on the road leading from Ballsbridge to Donnybrook. Beautifully restored period rooms, many with the original fireplaces still intact, and a great breakfast made entirely from home produce. Free parking available; child-friendly. Closed from December 15 to January 8. ⑥

Berkeley Court Hotel

Map 3, I7. Lansdowne Rd ☎660 1711, fax 661 7238.
Hideous exterior but the interior of this prestigious hotel combines conservative elegance with utter luxury. Five-star facilities include mini-gym and business centre. ⑨

Mrs Maureen Bermingham

Map 2, G5. 8 Dromard Terrace, Sandymount ℂ668 3861.

This is a family-run, value-for-money guesthouse in an ivy-covered period house near the beach; bus #3 or Sandymount DART station. Old-fashioned comfort, but no en-suite facilities. Non-smoking rooms. Child discount; baby-sitting. Open May–Sept. ②

Burlington Hotel

Map 3, H8. Upper Leeson St ℂ660 5222, fax 8496.

A massive modern four-star hotel in a pleasant location within walking distance of the city centre. Particularly well-equipped for conferences and tour groups – hence the Irish cabaret. ⑨

Lansdowne Hotel

Map 3, I7. 27 Pembroke Rd ℂ668 2522, fax 5585.

Popular with rugby fans because of its proximity to Lansdowne Road stadium, this small hotel, set in pleasant leafy surroundings within walking distance of the centre, has comfy rooms. Sports memorabilia decorate the hotel's small bar. Good-value deals are available for families and during low season. ⑦

Marian Stone

Map 2, G5. Lansa House, 68 Merrion Rd, Ballsbridge ℂ668 0416, fax 660 0803.

A mock-Tudor house opposite the Royal Dublin Society. Though without some of the frills of its neighbours, this guesthouse is clean, comfortable and friendly and one of the few value-for-money options in the area. Four en-suite rooms with TV and phone. Child discount and baby-sitting. Non-smoking. ④

DÚN LAOGHAIRE

Mrs Helen Callanan

Map 7, C3. 1 Rosmeen Gardens ℂ280 6083.

The first and one of the best of the many B&Bs off Summerhill

Road, midway between Dún Laoghaire and Sandycove and
Glasthule DART stations. Four basic non-smoking rooms with
TV, two of them en suite. ②

Mrs Anne Dalton
Map 7, C3. Annesgrove, 28 Rosmeen Gardens ℂ280 9801.
Another recommended option, further down Dún Laoghaire's
B&B street, with four basic but comfortable rooms, two of
which are en suite. Non-smoking. ③

Mrs Marie Dunne
Map 7, C3. 30 Rosmeen Gardens ℂ280 3360.
Three cosy rooms with shared facilities in a quiet cul-de-sac
near the DART station in Sandymount. Good value for
money; parking available. Open May–Sept. ③

Kingston Hotel
Map 7, C3. Adelaide St ℂ280 1810, fax 1237.
The facade doesn't do justice to the interior of this large
Victorian hotel; bedrooms are decorated in pale green and fitted with comfortable dark-wood furniture. Ask for a room
overlooking the bay. The cheerful and popular bar serves food
daily till 9.30pm. Wheelchair accessible; limited parking. ⑤

Lynden House
Map 7, C3. 2 Mulgrave Terrace ℂ280 6404.
A friendly family-run Georgian guesthouse five minutes' walk
from the car ferry terminus. Four comfortable rooms, two en
suite. The helpful owners offer a value-for-money service,
including early morning breakfasts for those catching the ferry.
Secure parking available. ③

The Royal Marine Hotel
Map 7, B3. Marine Rd ℂ280 1911, fax 1089.
A grandiose nineteenth-century hotel set in spacious grounds over-

looking Dublin Bay. Rooms are comfortable and facilities include bar, restaurant, 24hr room service, laundry service and parking. Up to fifty-percent reductions available some weekends. ⑨

Windsor Lodge

Map 7, D3. 3 Islington Ave, Sandycove ✆ & fax 284 6952.
Ideally located on a small street leading from the coast, near to Sandymount DART station. The non-smoking house with four en-suite rooms is especially suitable for families as it offers a child-minding service and generous concessions for older children. Secure parking. ③

DALKEY AND KILLINEY

Mrs Mary Barry

Map 2, I8. Church Rd, Killiney ✆285 2809.
One triple and one double room available in this fine family house set in large wooded gardens – perfect for those who prefer a bit of peace and quiet. Four minutes' drive from the ferry; parking available. ②

The Court Hotel

Map 2, I8. Killiney Bay, Killiney ✆285 1622, fax 2085.
Large Victorian mansion set in pleasant gardens overlooking Killiney Bay. Bedrooms have en-suite bathrooms and TVs, and some have sea-views. Two restaurants, one specializing in fish dishes, and a bar. Very handy for the DART; good weekend rates and child discounts. ⑦

Fitzpatrick Castle Hotel

Map 2, I8. Killiney ✆284 0700, fax 285 0207.
Once a stately home complete with battlements, now a comfortable four-star hotel, whose antique furnishings give it a traditional character, and position affords views over Dublin Bay. Facilities include indoor pool and crèche. Child discounts. ⑧

HOTELS AND B&Bs: DALKEY AND KILLINEY

211

Mrs Margaret Jackson
Map 7, G3. Desmar, 15 Railway Rd, Dalkey ℗285 8203.
Small B&B close to DART station. Good value, with four
rooms with shared bathrooms. Closed Nov–Feb. ②

HOSTELS

Although Dublin has always had its fair share of budget
options, the recent increase of young tourists has boosted
the amount of upmarket hostels you'll find around the city
– while some of these offer a very high standard of shared
accommodation, they do lack something of the traditional
communal feeling you associate with hostelling. Unless
we've specified otherwise, all the hostels listed are affiliated
to Independent Holiday Hostels (IHH). Hot showers, luggage rooms, payphones and TV lounges are standard; other
facilities vary.

THE SOUTHSIDE AND TEMPLE BAR

Ashfield House
Map 4, E4. 19–20 D'Olier St ℗679 7734, fax 0852.
A good option near College Green and Temple Bar. Spacious,
clean and friendly, with en-suite facilities throughout. Prices
include breakfast, though there is a £2 weekend supplement
on all rooms. Dorms sleeping fourteen (£11), six (£12.50) or
four (£14.50) persons; double (£27). Kitchen; laundry. Open
24hr.

Avalon House
Map 4, C8. 55 Aungier St ℗475 0001, fax 0303.
Friendly, traditional hostel with a pleasant café – excellent for
hanging out and meeting people – plus a large self-catering
kitchen, tip-top security and Internet access. Beds and bunks
come made up with fresh linen. Multi-bedded dorms

(£8–11); six-person dorms (£12–14.50); twin (£14–16) and four-bed (£11.50–13.50) rooms; breakfast included. Open 24hr.

Barnacles Temple Bar House

Map 6, E4.Temple Lane ℗671 6277, fax 6591.
Custom-made hostel right in the heart of Temple Bar. Excellent rooms all en suite, with efficient and friendly staff. All prices include continental breakfast. Be warned to book early as this is fast becoming the city's most popular hostel. Ten-bed dorms (£11), six-bed (£13), four-bed (£15); double rooms excellent value at £20 per person.

Brewery Hostel

Map 3, D5. 22–23 Thomas St ℗453 8600, fax 8616.
The unfashionable location of this hostel often means that while others are full it still has beds free. Housed in a converted library 10min walk along Thomas Street from Christ Church, the *Brewery* is friendly and offers good value for its en-suite rooms. One of the few city hostels that has secure parking. Ten-bed dorms (£10), eight-bed (£12) and twins (£22 per person). Breakfast included.

Kinlay House

Map 4, B6. 2–12 Lord Edward St ℗679 6644, fax 7437.
Cheerful USIT hostel near Christ Church Cathedral, though it can be a little noisy both from traffic and high-spirited guests. Multi-bedded mixed dorms (£10.50), dorms sleeping four to six (£12.50), some en suite (£14); twin rooms (£15), en suite (£17), and singles (£20). Free towel and soap. Café; kitchen; bike hire; laundry (£5). Open 24hr.

Oliver St John Gogarty's

Map 6, H3. 18–21 Anglesea St ℗671 1822, fax 7637.
Comfy and stylish, though a little expensive, this non-IHH

HOSTELS: THE SOUTHSIDE AND TEMPLE BAR

hostel is situated next to the eponymous pub in the heart of Temple Bar and, like the bar itself, is hugely popular. En-suite six- to ten-bed dorms (£17), four-bed (£16), triple (£18) and double (£22) rooms, plus snazzy four-person rooftop apartments (£140) with kitchen, TV and washing machine. No communal facilities.

THE INNER NORTHSIDE

Abbey Hostel
Map 4, E4. O'Connell Bridge, 29 Bachelors Walk ℗878 0700, fax 0719.

Just north of O'Connell Bridge this is a modern, well-equipped and friendly hostel. Rooms are fitted with a swipe card security system and have storage cages under every bed. Dorms range from twelve-bed to four-bed (£14 –17), all en-suite (the showers are excellent). Laundry and Internet facilities; breakfast included.

Abraham House
Map 4, F2. 82–83 Lower Gardiner St ℗855 0600, fax 0598.

A large, well-run non-IHH hostel whose facilities include a kitchen, laundry, bureau de change and secure parking. Ten-bed dorms (£8.50), six- to eight-bed (£12.00) or four-bed (£12.50); doubles (£20). En-suite four-bed dorms (£13.50) and doubles (£22.50). Bus #41 from the airport stops outside; open 24hr.

Cardijn House (or Goin' My Way)
Map 4, F2. 15 Talbot St ℗878 8484.

Small, family-run value-for-money hostel above a newsagents, close to O'Connell Street and the river. Eight- to twelve-bed dorms (£9), four-bed (£12) and twin rooms (£14), all including breakfast. Kitchen. No lockout, but a midnight curfew.

Celts House

Map 5, G2. 32–33 Blessington St ℂ & fax 830 0657.

The bright yellow Georgian door of *Celts House* marks the mood of this small, friendly hostel on a quiet cul-de-sac north of O'Connell Street. Prices are very competitive; eight-bed dorms (£9), four-bed (£10) and twin (£16). Limited facilities but no curfew.

Dublin International Youth Hostel

Map 5, G2. 61 Mountjoy St ℂ830 1766, fax 1600.

Way up near the Black Church and Upper Dorset St (bus #41 from the airport), the northside headquarters of An Óige is a well-equipped 460-bed hostel in an ex-convent that's barricaded against the 'hood. An Óige or Hostelling International members pay £9.50 for a dorm bed; non-members £10, plus a £1.25 surcharge. To stay here, you must have or hire a sleeping sheet.

Globetrotters Tourist Hostel

Map 4, F2. 46 Lower Gardiner St ℂ873 5893, fax 878 8787.

Well-run, comfortable hostel connected to the *Townhouse* B&B (p.205) whose cosy, tasteful dorms sleep six to ten people (£10–14), with security-coded doors and individual bed lights for a peaceful night's sleep. Their breakfast is the best you'll get in any hostel in Dublin, and the decor and standards are a lot higher, too.

Isaac's

Map 4, F3. 2–5 Frenchman's Lane ℂ874 9321, fax 1574.

A well-run modern hostel around the corner from the bus station, which had a reputation for being inflexible with its rules, but has become a little more relaxed of late (though it still enforces a lockout from 11am–2.30pm). Breakfast is not included but *Isaac's* has a good restaurant attached. Twelve-bed dorms (£7.95), six- to eight-bed (£9.25), four-bed (£13), triples (£14.50), twins (£16) and singles (£18.95).

Jacob's Inn

Map 4, G2. 21–28 Talbot Place ℭ855 5660, fax 5664.
Comfortable and stylish budget accommodation just north of
the bus station. Staff are friendly and security is first-rate with
swipe cards and excellent lockers. All rooms are en suite,
though breakfast is not included. Twins and doubles (£19.50),
triples (£16.50), four-bed dorms (£15.50), multi-bedded
dorms (£10.95). Non-IHH.

MEC Hostel

Map 5, H3. 44 North Great George's St ℭ878 0071, fax 874 6472.
Housing two converted listed Georgian buildings with most of
their original features intact, *MEC* is a non-IHH hostel 10min
walk from the bus station on a fine northside Georgian street.
Breakfast is served in a well-equipped basement kitchen where
the walls have been stripped to their original stonework.
Sixteen-bed dorms (£8.50), ten-bed (£10.50) and six-bed
(£11.50); four-bed dorms are £12.50 per person.

BALLSBRIDGE, DONNYBROOK AND SANDYMOUNT

Morehampton House

Map 3, I8. 78 Morehampton Rd ℭ668 8866, fax 8794.
A converted Victorian house in the embassy belt beyond the
Grand Canal, readily accessible by bus (#10, #46A or #46B
from Trinity College; #46A from Dún Laoghaire). En-suite
dorms sleeping twelve (£8), or four to six (£15.50); twin
rooms (£17.50); and larger family rooms (£50). Prices include
towel and soap, but not breakfast. Open 24hr. Garden, kitchen,
laundry and bike hire. Non-IHH.

DÚN LAOGHAIRE

Belgrave Hall

Map 2, H6. 34 Belgrave Square, Monkstown ℭ284 2106, fax 280 5838.

HOSTELS: BALLSBRIDGE, DONNYBROOK AND SANDYMOUNT, DÚN LAOGHAIRE

The best out-of-town option available, offering fine communal accommodation in a magnificent building next to the Irish Cultural Institute in Monkstown. Easily accessible from the city by DART and buses #7, #7A and #8. Ten-bed dorms (£13 per person), six-bed dorms (£15 per person) and doubles (£25 per person), all including breakfast. Non-IHH.

The Old School House

Map 7, B3. Eblana Ave ©280 8777, fax 284 2266.
A converted Christian Brothers school in a backstreet off the seafront, 10min walk from the ferry terminal, and 20min ride from Dublin by DART. Friendly, clean and cosy. Six-bed (£10) or four-bed dorms (£11), en suite for an extra £1.50, and double rooms (£14). Kitchen; meals served; bike hire. Open 24hr. Non-IHH.

STUDENT ACCOMMODATION

As an alternative to staying in a hostel or B&B, you can rent **student accommodation** during the summer holiday (mid-June to mid-Sept). They generally offer better facilities for self-catering than hostels, with a camaraderie arising from the fact that so many of the guests are foreign students attending courses – which makes it imperative to book months ahead.

Trinity College

Map 4, E5. College Green ©608 1177, fax 671 1267.
Not cheap, but the setting is unique and utterly central. Singles (£32) with a shared kitchen and bathroom, superior en-suite singles (£40) or four-bed rooms (£32) with a shared kitchen/lounge, in one of the many halls of residence on campus; twin en-suite rooms in the old college buildings (£36). Breakfast included.

Trinity Hall

Map 2, F6. Dartry Rd, Rathmines ✆497 1772.

A pleasant hall of residence in grounds near the Trinity College Botanical Gardens (bus #14 or #14A from Pearse Street near Trinity College). Single (£22) and twin (£27) rooms with shared facilities. Sports facilities available. Breakfast included.

UCD Village

Map 2, F5. Belfield ✆269 7111, fax 7704.

A complex of modern self-catering apartments on the UCD campus, about 5km south of the centre (bus #46), with single bedrooms at comparable rates to Trinity Hall's, plus a kitchen.

CAMPING

There are two **campsites** on the outskirts of Dublin, one in Clondalkin, the other between Killiney and Bray. Both are mainly aimed at caravaners, and relatively few backpackers use them for the simple reason that by the time you've taken fares into account it's unlikely to be any cheaper than staying in a hostel in Dublin – and involves far more effort.

Camac Valley Caravan and Camping Park

Map 2, A7. Corkagh Demesne, Clondalkin ✆462 0000, fax 0111.

On the southwest edge of Dublin, in a national park off the Naas road (bus #68 or #68A from town; 40min). An attractive setting and decent facilities. Campers pay £5 per tent plus £1 per person.

Shankill Caravan and Camping Park

Map 1, E6. Off Dublin Rd, Shankill ✆282 0011.

South of Killiney, 16km from the centre; access by DART (20min) and direct buses (#45, #45A, #46 or #84; 45min). Campers pay £6 per tent plus £1 per person. Pitches can't be booked in advance.

Eating

Dublin may not be the gastronomic capital of the world, but the phenomenal expansion in the range of **places to eat** since the 1980s means that almost any taste is nowadays catered for. Dubliners are now far more sophisticated in their eating habits than a decade ago, creating a virtuous circle of rising expectations and standards that shows every sign of continuing.

Most restaurants, bistros and upmarket cafés offer a **lunchtime** set menu of two to four courses for about half the cost of their evening fare. Alternatively, you could see what pubs have to offer; carvery lunches, seafood, steaks, hearty Irish stew and nourishing soups are typical, but you can find more exotic dishes at trendier bars on the southside.

While **dinner** offers the widest scope, you'd be wise to book a table if you're going to eat after 7.30pm, as the best places fill up fast. Many establishments have an "early-bird menu" before 7pm, which is often excellent value compared to what you'd pay later on.

If all else fails, **fast-food** outlets are rarely far away. O'Connell Street has the highest concentration, with *McDonald's*, *Wimpy*, *Burger King* and *Pizzaland* as well as a branch of *Beshoff's*, Dublin's traditional fish-and-chips emporium. Another home-grown fast-food chain is

Abrakebabra, a kebab eatery with outlets on the corner of Aston Quay and Westmoreland Street, by Merchant's Arch in Temple Bar, and at other locations around the city.

If you'd prefer to make your own meals, Dunnes Stores (see p.286) is one of the best places to buy food.

In the listings below, **prices** are indicated by the terms "cheap" (under £5); "inexpensive" (£5–10); "moderate" (£10–20); "expensive" (£20–30); and "very expensive" (over £30). For restaurants, these refer to the cost of a starter, main course and dessert for *one* person in the evening; for the places reviewed under the "Cafés and quick meals" heading, the classification generally refers to a basic one-course meal – the review will make it clear what you get for your money. The cost of **drinks** is not taken into account. Beer rarely costs much more than you'd pay in a pub, although it's not always available in restaurants. Wine is a lot dearer than anywhere else in Europe, owing to the high tax levied by the government.

A lot of restaurants include the **service charge** in their prices (if so it will be indicated on the menu); where they don't, a tip of 12–15 percent of the total bill is standard. All of the restaurants listed accept payment by **credit card**; cafés and pubs vary – we have indicated those that don't.

CAFÉS AND QUICK MEALS

The distinction between **cafés** and restaurants is often arbitrary, as many of the newer places that call themselves cafés are restaurants (or at least bistros) in all but name. This section is essentially a run-through of the best places to eat if what you want is a quick, unpretentious bite – and includes a couple of fine pubs. All the places listed are in the centre of Dublin – the majority of them on the southside.

Belgo

Map 6, C5.17–19 Sycamore St.

Mon–Thurs noon–3pm & 5–10.45pm, Fri & Sat noon–midnight, Sun noon–10.45pm. Inexpensive/Moderate.

Homage to all things Belgian, including mussels *à la marinière*, wild-boar sausages and mash, plenty of chips and 101 varieties of beer, served in a communal bierkeller. The lunchtime set menu is particularly good value (£5) as is the "Beat the Clock" session (Mon–Fri 5–7.30pm) when the price you pay is the time when you order your meal.

Bendini & Shaw

Map 4, D7. 4 St Stephen's Green North.

Mon–Fri 8am–5.30pm, Sat 9am–5.30pm, Sun 11am–3pm. Cheap.

Superior sandwiches, reasonably-priced, to take away or munch amidst the chrome and neon of the café's interior. Specialities include crispy bacon and avocado on walnut and rye, or pastrami with tomato and lettuce ciabatta. Handily located for picnicking on St Stephen's Green.

Beshoff's

Map 4, E4. 14 Westmoreland St.

Sun–Thurs 11am–11pm, Fri & Sat 11am–3am.

Map 4, D2. 7 Upper O'Connell St.

Daily 11am–3am. Cheap.

A Dublin institution, albeit not as grand as *Bewley's* (see overleaf). Ivan Beshoff was a survivor from the mutiny on the battleship *Potemkin*, who settled in Ireland and opened a fish shop in Howth and then a café in Dublin. There are now two city-centre *Beshoff's* with counter service. The menu varies with the catch, but you can be sure of getting a plate of fresh fish-and-chips for around £4. The O'Connell Street *Beshoff's* has a fine view from its upstairs windows. No credit cards.

CAFÉS AND QUICK MEALS

Bewley's Oriental Cafés

Map 4, D7. 78 Grafton St.
Mon–Thurs & Sun 8am–1am, Fri & Sat 7.30am–4am.
Map 4, E4. 11–12 Westmoreland St.
Daily 7.30am–7.30pm, Thurs until 9pm.
Map 5, G5. 40 Mary St.
Mon–Sat 8am–6pm. Cheap.

As integral to Dublin life as Guinness, *Bewley's* cafés have been a
meeting place for Dubliners for generations. Founded by a
Quaker family in 1840, they embody the ethos of the ordinary
made sublime: hearty hot breakfasts and lunches, sticky buns and
cakes, consumed on marble-topped tables in panelled rooms.
The smartening-up of the Grafton St branch has removed some
of its classless atmosphere, which is a pity, but it still retains Harry
Clarke's *Birds of Paradise* window. The Westmoreland St *Bewley's*
has a busy, lived-in atmosphere, along with wooden pews and
cosy fireplaces. Owing to its late opening hours, the one on
Grafton St attracts clubbers and nightbirds.

Blazing Salads II

Map 4, D6. Powerscourt Townhouse Centre, off Grafton St.
Mon–Sat 9am–6pm. Inexpensive.

Despite the excruciating pun, the food and setting are great. Its
marvellous vegetarian and vegan menu includes dairy-, gluten-
and sugar-free dishes, while the tables overlook the shopping
centre's atrium, adapted from the courtyard of a Georgian
mansion, where live music at lunchtime soothes shoppers and
diners (see *Live Music and Clubs*). No credit cards.

Café-en-Seine

Map 4, E7. 40 Dawson St.
Daily 10am–11pm. Inexpensive.

The café-bar that revolutionized Dublin's pub scene, inspiring a
host of imitators. A long elegant bar of *fin-de-siècle* design, with
tables on the pavement outside. Serves coffee and pastries all

day, carvery lunches, and a snack menu till 8pm. Their Sunday brunch (noon–5pm) features *oeufs Benedict* and other light French food, accompanied by live jazz (see p.257).

Café Irie
Map 6, F4. 11 Fownes St Lower.
Mon–Sat 9am–8pm, Sun noon–6pm. Cheap.
Hippie café that stuffs its baguettes, ciabattas and plain doorsteps with copious quantities of tapenade, avocado, hummus, salsa and various cheeses. Healthy breakfasts available till 11.30am during the week and all day at the weekend. Excellent value; no credit cards.

Café Java
Map 4, E7. 5 South Anne St.
Mon–Fri 7am–7.30pm, Sat 8am–6.30pm, Sun 9am–6.30pm.
Map 3, H8. 145 Upper Leeson St.
Mon–Fri 7.15am–5pm, Sat 8am–5pm, Sun 10am–5pm. Cheap.
Popular breakfast, lunchtime and coffee stop, offering such light meals as poached eggs with bacon or chicken with yogurt. The standard of coffee matches that of the food, and they serve wine too.

Café Kylemore
Map 4, D3. O'Connell St/North Earl St.
Mon–Sat 8am–9pm, Sun noon–8pm. Cheap.
Kylemore is a chain of bakeries, whose flagship café resembles a fusion of *Bewley's* and a motorway cafeteria, serving hot breakfasts all day and hearty lunches featuring chips with almost everything. To buttress the bistro-image purveyed by all the brass and bentwood chairs, they have a drinks licence.

Cobalt Café
Map 5, H3. 16 North Great George's St.
Mon–Fri 10am–6pm, Sat 11am–6pm. Cheap.

Converted Georgian townhouse whose eighteenth-century elegance and contemporary design give it a very relaxing atmosphere. Light menu including open sandwiches, chocolate cake and raspberry tart, plus cappuccinos, espressos and tea. Perfect for a refresher after visiting the James Joyce Centre.

Cornucopia
Map 4, D6. 19–21 Wicklow St.
Mon–Sat 9am–8pm, Thurs until 9pm. Inexpensive.
A wholefood shop and café of long standing, somewhat eclipsed by newer places like *Juice*, but still well regarded by veggies. Their hot breakfast (till 11am) includes vegetarian sausages. You can enjoy a good lunch here for £5.

Fitzer's
Map 6, F3. Temple Bar Square.
Mon–Sun noon–11.30pm.
Map 4, E7. 51 Dawson St.
Daily 9am–11.30pm.
Map 4, G7. National Gallery.
Mon–Sat 10am–5pm, Thurs until 8.30pm, Sun 2–4.30pm.
Map 2, F5. RDS, Merrion Rd.
Mon–Sat 12.30–11.30pm, Sun noon–3pm. Moderate.
A chain of cafés, each with an individual identity. The newest, in Temple Bar, has a cool high-tech design; Dawson Street's attracts a trendy crowd and has tables outside in the summer; while *Fitzer's* in Ballsbridge revels in the grandeur of the Royal Dublin Society dining rooms. The National Gallery branch is lacking in ambience, but the food is just as good. Menus change daily, so expect anything from calamari with pickled chillies to Cajun bean casserole. Lots of choice for vegetarians; sells alcohol.

Govinda's
Map 4, C7. 4 Aungier St.
Mon–Sat 11am–9pm. Cheap.

Great little vegetarian café serving whopping helpings of dahl and rice, pakoras with curry sauce, vegetarian kebabs and burgers, all for under £5. They also do mouthwatering lassis and desserts. No credit cards.

The Irish Film Centre
Map 6, D5. 6 Eustace St.
Mon–Fri 12.30–9.30pm, Sat & Sun 12.30–3pm & 5–9.30pm.
Inexpensive.
One of the coolest hangouts in Temple Bar. Its minimalist bar-restaurant is great for a lunchtime snack, or a full meal before the show. Serves bar food – including cakes and pastries – all day, and meals in the evening (Mon–Sat from 6pm). Plenty of vegetarian choice on an eclectic menu; vegetable pâtés, burgers, chicken, jambalaya with bananas all recommended.

Kilkenny Shop Café
Map 4, E6. First floor, 6 Nassau St.
Mon–Sat 9am–5pm, Thurs until 7pm, Sun 11am–5pm.
Inexpensive.
A popular self-service eatery and coffee spot above one of Dublin's slickest shops (see p.275). Does carvery lunches, tangy salads, freshly baked pies and a different stew each day. Packed at lunchtime, so be prepared to queue.

Leo Burdock's
Map 5, F8. 2 Werburgh St.
Mon–Sat noon–midnight, Sun 4pm–midnight. Cheap.
Dublin's best loved fish-and-chippie, near Christ Church Cathedral. Though the coal-powered fryer has gone, everything else remains the same. Great nosh and cheerful service. Queues at lunchtime, after work and during pub hours. Takeaway only; no credit cards.

CAFÉS AND QUICK MEALS

Odessa
Map 5, H7. 13–14 Dame Court, off Dame St.
Daily 5.30–11.30pm. Moderate.

Exotic snacks and outré decor make this one of the city's
trendiest cafés; good for gossiping in big squashy sofas and sampling cocktails. The menu features ceviche, tandoori chicken,
marinated tofu and other dishes "for cosmopolitan palates".
Brunch served at weekends from noon to 4.30pm (£7.50).

Panem
Map 4, C4. 21 Ormond Quay Lower.
Mon–Fri 9am–5pm, Sat 10am–5pm. Cheap.

Minuscule café serving excellent French and Italian snacks –
fresh soups, filled focaccia and sweet and savoury croissants. No
credit cards.

The Stag's Head
Map 5, H7. Dame Court, off Dame St.
Mon–Fri 12.30–3.30pm & 5.30–7.30pm, Sat 12.30–2.30pm. Cheap.

A mosaic of a stag's head on the pavement alerts you to the
presence of this delightful Victorian bar. Simple, inexpensive
pub grub: Irish stew, ham and cabbage, roast spuds and chips.
The hours above refer to when food is available; drinking
hours are longer, naturally (see p.253).

The Steps of Rome
Map 4, D7. Chatham Court, Chatham St.
Mon–Sat 10am–midnight, Sun noon–11pm.
Inexpensive/Moderate.

Tiny, crammed café serving excellent pizzas made by friendly
staff. You'll be lucky to get a table, but if you don't their takeaway slices are a treat. You can eat here at lunchtime for around
£5. Wine licence; no credit cards.

CAFÉS AND QUICK MEALS

Winding Stair Café

Map 4, C4. 40 Lower Ormond Quay.

Mon–Sat 10am–6pm, Sun 1–6pm. Cheap.

A secondhand book emporium on three floors; the staircase that links them (and the bookshop's name) was inspired by a Yeats poem. With wholesome soups, salads, sandwiches and cakes their café is good enough to stand on its own merits, and has large windows overlooking the Ha'penny Bridge so you can watch the world go by as you eat. A popular spot for lunch.

RESTAURANTS

The majority of Dublin's **restaurants** are in the centre of the city (defined here as anywhere between the Grand and Royal canals, though almost all of them are on the southside), but the suburbs and seaside resorts also feature a selection of places (listed separately, by location). Wherever they're situated, it's always advisable to book in the evenings.

CENTRAL

AYA

Map 4, D7. 48 Clarendon St ©677 1544.

Mon–Fri 7.30am–11pm, Sat & Sun 9am–11pm. Expensive.

Japanese restaurant with Dublin's first sushi conveyor-bar as its focal point – you eat what takes your fancy as it glides past; there's plenty of regular seating too. Open for European and Japanese breakfast till 11am, traditional Japanese lunch and a more contemporary style dinner menu that includes AYA duck – pan-fried duck breast with an orange soy glaze.

Bad Ass Café

Map 6, F4. 9–11 Crown Alley ℂ679 5981.

Daily 11.30am–midnight. Moderate.

Once deeply hip (Sinéad O'Connor was a waitress here), the *Bad Ass* is still popular with tourists and Dubliners on an evening out in Temple Bar. Snort at the puns on the menu while you work out what kind of pizza or pasta you fancy and see your order whizzed across the room by an overhead pulley.

Bruno's

Map 6, D4. 30 East Essex St ℂ670 6767.

Daily noon–11.30pm. Moderate.

Excellent French and Mediterranean cuisine with a contemporary edge, served in cool, modern surroundings. Try their fillet of oak-smoked beef with crushed Parma ham potatoes or lamb with pear and spinach timbale and garlic cream. Very popular.

Café Auriga

Map 6, F4. Temple Bar Square ℂ671 8228.

Tues–Sat 5.30–11.30pm. Moderate/Expensive.

Chic café on two levels, with glass walls overlooking the square outside. Light, contemporary-style food such as smoked salmon with mozzarella and roasted tomato, or pan-fried lobster tail with garlic and shallots in white and mustard cream. Early-bird two-course menu costs around £9.

Café Gertrude

Map 6, G2. 3–4 Bedford Row.

Sun–Wed 10.30am–11pm, Thurs–Sat 10.30am–midnight. Moderate.

Cosy bistro with a convivial atmosphere and accessible menu

RESTAURANTS: CENTRAL

including Thai chicken curry, beef and Guinness, and spinach lasagne. Best of the puddings is a fabulously sticky hot chocolate fudge cake. Sandwiches and salads at lunchtime; very little for vegetarians. Wine licence; no beer.

Chapter One

Map 5, G3. 18/19 Parnell Square North ℂ873 2266.
Tues–Fri 12.30–2.30pm & 6–10.30pm, Sat 6–10.30pm.
Moderate/Expensive.

A formal restaurant with an excellent reputation, housed in the atmospheric cellars of the Dublin Writers Museum. Starters include fricassé of lobster and confit of duck, and there's a selection of rich main courses fashioned around roast and grilled meat, fish and poultry.

The Cedar Tree

Map 4, D6. 11 St Andrew's St ℂ677 2121.
Daily 5pm–midnight. Moderate.

Located in a cavernous basement off Suffolk Street, *The Cedar Tree* is a great spot for a lively evening out. Its dazzling array of meze dishes are best appreciated by a group of friends, with lots of wine to wash it down. The diversity of dishes based on pulses and grains is perfect for vegetarians.

Chez Jules

Map 4, E4. D'Olier Chambers, 16A D'Olier St ℂ677 0499.
Mon–Fri noon–3pm & 6–11pm, Sat 1–3.30pm & 6–11pm, Sun 5–10pm. Inexpensive/Moderate.

Friendly, unpretentious French-style bistro with lots of seating for groups, close to *Ashfield House* hostel and Trinity College. They specialize in seafood and chargrilled steaks, but vegetarians can always find something decent on the menu. Good-value set lunches and early-evening meals (before 7pm).

RESTAURANTS: CENTRAL

Chicago Pizza Pie Factory

Map 4, D8. St Stephen's Green West ℗478 1233.

Mon–Wed noon–11pm, Thurs–Sat noon–1.30am. Moderate.

Another American-style place with rock associations: it stands on the site of the Dandelion Market, where U2 used to play before they made it big. Does tasty deep-pan fried pizzas. Youthful clientele. Full bar. Located next to the St Stephen's Green shopping centre.

Cooke's Café

Map 4, D6. 14 South William St ℗679 0536.

Mon–Sat 12.30–3.30pm & 6–11.30pm. Expensive.

Fashionable restaurant offering eclectic contemporary cuisine. Expect to find anything from veal kidney sautéed in brandy to scallops in Noilly Prat. *The Rhino Room* upstairs is less expensive, with a menu featuring New York chargrilled fare – seabream, swordfish and so forth.

Da Pino

Map 6, B6. 38–40 Parliament St ℗671 9308.

Daily noon–midnight. Inexpensive/Moderate.

One of the best of the many Italian restaurants in Temple Bar. Italians come here to enjoy spaghetti carbonara, *zuppa di cipolla* and other classic dishes. The welcome is warm and the decor sympathetic. The restaurant possibly stands on the site of the *Eagle Tavern*, where the notorious Hellfire Club (see p.64) was founded.

Dish

Map 6, F5. 2 Crow St ℗671 1248.

Daily noon–11.30pm. Expensive.

Chic and lively new restaurant swiftly gaining a great reputation for its imaginative menu. A strong bias towards Mediterranean flavours using fresh herbs, organic steaks and zingy pastas leavened by a more home-spun creativity – try their roast monkfish with leek and bacon mash. Good-value in the afternoon (till 5pm) and excellent Sunday brunch.

Don Angel
Map 4, E4. 7 D'Olier St ℂ679 3859.
Mon–Fri noon–11pm, Sat 1–11pm, Sun 1–10pm.
Inexpensive/Moderate.
Authentic Spanish café-restaurant with a no-nonsense interior and a full range of powerfully flavoured tapas, several paellas and, of course, wine. Definitely a place to settle in for the evening. Arguably the best coffee in Dublin too.

Eden
Map 6, D5. Sycamore St/Meeting House Square ℂ670 5372.
Tues–Sun noon–late. Expensive.
Tremendously chic, upmarket restaurant in the heart of Temple Bar, with seats out on the square during the summer. The menu offers classic Irish cuisine with a Mediterranean twist – try the braised lamb steaks with olives and lemon barley or organic steak with a rich béarnaise sauce. Very popular.

Elephant & Castle
Map 6, G3. 18 Temple Bar ℂ679 3121.
Mon–Fri 8am–11.30pm, Sat 10.30am–11.30pm, Sun noon–11.30pm. Inexpensive/Moderate.
A hit with Dubliners from the outset, its panache and informality has had a huge influence on the culinary scene in Temple Bar, and Dublin generally. Imagine a neighbourhood diner that just happens to be in the coolest part of town, and does gourmet burgers, breakfasts or late-night meals with a Cajun-Creole or Pacific Rim spin. Clubbers celebrate their hangovers with Sunday brunch at the *E&C*; on weekdays, you needn't feel ashamed of ordering the spicy chicken wings as a snack for two.

RESTAURANTS: CENTRAL

Good World Restaurant

Map 4, C6. 18 South Great George's St ℂ677 5373.

Daily 12.30pm–midnight. Moderate.

Sited near several pubs off Dame Street, its late hours ensure a boisterous clientele after closing time, and the reputation of its dim sum packs patrons in by day. Dublin's Chinese community is divided on whether the *Good World* or the *Imperial* (see opposite) does better dim sum, but relishes putting both to the test. Come here early on a Sunday to get a place upstairs.

The Gotham Café

Map 4, D7. 5 South Anne St ℂ679 5266.

Mon–Sat noon–midnight, Sun 10.30am–1pm. Moderate.

Buzzy, child-friendly café specializing in Cal-Ital food. Does great pizzas, chargrilled chicken with peanut sauce, spicy prawn salad, and other yummy concoctions. You can enjoy lunch for under £10, and dinner for less than £15.

Halo

Map 4, C4. *Morrison Hotel*, Ormond Quay Lower ℂ887 2421.

Daily 12.30–2.30pm & 6.30–10.30pm. Expensive/Very expensive.

Cutting-edge interior design makes this a very fashionable place to eat. Expect the fresh, crisp flavours of Asian-fusion cuisine delivered with flair. Starters include fresh oysters, sushi and crab won ton soup; main courses also revolve around seafood – try the steamed aromatic sea bass with tamarind sauce.

Il Baccaro

Map 6, D5. Meeting House Square ℂ671 4597.

Mon–Fri & Sun 6–11.30pm, Sat 2.30–11.30pm. Inexpensive/Moderate.

Lively, informal cellar-osteria serving traditional rustic Italian food. No one minds whether you just fancy a starter or a full meal – wine flows straight from the barrel and the musicians play. A great spot for a party.

Imperial Chinese Restaurant

Map 5, H8. 12A Wicklow St ℗677 2580.

Daily 12.30pm–midnight, Fri & Sat until 12.30am. Moderate.

A large room buzzing with Chinese customers, who generally rate it the best restaurant in Dublin. Others, too, have discovered the joys of its superb dim sum (served 12.30–5pm), and a Sunday brunch at the *Imperial* rivals brunch at the *E&C* as a sociable experience. À la carte in the evening is dearer, but the ingredients and cooking are so fine that you won't complain.

Juice

Map 4, C6. South Great George's St ℗475 7856.

Mon–Wed 9am–11pm, Thurs & Fri 9am–4am, Sat noon–4am, Sun 12.30–11pm. Moderate.

Juice is a chic vegetarian eating place with not a sweaty sandal in sight. Its imaginative menu takes in a range of vegetarian and vegan fare, including orange shiro stir fry, Thai curries, stroganoff and aduki bean Juiceburgers; the drinks list features juices, lassis and organic wines. Early-bird menu (Mon–Sat 5–7pm) around £9.

La Paloma

Map 6, G2. 17B Asdills Row ℗677 7392.

Daily noon–1am. Inexpensive/Moderate.

A cosy, friendly Spanish restaurant just off the main drag in Temple Bar. Taped flamenco music, hot pink walls and a yellow ceiling contribute to the Iberian ambience, a stone's throw from the Liffey. Does good, cheap tapas and pricier paellas and tortillas.

La Stampa

Map 4, E7. 35 Dawson St ℗677 8611.

Mon–Fri 12.30–2.30pm & 5.30pm–midnight, Sat 6pm–midnight, Sun 6.30–11.30pm. Expensive.

A nineteenth-century ballroom extravagantly decked with

RESTAURANTS: CENTRAL

flowers forms the setting for this much-praised award-winning restaurant. The varied European-style menu includes Bayonne ham, melon and mango salad as a starter followed by pan-fried halibut, *pommes a l'huile* and salsa. Early-bird menus are available (Mon–Fri).

The Latchford Bistro
Map 4, H9. 99/100 Lower Baggot St ℅676 0784.
Mon–Sat 12.30–3pm & 6–11pm. Moderate/Expensive.
Elegant, intimate restaurant in a delightful Georgian townhouse with a menu offering richly flavoured international cuisine. Crisp confit duck with steamed pancakes, peppered fillet of salmon with lime butter, and pan-fried sirloin steak all feature on the set dinner menu at £21.95, and the early-bird and lunch menus are similarly enticing.

Lord Edward Seafood Restaurant
Map 4, A6. 23 Christchurch Place ℅454 2420.
Mon–Fri 12.30–2.30pm & 6–10.45pm, Sat 6–10.45pm. Moderate/Expensive.
Around the corner from *Leo Burdock's*, the legendary chippie, the *Lord Edward* represents the other end of the pescatorial scale. Dublin's oldest seafood restaurant, above a pub opposite Christ Church Cathedral, it is a venerable club-like institution dedicated to simple cooking with the very freshest fish, savoured by barristers.

The Mermaid Café
Map 6, C6. 69–70 Dame St ℅670 8236.
Mon–Sat 12.30–2.30pm & 6–10.30pm, Sun 12.30–3.30pm & 5–9.30pm. Expensive.
An airy, chic spot with austere contemporary furnishings. Great food from an eclectic menu which includes New England crab cakes with picquant mayonnaise and chargrilled aubergines with ricotta, herbs and sweet chilli relish.

La Mezza Luna

Map 6, E5. 1 Temple Lane South ℗671 2840.

Mon–Thurs noon–11pm, Fri & Sat noon–11.30pm, Sun noon–10.30pm. Moderate.

Overlooking Dame Street, but entered from the lane around the corner, this popular and lively Italian restaurant does a variety of pizzas and pasta dishes. Particularly good value is their three-course early-bird menu (3–7pm) for under £10.

Milano

Map 4, E7. 61 Dawson St ℗670 7744.
Map 6, D4. 19 Temple Bar ℗670 3384.

Both daily noon–midnight. Moderate.

The first venture of the British *Pizza Express* chain in Ireland, *Milano* offers a familiar and affordable range of tasty pizzas and pastas in a ritzier setting than one associates with *Pizza Express*. Currently an "in" place to eat and be seen for the bright young things around town. You can lunch here for under £10.

Mongolian Barbecue

Map 6, H4. 7 Anglesea St ℗670 4154.

Mon–Fri noon–3pm & 6–10pm, Sat noon–10pm, Sun 1–10pm. Inexpensive/Moderate.

On the strength of this cheery theme-restaurant, you can't help feeling that if the Mongols had eaten this well at home, they wouldn't have bothered to carve out an empire. All you can eat of noodle stir-fries, composed from a wide range of exotic ingredients and fried on the spot. Great value at lunchtime (£5.95; Sun £7.95) or at the buffet in the evenings (£9.95), when you'll never get a table without booking.

Morel's Bistro

Map 4, F10. 14–17 Lower Leeson St ℗662 2480.

Mon–Thurs 12.30–2pm & 6–9.30pm, Fri 12.30–2pm & 6–10pm, Sat 6–10pm. Expensive.

Snazzy, eclectic bistro beneath the *Stephen's Hall Hotel*. The bright decor complements such zestful dishes as monkfish tempura with lime and coriander, or wood pigeon with roast shallots and crispy bacon. The service and wines are fine too. Child-friendly; highchairs provided.

Nico's

Map 6, E6. 53 Dame St ℗677 3062.

Mon–Fri 12.30–2.30pm & 6pm–midnight, Sat 6pm–midnight. Moderate/Expensive.

A highly successful Italian restaurant popular with theatre-goers and courting couples. The food is good solid stuff like carbonara and risotto, but the real secret of its success is the atmosphere, enlivened by the dramatic flounces of the waiters, and piano music as the night wears on.

The Old Dublin

Map 3, E6. 90–91 Francis St ℗454 2028.

Mon–Fri 12.30–2.15pm & 6–11pm, Sat 6–11pm. Moderate/Expensive.

Long established amid the antiques shops of the Liberties, *The Old Dublin* offers a hybrid of Irish, Scandinavian and Russian cuisine, with zestfully prepared dishes like coddle, gravadlax, borscht and blinis, that work well together. Particularly good for vegetarians.

101 Talbot

Map 4, F2. 100–101 Talbot St ℗874 5011.

Mon 5–10pm, Tues–Sat 5–11pm. Moderate.

One of the very few good restaurants on the inner northside, conveniently close to the Abbey Theatre. Seedy Talbot Street is left behind as you climb the stairs to a lovely spacious dining room, where flavoursome dishes like mung bean and aubergine stew keep vegetarians coming back, and the service never falters.

RESTAURANTS: CENTRAL

Pasta Fresca

Map 4, D7. 3–4 Chatham St ℂ679 2402.
Mon–Fri 11am–11.30pm, Sat 10am–midnight, Sun 12.30–10pm.
Moderate/Expensive.

Ireland's first fresh pasta shop when it opened a decade ago,
Pasta Fresca still delights the ciabatta-loving classes. Informal
restaurant with a few tables and chairs in the window, serving
fresh pasta and other Italian dishes; always busy at lunchtime,
when two courses cost around £7.

Patrick Guilbaud

Map 4, G8. 21 Upper Merrion St ℂ676 4192.
Tues–Sat 12.30–2.30pm & 7.30–10.15pm. Very expensive.

An elegant French restaurant that once stunned foodies with its
flair and prices, this modestly eponymous establishment still has
bags of cachet. Many critics hold *Guilbaud*'s nouvelle cuisine to
be the best in Dublin – certainly a serious contender among
the culinary heavyweights.

Peacock Alley

Map 4, D8. *Fitzwilliam Hotel*, St Stephen's Green West ℂ478 7015.
Mon–Sat 12.30–3pm & 6.30–11pm. Very expensive.

Ultrafashionable restaurant dedicated to modern Irish cuisine
with lots of Mediterranean touches. Ravioli with lobster and
goat's cheese appears at lunch, while the evening menu features
rack of lamb with rosemary mashed potatoes, chicken stuffed
with organic greens, and other treats. Worth a serious splurge.

The Rajdoot Tandoori

Map 4, D7. Westbury Centre, 26–28 Clarendon St ℂ679 4274.
Mon–Sat noon–2.30pm & 6.30–11.30pm, Sun 6.30–11.30pm.
Moderate.

Despite being in the Westbury Mall off Grafton Street, and far
plusher than other Indian restaurants, the *Rajdoot* keeps a keen
eye on its rivals, so you'll be pleasantly surprised by the prices –

RESTAURANTS: CENTRAL

especially at lunchtime. Lots of choice for vegetarians, and excellent service.

Romano's

Map 4, B4. 12 Capel St ℡872 6868.

Mon–Sat 12.30–10pm. Moderate.

Unpretentious and welcoming Italian restaurant serving excellent healthy meals – home-made pizza and pasta using free-range eggs, organic flour, and herbs and fresh veg from the market a street away. The area isn't great, and women should be careful when walking here at night, but this said, it's well worth a foray. The lunch special costs around £6.

The Shalimar

Map 4, C6. 17 South Great George's St ℡671 0738.

Daily noon–2.30pm & 5pm–midnight. Inexpensive/Moderate.

A long-established rival of the *Rajdoot's* that's opened a balti house in its basement. You can choose between tandooris, biryanis and other classic Punjabi dishes, or a simpler keema or kofta downstairs – both with lots of options for veggies. Always busy, but especially as the pubs close.

South Street Pizzeria

Map 4, C6. South Great George's St ℡475 2273.

Daily noon–1am. Moderate.

Sited across the road from Exchequer St, the *South Street Pizzeria* is one of the most popular hangouts on a street noted for its pubs and restaurants. Relaxed and friendly atmosphere, smashing pizzas, a wine bar and cheap lunchtime specials.

Tante Zoe's

Map 6, F5. 1 Crow St ℡679 4407.

Daily noon–4pm & 5pm–midnight. Moderate.

The first Cajun/Creole restaurant to open in Temple Bar, it remains popular for continuing to serve decent food at affordable prices and managing to be fun. Go for the inexpensive lunchtime or early-bird menu and you won't regret it.

The Tea Rooms

Map 6, B4. *The Clarence Hotel*, 6–8 Wellington Quay ©670 7766.
Mon–Fri 12.30–2pm & 6.30–10pm, Sat 6.30–10pm, Sun 6.30–9pm.
Expensive/Very expensive.

Dublin's most stylish hotel, *The Clarence* (see p.199), has a fabulous restaurant that's one of the coolest places to be seen in town. Its stunning design provides a perfect foil to the eclectic menu, offering ten different starters and a dozen main courses, from Thai soup to steamed cod with aubergine blinis. For the ultimate splurge this is definitely the place.

Tosca

Map 4, D6. 20 Suffolk St ©679 6744.
Daily noon–11.30pm. Moderate/Expensive.

Located between Grafton Street and the Dublin Tourism Centre, this modernist temple to southern European food and wine has won over those who expected to see its owner, Norman Hewson (brother of U2's Bono), fall flat on his face. Aside from its cool halogen spot-lit interior, *Tosca* is known for its zestful salads and pastas, with lots of choices for vegetarians. The menu changes daily, and the wine list is imposing. Though quite laid-back at lunchtime, it gets very busy at night.

Trocadero

Map 4, D6. 3 St Andrew's St ©677 5545.
Mon–Sat 6pm–midnight, Sun 6–11.15pm. Moderate/Expensive.

Looks like an obnoxiously rich trattoria, but in fact is pleasant, friendly and has excellent food. One of Dublin's oldest Italian restaurants, its walls are hung with plaudits in the form of signed photographs of visiting showbiz luminaries. The place comes into its own late at night when it fills up with theatre folk. There's an early-bird menu for those who'd rather save money than socialize.

Unicorn

Map 4, F8. Merrion Court, off Merrion Row ©622 4757.
Mon–Sat 12.30–3.30pm & 6–10.30pm. Moderate/Expensive.
This Italian haunt of *bien pensant* media folk and politicos was run for decades by the Sidoli family. Following the trauma of a change of ownership, its regulars are happy to find that the trattoria fare and plain, no-nonsense interior haven't altered, and their interactions still make the *Unicorn* what it is – a Dublin institution.

Wagamama

Map 4, D7. South King St ©478 2152.
Daily noon–midnight. Inexpensive/Moderate.
Ultrahealthy Japanese-style meat and vegetarian noodle dishes served in a near-clinical atmosphere of long benches, crisp lighting and clean air. Non-smoking.

Yamamori Noodles

Map 4, C6. 71–72 South Great Georges St ©475 5001.
Mon–Sat 12.30–2.30pm & 5–11pm, Sun 5–11pm. Moderate.
Trendy, fun Japanese restaurant in the heart of publand. Delicious noodles, teriyaki, tempura, sushi and sashimi. You can eat well at lunch for under £10; in the evenings you must get there early (or book) to stand any chance of getting a table.

BRAY

Tree of Idleness

Map 1, F6. The Strand ©286 3498.
Tues–Sat 7.30–11pm, Sun 7.30–10pm. Moderate/Expensive.
An award-winning Greek-Cypriot restaurant on the seafront, serving the freshest seafood, wonderful moussaka and suckling

RESTAURANTS: BRAY

pig, accompanied by a great wine list and excellent service. Such is its reputation, people travel right out from Dublin to dine here.

DALKEY

Guinea Pig Fish Restaurant

Map 7, G3. 17 Railway Rd ©285 9055.

Daily 6pm–midnight. Expensive.

Just downhill from the DART station, en route to Dalkey's high street, this little award-winning seafood restaurant offers a five-course meal of asparagus, salmon, crab, seafood chowder and dessert for £27. You can pay well over £30 going à la carte, so it's certainly a tempting deal, as is the early-bird menu at £13.50.

P.D.'s Woodhouse

Map 7, G2. 1 Coliemore Rd ©284 9399.

Mon–Sat 6–11pm, Sun 1–9.30pm. Moderate/Expensive.

A pub-like restaurant that's currently cool in Dalkey, with garden tables for those balmy summer days. Chargrilled steaks are a speciality; the kebabs, seafood, baked potatoes and crunchy salads are also fine.

BLACKROCK, DÚN LAOGHAIRE & SANDYCOVE

Ayumi-Ya

Map 2, H6. Newpark Centre, Newtownpark Ave, Blackrock ©283 1767.

Mon–Sat 6–11.30pm, Sun 5.30–9.45pm. Moderate.

It's worth a trip to neighbouring Blackrock to sample the delights of this traditional Japanese restaurant. The huge and varied menu includes excellent sashimi, tempura and sushi, plus more exotic dishes. You can get there from Dún Laoghaire by DART (to Blackrock station, then bus #114 to the Newpark

RESTAURANTS: DALKEY, BLACKROCK, DÚN LAOGHAIRE & SANDYCOVE

Centre) or bus #45 (to the corner of Stradbrook Road and Newtownpark Avenue).

Brasserie na Mara

Map 7, B3. The Harbour, Dún Laoghaire ✆280 6767.

Mon–Fri 12.30–2.30pm & 6.30–10pm, Sat 6.30–10pm. Expensive.

A successful venture into restauranting by Irish Rail, in the former station buffet uphill from the ferry terminal. Giant drapes and mirrors create a stylish setting to enjoy Paul Keogh's cooking. As the name suggests, seafood is his forte – try the deep-fried hake in a tortilla crust. Dining à la carte costs around £20, and there's a set menu for slightly less than that.

Odell's

Map 7, D3. 49 Sandycove Rd ✆284 2188.

Mon–Sat 6–10.30pm, Sun 6–9.30pm. Moderate.

Sadly only open in the evenings, this friendly bistro is noted for its generous helpings of Cajun dishes given a Mediterranean workover or a pinch of Chinese spicing. Check out the early-bird menu.

HOWTH

Adrian's

Map 8, G3. 8 Abbey St ✆839 1696.

Mon–Sat 12.30–2pm & 6.30–9.30pm, Sun 12.30–7.30pm. Moderate.

Just uphill from Harbour Road in a converted house painted to resemble a giant aquarium. The food is as playful as the exterior, ranging from a chowder-snappy spliced with whiskey to a curried chicken garnished with fried banana. There are some nice dishes for vegetarians, too.

Casa Pasta

Map 8, G3. 12 Harbour Rd ℂ839 3823.
Mon–Thurs 6pm–midnight, Fri 12.30–3pm & 6pm–midnight, Sat & Sun 12.30–10.30pm. Moderate.

With views of the harbour and great Italian cooking this place has been a big success since it opened in 1993. Pasta with shrimps, fetuccine with pesto, spicy chicken wings and deep-fried brie are only some of the treats on offer.

El Paso

Map 8, G3. 10 Harbour Rd ℂ832 3334.
Mon–Sat 6–11pm, Sun 2–10pm. Moderate.

Though it seems a bit incongruous to find a Tex-Mex steak-house on the seafront of a fishing town, the *El Paso* is the Real McCoy for delicious steaks, nachos, tortillas and all the rest (including vegetarian dishes).

King Sitric's Fish Restaurant

Map 8, H3. East Pier ℂ832 5235.
Mon–Sat 6.30–11pm; May–Sept Mon–Sat also noon–3pm.
Expensive/Very expensive.

Howth's equivalent of the *Lord Edward* in central Dublin, *King Sitric's* is a fine, old-fashioned seafood restaurant whose ingredients are landed at the pier nearby. Don't expect exotic sauces or vegetables, just the fruits of the sea, perfectly cooked and presented.

Drinking

"Good puzzle would be cross Dublin without passing a pub"
– James Joyce, *Ulysses*

Dubliners boast, with ample justification, that the best **pubs** in the world are to be found in their city. The public house stands at the very centre of Irish social life, and any visitor seeking the "craic" for which Dublin nightlife is so famous should have little trouble tracking it down in one of the city's hundreds of pubs and bars.

In general, pubs are open from 10.30am or 11.00am to 11.00pm during the winter months, and until 11.30pm in the summer, but in recent years some flexibility has been introduced into Ireland's arcane licensing laws and it is increasingly common for city-centre pubs to keep serving until well after midnight.

All pubs serve draught beers (a half-pint is invariably referred to as "a glass"), with pride of place being reserved for the city's most famous tipple, Guinness, which really does taste infinitely superior in its hometown, where it's always granted the requisite seven minutes settling time, however busy the barman or thirsty the customer. You'll also find Irish whiskey like Paddy's, Powers and Jameson's, as well as a variety of other spirits and, depending on the premises, a wide range of the imported bottled beers, "alcopops" and wines.

The economic boom which Dublin has enjoyed of late has had some negative consequences for the city's pub culture. A trend towards "quaintification" has seen many modest old pubs gutted and refitted with bulk-purchased turf baskets, moth-eaten books and blackened fire-irons, and practically every fortnight another soulless pastiche opens in Temple Bar or the Grafton Street area. Nevertheless, there are many genuinely historic licensed premises still trading in more or less the same condition that Joyce's hero Leopold Bloom would have found them in 1904.

In recent years these traditional pubs have been joined by a huge array of more youth-oriented and cosmopolitan bars. The new and old coexist quite happily and the compact nature of the city centre means that you can find yourself careening between a succession of nicotine-stained Victorian snugs and ultrahip designer watering-holes in the course of a single riotous evening.

The Brazen Head

Map 5, E7. 20 Lower Bridge St.

Northwest of Christ Church and just across the river from the Four Courts stands the pub which is a leading contender for the impressive title "oldest pub in Europe". There has been a tavern on the site of the *Brazen Head* since Viking times, and it is said to be haunted by the ghost of one of Ireland's greatest martyred patriots, Robert Emmet. Traditional Irish music sessions are held here in the evenings (Wed–Fri) and on Sunday (1–3pm).

Café-en-Seine

Map 4, E7. 40 Dawson St.

This swanky, high-ceilinged bar is where thrusting young professionals come to ogle haughty teenage models. The raised benches that line its walls make it an ideal location for people-watching, talent-spotting and gossip-causing. Good coffee and sandwiches at lunchtime (see p.223).

The Chocolate Bar
Map 4, D10. Harcourt St.

Nestling in the armpit of one of Dublin's most stylish night-clubs, this Gaudi-inspired watering-hole is where Dublin's truly trendy young things congregate to swig alcopops and imported bottle beers before swaggering around to the club. Mean cocktails and wonderful sink-into sofas.

Davy Byrne's
Map 4, E6. 21 Duke St.

Davy Byrne's "moral pub" receives a particularly honourable mention in Joyce's epic novel as the place where Leopold Bloom takes a break from his famous perambulation across Dublin for a Gorgonzola sandwich and a glass of Burgundy. It's been extensively redecorated over the years, so little of its 1904 ambience remains, but it's still a popular place for both natives and visitors.

The Dockers
Map 3, J4. 5 Sir John Rogerson's Quay.

Rock fans from around the world make pilgrimage to this cosy establishment, located on the somewhat dilapidated quays east of the centre, just around the corner from the original site of Windmill Studios, where U2 recorded their early albums. Although the studio itself has now moved, Bono and the boys are still known to drop by for the occasional pint between tours.

> U2 fans may also want to visit the **Windmill Lane wall**, off Creighton St, where, for the past decade, devotees have been recording their love of the band.

Doheny and Nesbitt

Map 4, G9. 5 Lower Baggot St.

This tiny, atmospheric, smoke-filled room looks as if it's hardly changed since the beginning of the century. Its cosy snugs are frequently packed, but if you can't stand the pace here, there's a slightly less hectic lounge upstairs.

The Front Lounge

Map 6, A5. Parliament St.

One of Temple Bar's runaway success stories, this enormous and airy bar has been thronged since the day its doors first opened a couple of years ago. The designer watering-hole of choice for arty Dubliners, gay and straight alike, with comfortable sofas and good coffee. As New York as Dublin pubs get.

The Globe

Map 4, C6. 11 South Great George's St.

Outrageously popular with the sassy and fashion-conscious youth of Dublin, this loud and lively bar is invariably packed at weekends, and busy every night. It is pleasantly dark-wooded and discreetly lit, with an upbeat, sociable atmosphere that makes it a perfect prequel to a night's clubbing.

Grogan's

Map 4, D6. 15 South William St.

Lively, popular bar where works by well-known local artists hang on the walls and from the ceiling, and a new generation of painters and poets nurse their pints, dreaming perhaps of one day being added to the fantastic stained-glass celebration of famous *Grogan's* regulars from the past.

Hartigan's

Map 4, F10. 100 Lower Leeson St.

Latterly the stomping ground of students from the nearby medical schools of UCD and College of Surgeons, this bar has made few concessions to the passage of time or modern notions of comfort. But what it lacks in decor and seating is more than made up for in history and attitude. And, given the good-natured riotousness that frequently erupts (especially after college rugby matches), the lack of breakable furniture is perhaps understandable.

Hogan's

Map 4, C6. 35 South Great George's St.
Another favoured haunt of the city's bright young things, this large and extremely busy bar is not for those seeking a quiet contemplative drink. The volume of the eclectic music mix often renders meaningful conversation well-nigh impossible, but the excitable crowd that throng this lively joint seem to manage more than adequately with sign language and knowing looks.

The Horsehoe Bar

Map 4, E8. St Stephen's Green.
The Horsehoe Bar in the magnificent *Shelbourne Méridien Hotel* (p.202) is the place where politicians, gossip columnists, solicitors and advertising executives repair every Friday evening to flirt, swagger and carve up the world. The back bar attracts a somewhat younger crowd of suit-wearers and mobile-phone-owners, while the more civilized drawing room provides a welcome respite from the gossip and the crowds.

Hughes's

Map 5, E6. 19 Chancery St.
The local for habitués of the neighbouring Four Courts, this venerable establishment quenches the thirst of barristers, litigants, and Guards (as the police force, officially the Gardaí, are generally known) without fear or favour. In the evening it hosts excellent traditional music sessions.

The International Bar
Map 5, H8. 23 Wicklow St.

On three compact floors, this charming and civilized old pub is an unspoilt gem within a stone's throw of Grafton Street. The magnificent carved shelving behind the ground floor bar are worth a visit alone, and the gently reclining red velour seats support the bottoms of both ordinary Dubliners and the comedians, songwriters and musicians who perform in the tiny and informal venue upstairs.

The Irish Film Centre
Map 6, D5. 6 Eustace St.

Another oasis of calm in the commercial storm: the narrow passageway entrance opens up into an ancient courtyard now covered and converted into a room three storeys high. Spacious and cultured, this is a pleasant spot for a pint and a cappuccino at any hour of the night or day, and film buffs can browse the specialist bookshop or view cult movies in the adjoining cinema (see p.267).

Keogh's
Map 4, D7. 9 South Anne St.

Until a few years ago the family whose name adorns this wonderful old establishment lived upstairs, reputedly the last resident publicans in the city centre. To the collective relief of Dublin's more discerning drinkers, the new owners have scarcely touched the wonderful mahogany interiors, and there are few happier places to be than in the innermost seat of the tiny snug, with a pint settling on the table in front of you.

The Long Hall
Map 4, C7. 51 Aungier St.

Wonderfully ornate Victorian pub, with deep-red walls and plasterwork, glittering mirrors, and, as you might expect, a very long wooden bar. Popular with a good mix of tourists and locals.

McDaid's

Map 4, D7. 3 Harry St.

One of Dublin's best known literary pubs, this small, high-ceilinged bar boasts the dubious distinction of having been the preferred watering-hole of Ireland's most famously dipsomaniac writer, Brendan Behan (see p.120). It remains more-or-less intact, and is highly popular with locals and visitors alike.

Morrison

Map 4, C4. *Morrison Hotel*, Lower Ormond Quay.

Minimalist and extra-chic, but nonetheless very mellow bar; a great place to chill out, chat and play chess. The clientele is a fairly regular mix of locals and visitors, so don't be put off by the arch-cool exterior.

Mulligan's

Map 4, E4. 8 Poolbeg St.

This establishment is generally accepted to be the home of "the best pint in Dublin", an accolade which alone justifies a visit to its low-ceilinged premises. A favoured haunt of print workers and journalists, this no-nonsense two-room bar is the genuine article, unaffected by either fashion or prosperity.

The Octagon Bar

Map 6, B4. *The Clarence Hotel*, Wellington Quay.

As you might expect, the wood-panelled, octagonal bar of *The Clarence* (see p.199) is the epitome of studied cool, eerily illuminated by artificial daylight, however late the hour. This said, it attracts a mixed crowd – though you might spot the occasional celeb who's wandered down from their penthouse suite for a nightcap.

The Odeon

Map 4, D10. Harcourt St.

Housed in a converted railway station this is one of Dublin's trendiest new bars, with potted palms, Art Deco fittings and a fabulously ornamental bar salvaged from a Barcelona bank. Heaving at night; hip young chill-out session on Sunday – if you're there at 6pm you'll see the kitschest Virgin Mary this side of Lourdes, an image projected onto the back wall to coincide with the Angelus. Late opening (Thurs–Sat till 1.30am).

O'Donoghues

Map 4, F8. 15 Merrion Row.

One of Dublin's most famous musical pubs, where many of Ireland's foremost traditional and folk groups (the Chieftains and the Dubliners, to name but two) began their musical careers squashed in together at the window seat. The sessions are as energetic as ever, and as popular – if you want a good seat get there early.

O'Neill's

Map 5, H7. 2 Suffolk St.

A series of interconnecting rooms knocked together, this large pub has been a home from home for generations of students and lecturers from nearby Trinity College. Also much favoured by office workers as a lunching spot, who come for the healthy portions of buffet food and sandwiches served.

The Palace Bar

Map 4, E5. 21 Fleet St.

An elegant and sociable outpost of Old Dublin on the eastern boundary of Temple Bar, this handsome bar attracts a mixed crowd of drinkers drawn in by the quality of the pint and the relative tranquillity of its ambience compared with the surrounding piped-music tourist traps.

The Porter House

Map 6, B5. 16 Parliament St.

Dublin's first microbrewery serves a wide selection of its excellent and playfully monikered own-brand beers on three busy floors, attracting both curious locals and visitors enticed by the bright, bustling interior. Check out a sample tray of all eight beers for £6, a great way to establish your chosen pint before settling in. Live music most nights; late opening (Thurs & Fri till 1.30am, Sat till 1am).

Pravda

Map 4, C4. Liffey St/Ormond Quay.

Immensely trendy super-bar. Don't miss the upper floor, where the walls are covered in a combination of huge Revolutionary murals and gilt-rimmed Russian orthodox icons; plenty of sofas mean you can survey the scene in comfort. Food available; late opening (Wed–Fri till 1.30am).

Ryan's

Map 5, A6. 28 Parkgate St.

Situated near the entrance to the Phoenix Park, this stately establishment can fairly claim to be the "president of Ireland's local". The quality of its Guinness is legendary, and its regulars hotly dispute the claim of *Mulligan's* of Poolbeg St to the city's finest pint. The sensitive and notoriously travel-sickness-prone liquid, they triumphantly point out, has by far the shorter distance to travel to reach *Ryan's*, the St James St Brewery being a mere river-breadth away.

Slattery's

Map 4, B3. 129 Capel St.

This cheery and unpretentious pub has been hosting excellent traditional music sessions for many years, and is well worth the short walk across Capel Street Bridge away from the more self-conscious establishments that proliferate in the Parliament Street area. This is where real Dubs come to hear their ballads. That said, it's not the safest of areas and women in particular should take care here.

The Stag's Head
Map 5, H7. 1 Dame Court.
One of Dublin's prettiest old bars, favoured by students and workers alike. Its dark woods and stuffed fauna evoke the ambience of a slightly scruffy hunting lodge. Extremely lively at weekends when the crowds overflow out onto the pavements, eventually turning the narrow street into a traffic-impassable beer garden. Decent pub food too.

Thomas Read's
Map 6, B6. 1 Parliament St.
Actually two bars knocked into one, this lively establishment serves a globe-spanning selection of bottled and draught beers to its youngish regulars. By day, its large windows and strategic location on the corner of Parliament and Dame streets, just opposite Dublin Castle, make it the perfect place to while away a few hours watching the city flow by outside.

Toners
Map 4, G9. 139 Lower Baggot St.
This Victorian bar, just across the road from *Doheny and Nesbitt*, is one of Dublin's finest. Dark and cosy with a refreshingly plain exterior, its snugs and glazed partitions are perfect for making and breaking confidences. Amazingly efficient service, despite the crowds.

The Welcome Inn
Map 5, H3. Parnell St.
No-nonsense boozer colonized by students. A good spot for serious and impassioned banter in a tatty northside location – worth a hop if you're staying at the *MEC* hostel.

Zanzibar
Map 4, C4.1 Lower Ormond Quay.
Gargantuan African-themed bar whose flamboyant interior,

decked out with lanterns, pots and palm trees, attracts a mixed and fashionable crowd. Serves a bewildering array of cocktails – but they're pricey, as is the beer. Crammed to the rafters at weekends

Live music and clubs

The international success of artists like Sinéad O'Connor, Hothouse Flowers and, particularly, U2 has created a huge boom in the Irish **music** industry, and Dublin can fairly claim to be Europe's Second City of Rock after London. The capital's proximity to London, and its reputation as a music-friendly town, means that most international rock, pop and country acts include a Dublin date on their tours, and the vibrant local music scene throws up a seemingly inexhaustible supply of young guns. Any night of the week you'll find a wide variety of music listed in the pages of magazines like the iconoclastic *Hot Press*, the lively *In Dublin* and the excellent and widely available freesheet *Dublin Event Guide*. For larger shows, you may need to book in advance – the ticket shop at HMV on Grafton Street is your best bet. At smaller venues you can generally pay at the door; prices vary from about £5 to £15 depending on the act.

Some of the best Irish traditional music can be heard for nothing at the informal sessions that take place in various pubs (see Chapter 12, *Drinking*).

For many years Dublin's **club** scene comprised a cluster of cramped, expensive and mostly unlicensed basements on Leeson Street. "The Strip", as the Leeson Street clubs are collectively known, still exists to snare the unwary. These days, however, there are many better options for those looking to keep the night alive. After a somewhat late start, club culture has now arrived in Dublin with a vengeance. Venues crop up or disappear so rapidly that the only way to find the hottest draws is to pick up one of the listings mags. The places we've listed are the pick of the durable clubs. Generally you can expect to pay anything from £5 to £12 for entrance, depending on the coolness of the club and the reputation of the DJ, but on special nights, with an international DJ, you can pay as much as £25.

> **Many of Dublin's pubs and live music venues turn into clubs on selected nights, notably the *Mean Fiddler*, *Whelans*, the *Music Centre*, the *Irish Film Centre* and the *DA Club*.**

The **classical music** scene in Dublin isn't too hot, but the RTE Symphony Orchestra gives regular performances at the National Concert Hall in Earlsfort Terrace (©671 1533), the main venue for classical concerts. In addition, concerts are often held in Powerscourt Townhouse, the Bank of Ireland in Foster Place, the RDS in Ballsbridge and at the Municipal Gallery of Modern Art on Parnell Square. Operas are performed at The Gaiety Theatre on South King Street twice yearly and both St Patrick's and Christ Church cathedrals host organ recitals, while lunchtime performances can be heard at St Ann's on Dawson Street. Choral and organ recitals are given occasionally at Trinity and UCD, and you can hear the best of the city's students at the schools of music in Chatham Street and Westland Row.

Although Dublin has never been renowned for its **jazz** music the city's increasing cosmopolitanism is reflected in the number of venues now hosting jazz concerts. The most stylish location to hear live jazz is *Café-en-Seine* on Dawson Street, though *Alfie Byrnes'* bar in the *Conrad Hotel* has a local reputation for its jazz night on Saturdays. Other bars that feature jazz throughout the week are *McDaid's* on Harry Street and *J.J Smyth's* on Aungier Street.

LIVE MUSIC VENUES

The DA Club

Map 3, I2. 3–5 Clarendon Market, off South William St ✆671 1130. The small but perfectly formed *DA Club* hosts a variety of musical styles on its two floors. Its adventurous booking policy means that some of Dublin's hottest young talent can be found strutting their stuff on the extremely tiny stage, and serenading you through the surprisingly sophisticated sound system.

Eamon Doran's

Map 6, G4. 3A Crown Alley ✆679 9114. A large, rather soulless joint, but young bands can be heard here most nights, often two or three per evening. You're unlikely to have heard of any of them before, and with an occasional honourable exception, you're unlikely to hear of them again. Still, if you can deal with the wildly varying standards of the performers, the venue itself is clean and the crowd are out for a good time.

The Furnace

Map 4, D4. 2 Aston Place ✆671 0088. As you might expect of a venue run by the Union of Students in Ireland, the beer in this mid-size venue is cheap and the

LIVE MUSIC VENUES

often quite well-known bands booked tend to be at the noisier and more youth-oriented end of the spectrum. High spirits and plastic glasses abound.

HQ at the Hall of Fame

Map 4, D3. 57 Middle Abbey St ℡878 3345.

Dublin's newest venue is well-conceived, catering to a slightly older clientele with a preference for retrospective rock and pop. Prices for tickets are generally above average, but it's worth paying the extra for the full-table service and intimacy of the venue.

IFC Bar

Map 6, D5. 6 Eustace St.

The place to go on Friday and Saturday nights if you want to quietly savour the best jazz and blues in the city. After 11.30pm the main foyer converts into the perfect venue, where a relaxed and discerning crowd listens to renowned local and international artists.

The International Bar

Map 5, H8. 23 Wicklow St ℡677 9250.

For those who want to spot the next great Dublin songwriter taking his or her first faltering steps towards superstardom, every Tuesday young hopefuls come out to play a song or two at the unamplified "Songwriter's Night", held upstairs at *The International Bar*. If some of the songs seem woeful, don't worry – with up to twenty performers per night, there'll be somebody better along in a minute.

The Mean Fiddler

Map 4, C9. 26 Wexford St ℡475 8555.

This trendy, 800-capacity venue with a seriously cool interior is part of London's *Mean Fiddler* chain, and many burgeoning international acts touring their UK halls are routinely booked for a date here. Excellent sightlines and sound system.

The Music Centre

Map 6, E5. Curved St ℂ679 0533/4.

This is one of the jewels in Temple Bar's crown – a custom-built facility whose amenities include an impeccable, if slightly antiseptic venue for audiences of up to 650. The bar area outside also features frequent free shows by up-and-coming songwriters.

The National Stadium

Map 3, E8. South Circular Rd ℂ453 3371.

Frequently used medium-size venue holding between 1000 and 2000 people, depending on whether or not the seats are taken out. As you'd expect of an ageing hall designed primarily to host boxing matches, the facilities for audiences are fairly spartan, but the excellent sightlines and acoustics compensate.

Olympia Theatre

Map 6, C6. 72 Dame St ℂ677 7744.

This wonderful old Victorian theatre is frequently used for live music – quieter and more established international and Irish acts tend to play early-evening sets, with late-night gigs on Fridays and Saturdays, known as "Midnight at the Olympia", reserved for more good-time performers to entertain the audience drawn in by the promise of the theatre's late alcohol licence (see p.266).

Point Theatre

Map 3, J4. East Link Bridge, North Wall Quay ℂ836 3633.

The venue of choice for most visiting superstar acts, the cavernous Point Theatre is a huge and charmless converted warehouse on the north bank of the Liffey, about one mile east of O'Connell Street, with a capacity of between 4000 and 7000, depending on whether the show is seated or standing. The acoustics and sightlines are good, but considering its size and status, the venue is surprisingly bereft of facilities for the humble punter.

LIVE MUSIC VENUES

The SFX
Map 5, H1. 28 Upper Sherrard St ℂ874 5227.

This 1500-capacity hall is one of Dublin's oldest and most popular rock venues, and has hosted some of the city's best rock and pop gigs over the last two decades. The advent of new venues and *The SFX*'s unfashionable location has diminished its popularity somewhat, but it's still a great place to see quality acts.

Vicar Street
Map 5, D8. Thomas St ℂ454 5533

Opposite John's Lane Church *Vicar Street* is one of the city's newer venues, with a good restaurant and bar attached. The 650-capacity arena plays host to an eclectic mix of entertainers, from established rock bands to alternative comedians.

Whelans
Map 4, C9. 25 Wexford St ℂ478 0766.

With its welcoming 350-capacity, two-level room, this is perhaps the city's best place to see live music up close. Its intimate atmosphere makes it a particularly ideal venue for acoustic and roots music, and the list of international stars who've graced its compact stage is a mile long.

CLUBS

The Andrew's Lane Theatre
Map 4, D6. 9 Andrew's Lane, off Trinity St.
Thurs–Sun 11pm till late.

On weekend nights, after the last play-goer has gone, this small modern theatre throws its doors open to a very different public. Expect user-friendly trip-hop and jazzy beats. Saturday night's "Club Absinthe" is proving hugely popular and look out for the monthly drum-and-bass night.

CLUBS

Break for the Border
Map 4, C7. Lower Stephen's St.
Wed–Sat 11pm–2am.

This enormous Western-themed restaurant attracts hundreds of good-natured punters in pursuit of dance, drink and the opposite sex. The mainstream music policy is more than compensated for by the clientele's impressive dedication to the pursuit of a good time.

The Funnel
Map 4, G4. 24 City Quay.
Fri & Sat 9pm–2am.

A little out of the city centre, *The Funnel's* cool, modern bar downstairs contrasts with a small, dark and sweaty dance venue upstairs, which plays host to some of the best local and international techno in the city. Saturday nights, featuring resident DJs, are gaining a loyal following.

The Gaiety Theatre
Map 4, D7. South King St.
Fri & Sat 11.30pm–2.30am.

On Friday and Saturday nights Dubliners out for a good night throng the beautiful old Gaiety Theatre for the highly popular "Velure", a multievent club night which offers live bands (predominantly jazz and samba), DJs and even film screenings in the array of backstage bars and green rooms.

The Kitchen
Map 6, C4. East Essex St.
Mon–Wed 11.30pm–2am, Thurs–Sun 11pm–2am.

Housed beneath the *Clarence Hotel* (see p.199), *The Kitchen* is equally trendy in design but it's not a place for posing; big beats hammered out by resident DJs on Thursday and Saturday nights attract a hugely enthusiastic crowd, resulting in it being arguably the most popular dance venue in the city.

CLUBS

Unsurprisingly, gaining entry can be tricky, and you'll almost certainly have to queue.

Lillie's Bordello
Map 4, E6. Adam Court, Grafton St.
Mon–Sun 11pm till late.

Rock stars – would-be, has-been and actual – quaff and bitch with supermodels in the velour-bedecked *Lillie's Bordello*. Don't worry unduly if you're asked whether or not you're a member – practically nobody is. Regulars get priority and rarely pay the reasonably hefty entrance fee (£8), but if you beat the after-pub crowd, act relaxed and don't look too dishevelled you should get in easily enough. If you do gain admittance you'll have the dance floor more or less to yourself: the regulars are far too cool to boogie.

The POD
Map 4, D10. 35 Harcourt St.
Wed–Sat 11pm–2.30am.

The phenomenally popular *POD* (short for Place Of Dance) on Harcourt Street is a match for anything that New York, Berlin or Tokyo has to offer, boasting ultramodern decor and a tooth-loosening sound system. *The POD* is home to the hottest local DJs, the most popular venue for international dance acts, and the hangout of choice for many a visiting celebrity. The clientele are intimidatingly chic, and the door policy, especially at weekends, can be tough. Dress to impress and get there early.

Red Box
Map 4, D10. 35 Harcourt St ©478 0225.

Far more plush than other similar-size dance venues in the city, *Red Box* is a tailor-made and lovingly designed 1000-capacity hall located upstairs from *The POD* nightclub, but with a more relaxed and less style-conscious atmosphere.

Renard's

Map 4, F6. South Frederick St.

Mon–Sun 11.30pm–3am.

Popular with Dublin's small but self-important music and media pack. Claustrophobes may find the ground-floor bar preferable to the sweaty basement dance floor.

Rí-Rá

Map 4, C6. South Great George's St.

Thurs–Sun 11.30pm–2.30am.

The records spun at *Rí-Rá* (pronounced Ree-Raw) can range from trip-hop to world music to hard funk, depending on night and mood: this club manages to be both informal and fashionable and draws an eclectic and friendly crowd.

System

Map 4, D7. 21 South Anne St.

Fri & Sat 11pm–3am.

Younger and less elitist than many of the city's new breed of nightclub, *System* specializes in hard, fast techno, served up at a deafening volume. Dress light, or you'll expire.

Temple Theatre

Map 5, H2. St George's Church, Temple St.

Fri & Sat 9pm–2am.

The *Temple Theatre*, housed in an enormous restored church and clearly inspired by UK mega-clubs like *Cream* and *Ministry of Sound*, has had some difficulty finding its feet not least because of its unfashionable location. After a short closure it has reoriented itself somewhat away from the furious dance music that was its mainstay and now promotes a funky Seventies retro night on Fridays.

CLUBS

Theatre and cinema

As befits a city with a rich literary past, **theatre** flourishes in Dublin. The traditional diet of Irish classics at the "establishment" theatres is now spiced by experimental or fringe programmes at newer, smaller venues. Theatres operate from Monday to Saturday; evening performances usually begin at 7.30pm or 8pm, and there may be matinées, too. Credit-card booking is widely available – expect to pay £8–10 per ticket for fringe theatre, £10–16 for mainstream. For the budget-conscious it's worth enquiring about stand-by tickets on weekdays and cut-price Monday- and Tuesday-night shows, and students with ID can sometimes find good reductions. Highlights of the year include the **Dublin Theatre Festival** in early October and the **Dublin Fringe Festival** which runs from late September to mid-October (see p.292 for both).

Dublin has numerous **cinemas** showing mainstream films (which are often released earlier in Ireland than in Britain); most of them are in or around O'Connell Street, such as the Ambassador (℡872 7000) and the Savoy (℡874 8487). For art-house cinema the Irish Film Centre and Screen are the chief venues. The **Dublin Film Festival** in March/April is well worth checking out (see p.288). All cinemas operate a policy of cheap seats before 5pm (6.30pm in some cases), seven days a week, during which time tickets cost around £3 – after this they cost about £5; student discounts are also often available. Check *In Dublin*, *The Event Guide* or the *Irish Times* for details of what's on.

THEATRES

The Abbey Theatre
Map 4, E3. Lower Abbey St ℗878 7222.
This is the National Theatre of Ireland, founded by W.B. Yeats and Lady Gregory in 1902. The original building was destroyed by fire in the 1950s and replaced by the current, ugly building in 1966. It tends to show Irish classics (by Synge, Sheridan, O'Casey, Wilde, etc), plus new offerings by contemporary playwrights such as Brian Friel, Marina Carr, Bernard Farrell and Tom Murphy (see also Peacock Theatre, p.267).

Andrew's Lane Theatre
Map 4, D6. Between St Andrew's St and Exchequer St ℗679 5720.
Situated just off Dame Street, this theatre specializes in contemporary drama, and generally has two shows on the go at once. The studio upstairs presents a mix of fringe and amateur theatre.

Crypt Arts Centre
Map 4, B6. Dublin Castle ℗671 3387.
A small venue in the crypt of the Chapel Royal, it's managed by a company called *íomhá Ildánach* (roughly translated as "varied image") who stage a number of plays throughout the year, generally fringe pieces. Occasional art exhibitions are also held here.

Focus Theatre
Map 3, H8. 6 Pembroke Place, off Sussex Rd ℗676 3071.
Founded by Deirdre O'Connell, a student of Lee Strasberg at

THEATRES

the Actors' Studio in New York, this diminutive but important venue stages powerful European and American modern drama and occasional fringe plays.

Gaiety Theatre

Map 4, D7. South King St ℂ677 1717.

An old-style playhouse with velvet curtains and gilded boxes, that usually hosts musicals, pantomimes and other family entertainments. On Fridays and Saturdays it becomes an after-midnight club (see p.261).

Gate Theatre

Map 4, D1. Cavendish Row, beside the Rotunda Hospital on Parnell Square ℂ874 4045.

Founded in 1928 by Micheál MacLiammóir and Hilton Edwards (see p.116). The Gate has a reputation for staging adventurous experimental drama as well as established classics, in a stark auditorium.

The Lambert Puppet Theatre

Map 7, A5. 5 Clifton Lane, Monkstown ℂ280 0974.

Dublin's only puppet theatre, producing shows of very high quality every Saturday and Sunday at 3.30pm. Great for kids, though during the International Puppet Festival in early September there are also performances for adults.

Olympia Theatre

Map 6, C6. 72 Dame St ℂ677 7744.

Somewhat similar to the Gaiety, this old-style music hall has been through many incarnations since it opened in 1749, with a roll-call of luminaries from Charlie Chaplin and Noel Coward to Mary Black and Jack Dee. Nowadays it hosts musicals, stand-up comedy shows and medium-size gigs, with late-night Friday and Saturday concerts (see p.259).

THEATRES

Peacock Theatre

Map 4, E3. 26 Lower Abbey St ℺878 7222.
The Abbey's smaller sister theatre, in the basement, produces
new Irish drama in both Gaelic and English, and can often be a
goldmine for great entertainment and new talent.

Project Arts Centre

Map 6, C5. 39 East Essex St (℺679 6622 or 1850 260027).
Renowned for its experimental and often controversial Irish
and international theatre, the Project was closed at the time of
writing but will reopen in March 2000 with two performance
venues. The centre also hosts dance and contemporary music
performances, and art exhibitions.

Samuel Beckett Theatre

Map 4, E6. Trinity College ℺608 2461.
A small venue used for Trinity College student productions and
on a commercial basis by a broad range of theatre, dance and
opera companies, both Irish and international.

Tivoli Theatre

Map 5, E8. Francis St ℺454 4472.
A modern theatre in the Liberties, with hard seats on three
sides of a raised stage. The Tivoli produces a lot of Shakespeare,
popular comedy and contemporary drama and also acts as a
venue for rock and traditional music gigs.

CINEMAS

The Irish Film Centre

Map 6, D5. 6 Eustace St ℺679 3477.
Art-house cinema with two screens and an excellent restaurant
(see p.225), as well as a film-related bookshop and dance club

on Fridays and Saturdays. Films include new, low-budget Irish works plus a good range of world and gay cinema.

The Screen Cinema

Map 4, E4. D'Olier St ℗872 3922.

A fairly old-fashioned, low-key venue with three screens; a good place to catch art-house films, plus occasional screenings of international and mainstream films.

Gay Dublin

With attitudes to homosexuality in Dublin becoming more liberal since the mid-Nineties, the capital's **gay** community has grown in confidence, and a vibrant scene is now developing in parts of the city.

A good starting point for finding out the latest on gay **events** and venues in Dublin is the drop-in centre at the Outhouse, 6 William Street (daily 11am–6pm; ℂ670 6377), which has plenty of up-to-date information, plus a café (on the second floor) and small library, or Lesbians Organizing Together, which has a drop-in centre at 5 Capel Street (Mon–Thurs 10am–6pm, Fri 10am–4pm; ℂ872 7770). Alternatively you could call Gay Switchboard Dublin (Mon–Fri & Sun 8–10pm, Sat 3.30–6pm; ℂ872 1055).

It's also a good idea to pick up a copy of the free monthly *Gay Community News*, which has detailed listings of upcoming events and all the vital info you need to enjoy yourself. These are stocked in the gay-friendly Books Upstairs opposite the main gate of Trinity College, The Winding Stair Bookshop on Bachelors Walk, or the Temple Bar information centre on Eustace Street. The number of permanent fixtures on the scene is small but growing; most of the real action happens at the gay nights in the straight venues. Most **pubs** around Temple Bar and South Great

George's Street have a mixed clientele and a keen eye on the pink pound, while several mainstream **clubs** have theme nights and gay events.

PUBS

The Front Lounge
Map 6, A5. Parliament St.
Not "officially" gay, but many gay men and lesbians relish its classy, bouffant hair-styled atmosphere.

The George
Map 4, C6. 89 South Great George's St.
Ireland's first gay pub when it opened sixteen years ago, *The George* remains as popular as ever. Its original bar (known as Jurassic Park due to its older clientele) is quite dowdy but full of character; the newer half is bright and breezy, serving good meals during the day. Besides *The Block* (see opposite) upstairs, it has a weekly men-only leather/denim/uniform club on Fridays.

Hogans
Map 4, C6. 11 South Great George's St.
Just up the road from *The George*, this cool, dark modern bar caters to a stylish mixed crowd. Lively and noisy, but not the best place to make friends.

Out on the Liffey
Map 5, F6. 27 Upper Ormond Quay.
Dublin's other gay pub is a nice relaxed place for a midweek drink or to warm up for a weekend session. Equally popular with gays and lesbians, with late hours and events (quizzes, etc) advertised in *GCN*. Just beware of your safety in the back-streets.

CLUBS

The Block
Map 4, C6. 89 South Great George's St.

Wed–Sun 11pm–2am.

The George's swinging alter ego. Has four sections linked by *Gone with the Wind* stairways and a small dance floor. Wednesday night is karaoke. Thursday's Seventies. On Fridays and Saturdays there's a dance club with full bar. Heavy-handed security.

Candy Club
Map 6, C4. *The Kitchen*, East Essex St.

Mon 11pm–late.

Not exclusively gay but a fun night frequented by the city's hedonists who refuse to acknowledge that the weekend has finished.

Freedom at the Mission
Map 6, **D4**. Eustace St, Temple Bar.

Mon 11pm–2am.

This is the place to go if you want to meet people. Good commercial dance music in a no-nonsense nightclub setting. Roomy chill-out area upstairs.

Furnace: getOUT!
Map 6, F2. 1–2 Aston Quay.

Every second Sat 9pm–1am.

Monthly dance club catering to all tastes, with a young crowd. The venue is owned by the Union of Students of Ireland. Come early to get an elevated seat for a good view of the dance floor.

H.A.M. (Homo Action Movies)
Map 4, D10. *POD*, 35 Harcourt St.

Fri 11pm–3am.

Gay night at Dublin's trendiest club. The main dance floor

looks like a Duran Duran video shoot, and the Art Deco ante-room is for chilling out and watching the movie. Definitely an occasion for dressing up. Totally queer door policy; mostly males.

The Playground

Map 4, A5. Upper Ormond Quay.

Sun 10.30pm till late.

A cruisy dance-oriented club for those who've still got some energy left by Sunday night. Good music but bland surroundings. You can buy hot snacks or partake of the free bowls of fruit.

Powderbubble

Map 4, D10. *Red Box* (above *POD*), 35 Harcourt St.

11pm–3am.

Monthly club that's very nearly a full-blown rave; the balcony is for those who prefer talking. Special features include exotic-looking creatures waving sparklers, complimentary candyfloss, and a false nail and eyelash implant service. The Alternative Miss Ireland is held here. Pricey (£12–15) but brilliant.

StoneWallz

Map 3, E8. Griffith College, South Circular Rd.

Sat 9pm–12.30am.

Very friendly women-only club in unusual surroundings. Extremely popular, so get here early (bus #16 from Dame St or George's St).

Wonder Bar

Map 6, E5. Temple Bar Music Centre, Curved St.

First and third Sat each month; 9.30pm–2.45am.

The spiritual home of the pleasuredome kids, with a stage for acts ranging from standard drag to bizarre passion plays on the life of Alison Moyet. Open door policy, mixed crowd.

Shopping

Dublin's recent prosperity is reflected in the development of the city centre's shops, but north and south of the Liffey are two distinct areas. The southside, focusing on Grafton Street's swish stores and the design culture of Temple Bar, is fashion and form incarnate, while the north, based on O'Connell Street and the grid of surrounding streets, is all function. You buy what you need north of the river and what you want on the south.

Our listings are grouped into the following categories: antiques (p.274); art, crafts and design (p.274); books (p.276); clothing and fashion (p.279); jewellery (p.281); markets (p.282); records (p.284); shopping centres and department stores (p.285).

Dublin shops generally open from 9am to 5.30pm or 6pm Monday to Saturday, with late shopping until 7pm or 8pm on Thursday evenings, and many places (though not food stores, generally) open on Sunday from around noon to 5pm or 6pm. The exception is Temple Bar, where businesses may not open until at least an hour later. Most shops, except small food stores, market stalls and secondhand shops, accept credit cards. Visitors from non-EU countries can claim tax back on most items purchased (see p.304).

ANTIQUES

You're unlikely to find quality **antiques** at bargain prices anywhere in Dublin – many dealers import from Britain and Germany, so prices tend to be high. **Francis Street** in the Liberties forms the hub of the city's antiques trade, catering for all budgets, with a spread of shops dispensing everything from old beer trays to expensive oriental rugs and *objets d'art*. The Antiques Gallery in the Powerscourt Centre (see p.286) has a great concentration of quality outlets, offering a large selection of jewellery, porcelain, silverware and small pieces of furniture. An antique collectors' fair takes place fortnightly at Newman House (see p.40) on Sundays from 11am to 6pm (✆670 8295 for information).

ART, CRAFTS AND DESIGN

Dublin's **art and design** scene is thriving, and there are now several reliable outlets for buying work of a very high standard, the best of which are listed below. Examples of Irish **crafts** geared specifically towards the tourist market may be found in several of the knitwear shops on Nassau Street.

The Bridge Art Gallery

Map 4, B4. 6 Upper Ormond Quay ✆872 9702.
Mon–Sat 10am–6pm, Sun 2–5pm.
One of the very best places in Dublin for contemporary art and crafts including ceramics, hand-blown glass, prints, mirrors, paintings and sculpture, with many pieces very competitively priced. Monthly exhibitions are displayed in the gallery to the rear.

DESIGNyard

Map 6, C4. 12 East Essex St ✆677 8453.
Mon & Wed–Sat 10am–5.30pm, Tues 11am–5.30pm.
A major showcase for excellence in Irish design, applied art

and crafts, including stunning collections of contemporary jewellery. The place to head for if you want to commission a unique work from an Irish designer.

Gallery of Stone

Map 6, E5. 2 Temple Lane ℂ671 5107.
Mon–Sat 10am–5pm.

Contemporary Zimbabwean sculpture, including some tremendous pieces depicting human and animal forms emerging from stone. As well as the larger works they keep a small range of inexpensive gifts: batiks, hand-painted wallhangings and small carved items.

Giles Norman Gallery

Map 4, D6. Ground floor, Powerscourt Centre ℂ677 3455.
Mon–Sat 10am–6pm, Thurs till 8pm, Sun noon–6pm.

Black-and-white photographs of Ireland – largely rural subject-matter, but the collection does include some atmospheric shots of Dublin.

The Kilkenny Shop

Map 4, E6. 6 Nassau St ℂ677 7066.
Mon–Sat 9am–6pm, Thurs till 8pm, Sun 11am–6pm.

A superb range of Irish crafts, particularly pottery and glassware. Look out for decorative pottery by Nicholas Mosse, Bernard Kavanagh's' vibrant blue glazes and Stephen Pearce's classic natural earthenware. Best of the glassware includes colour-dappled Jerpoint Glass and Waterford Crystal.

Louis Mulcahy

Map 4, E7. 46 Dawson St ℂ670 9311.
Mon–Sat 10am–6pm, Thurs till 8pm.

Hand-thrown pots, urns and vases from one of Ireland's most famous potters, plus a selection of hand-woven wool tapestries.

ART, CRAFTS AND DESIGN

Merrion Square

Map 3, H6.

Sat & Sun 10am–6pm (approx).

Original paintings are sold by the artist in person from the railings around the square. There's no shortage of doe-eyed maidens and dewy glens, but there's a huge range and some of it is very good. Mainly cash transactions.

Original Print Gallery

Map 6, E4. Temple Bar ℂ677 3657.

Tues–Fri 10.30am–5.30pm, Sat 11am–5pm, Sun 2–6pm.

One of the best places in town for contemporary etchings, lithographs and screen prints, mainly Irish. A well-run gallery with plenty of variety and work of a very high standard.

The Solomon Gallery

Map 4, D6. Second floor, Powerscourt Centre ℂ679 4237.

Mon–Sat 10am–5.30pm.

A spacious commercial gallery showing predominantly Irish paintings and sculpture, along with a handful of pieces by British artists.

Urbana

Map 6, E4. 43–44 Temple Bar ℂ670 3083.

Mon & Fri 11am–6pm, Tue & Wed 11am–7.30pm, Sat 10am–6pm, Sun noon–6pm.

Several outfits under one roof, selling novelty household gear; retro crockery, furniture, glassware and a small selection of distinctive Irish linen.

BOOKS

Dublin's literary life is well-supported by its numerous new and secondhand bookshops, ranging from large general stores such as Eason's and Waterstone's to specialist outfits such as Connolly Books.

Books Upstairs

Map 4, E5. 36 College Green ✆679 6687.

Mon–Fri 10am–7pm, Sat 10am–6pm, Sun 1–6pm.

Strong selections of Irish poetry and drama, as well as books on psychology, philosophy, women's studies and gay literature. You'll also find keenly-priced American imports and a good range of periodicals.

Cathach Books

Map 4, E6. 10 Duke St ✆671 8676.

Mon–Sat 9.30am–5.45pm.

Cathach specializes in rare first editions and antique maps of Irish interest; in the window you might find signed first editions of Yeats's poetry or a 1922 edition of *Ulysses*. The basement is the place to pick up original mounted illustrations at reasonable prices.

Connolly Books

Map 6, B5. 43 East Essex St ✆671 1943.

Mon–Sat 9.30am–5.30pm.

The red frontage and its title give the game away about the nature of this excellent bookshop. Its shelves are filled by works on Irish political history, including a number by James Connolly himself, plus modern fiction, music and the arts. New books are often discounted.

Dublin Bookshop

Map 4, D7. 24 Grafton St ✆677 5568.

Mon–Fri 9am–10pm, Sat & Sun 9am–6pm.

General bookshop offering a broad range of titles, including an extensive Irish section. Specializes in books relating to the mind and body.

Eason's

Map 4, D2. 40 Upper O'Connell St ✆873 3811.

BOOKS

Mon–Sat 8.30am–6.45pm, Thurs till 8.45pm, Fri till 7.45pm, Sun 12.45–5.45pm.

The best general bookshop north of the Liffey, Eason's stocks a wide range of books, cards and stationery, as well as having one of the largest magazine sections in Ireland.

Fred Hanna's

Map 4, E6. 27–29 Nassau St ℂ677 1255.

Mon–Sat 9am–6pm, Thurs till 8pm.

One of Ireland's leading independent booksellers, Fred Hanna's has a great range of academic titles, new and secondhand, and specializes in books on Ireland and Irish literature. Good selection of maps and guidebooks.

Greene's

Map 4, G7. 16 Clare St ℂ676 2554.

Mon–Fri 9am–5.30pm, Sat 9am–5pm.

A long-standing Dublin bookshop just around the corner from the National Gallery, selling new and secondhand books. The barrows under its distinctive wrought-iron canopy hold all sorts of treasures. Also contains a small post office.

Hodges Figgis

Map 4, E7. 56–58 Dawson St ℂ677 4754.

Mon–Fri 9am–7pm, Thurs till 8pm, Sat 9am–6pm, Sun noon–6pm.

Founded in 1768, Hodges Figgis is a Dublin institution. Although the breadth of its coverage is huge, its emphasis is instantly apparent – directly opposite the door is a comprehensive Irish fiction section, while other shelves are dedicated to contemporary and historical Ireland, its language, art and culture. Upstairs there are book bargains and a café.

Hughes & Hughes

Map 4, D7. St Stephen's Green Shopping Centre ℂ478 3060.

Mon–Sat 9.30am–6pm, Thurs till 8pm.

A long-established family bookshop, with additional outlets in Dublin airport, covering a broad range of titles including children's books and a comprehensive travel section (the shop stocks every book published about Dublin).

Waterstone's

Map 4, E6. 7 Dawson St ℂ679 1415.
Mon, Tues & Fri 9am–8pm, Wed 9.30am–8pm, Thurs 9am–8.30pm, Sat 9am–7pm, Sun 11am–6pm.

Large general bookstore on five levels, with a huge range of fiction, books of general and Irish interest, and academic and business titles.

The Winding Stair

Map 4, C4. 40 Lower Ormond Quay ℂ873 3292.
Mon–Sat 10am–6pm, Sun 1–6pm.

A pleasantly relaxed secondhand bookshop, particularly good for Irish literature, with its own café where you can settle down with your recently-purchased well-worn tomes.

CLOTHING AND FASHION

Grafton Street is *the* place for high-street fashions and designer clothes. British chains such as Next, Miss Selfridge and Jigsaw dominate, but here too you'll find Dublin's most famous department store Brown Thomas (see p.285), with its superb range of designer labels, and the nearby Powerscourt Centre; other department stores and shopping malls are also worth exploring. For trendy secondhand, ethnic and club gear, try Temple Bar or the Market Arcade (see p.283), and for knitwear and tweed shops check out Nassau Street (The Kilkenny Shop – see p.275 – also has a fine selection of clothes). For cheap, serviceable clothing, Penney's and Dunnes Stores are hard to beat – branches are on O'Connell Street and in the St Stephen's Green Shopping Centre respectively.

A:Wear

Map 4, D7. 26 Grafton St ℂ671 7200.

Mon–Sat 9.30am–6.30pm, Thurs till 8.30pm, Sun noon–6pm.

Inexpensive women's High-Street fashion chain geared towards the teens and twentysomethings. Irish designers Quin and Donnelly are particularly well represented.

Cleo Limited

Map 4, F8. 18 Kildare St ℂ676 1421.

Mon–Sat 9am–5.30pm.

Small shop crammed with clothes made of traditional Irish textiles, including replicas of Aran waistcoats, hardy wool-lined trousers, casual linen shirts and hand-knitted sweaters. Generally rather expensive.

Design Centre

Map 4, D6. First floor, Powerscourt Centre ℂ679 5718.

Mon–Sat 9am–6pm, Thurs till 8pm, Sun noon–6pm.

The Design Centre's ever-changing panoply of stalls represents the cream of young Irish designers of women's fashion, including Louise Kennedy, Lyn-Mar, Deirdre Fitzgerald and Ciarán Sweeney.

Eager Beaver

Map 6, G4. 17 Crown Alley ℂ677 3342.

Mon–Sat 9.30am–5.30pm, Thurs till 7pm, Fri & Sat till 6pm.

Two-storeyed shop stocking a huge range of secondhand clothing, which offers discounts to the unemployed and senior citizens. Garments packing the rails include combats, Seventies gear, flares and leather coats.

Flip, Short's Ville and The Real McCoy

Map 6, F5. Spranglers Yard, Fownes St Upper ℂ671 4299.

Mon–Sat 9.30am–6pm, Thurs till 7pm.

Trio of secondhand clothes stores, all run by the same people.

Items include imports of US workshirts, sports tops, leather jackets and plenty of retro and club gear.

The House of Ireland
Map 4, E6. 37–38 Nassau St ©677 7949.
May–Sept Mon–Sat 9am–7pm, Thurs till 8pm, Sun 10.30am–6pm;
Oct–April Mon–Sat 9am–6pm, Thurs till 8pm,
Sun 10.30am–5.30pm.

Spacious, quality tourists' shop stocking Arans, hand-knits, colourful Ireland's Eye sweaters and tailored tweed jackets.

Kevin & Howlin
Map 4, E6. 31 Nassau St ©677 0257.
Mon–Sat 9.30am–5.30pm.

Tweed heaven – jackets, caps, waistcoats, hats, ties, suits, all expertly tailored in Donegal tweed. Both men's and women's clothing.

JEWELLERY

Dublin offers jewellery to suit all tastes and budgets. Some of the most expensive outlets cluster along Johnson's Court (which runs between Grafton Street and the Powerscourt Centre) and off here in Westbury Mall. For the best in contemporary design pieces check out the DESIGNyard (see p.274).

Angles
Map 4, D7. 10 Westbury Mall, off Grafton St ©679 1964.
Mon–Sat 10am–6pm, Thurs till 7pm, Sun noon–6pm.

This tiny store sells intriguing contemporary jewellery, providing a showcase for Irish designers alongside international collections. The emphasis is very much on design, with many pieces in silver, some with semi-precious stones or gold detailing.

JEWELLERY

Equinox

Map 4, D6. Ground floor, Powerscourt Centre ℂ670 5400.

Mon–Sat 10am–6pm.

Varied selection of contemporary jewellery, including the fish-laden silver of Clio Blue, Wright & Teague's solid, stylish rings and earrings, pearls and gemstones from Babylone, and quirky pieces by Jean-Paul Gaultier. Closed Sun.

Taboo

Map 6, F5. Unit 13, Spranglers Yard, Fownes St Upper ℂ671 6871.

Mon–Sat 10am–6pm, Thurs till 7pm.

Inexpensive gift shop offering a huge range of affordable jewellery for the teens to twenties market.

MARKETS

Dublin's once-thriving street markets have all but disappeared and the few that remain have moved into adopted homes under cover. Despite this, all the places listed below are well worth a visit.

Blackrock Market

Map 2, H6. Off main street (Blackrock DART).

Sat 11am–5.30pm, Sun noon–5.30pm.

A delightful, little, partially-covered market well worth browsing. Plenty of variety, including rugs, hats, secondhand books, clothes and crafts, plants and CDs, plus an excellent cheap café.

The Liberty Market

Map 3, E5. Meath St.

Thurs–Sat, 10am–5pm.

The Liberty's stalls are crammed, maze-like, into a small indoor hall halfway along a vibrant local shopping street. You can buy anything here from Boyzone bangles to WD40, but most people come for the cheap clothing and footwear.

The Market Arcade
Map 4, C6. South Great George's St.
Mon–Sat 10am–6pm, Sun 1–6pm.

A covered market with an excellent laid-back, rough-and-rummage atmosphere. Immensely popular for its secondhand book and record stores, used and period clothing and its olive stall – one of the cheapest places to get a nutritious snack. There's also a good café.

Moore Street Market
Map 4, D3. Off Henry St.
Mon–Sat 10am–6pm.

A long-established, lively and colourful market selling fruit, veg and flowers. One of the few places in Dublin where you'll catch sight of produce being unloaded off a horse-drawn cart, as well as old women in slippers selling bananas from babies' prams.

Mother Redcap's Market
Map 3, E5. Back Lane, off High St.
Fri, Sat & Sun 11am–5.30pm.

Mother Redcap's packs around fifty stalls and small shops into its indoor setting. Things on offer range from the mundane (valve radio repairs, ironmongery, wholefoods and secondhand books) to the arcane (African carvings, nail-biting and cuticle problem-solvers, Thai goods, the Reptile Shop, tarot readings and numerology). There's a cheap café in the centre.

Temple Bar Market
Map 6, D5. Meeting House Square.
Sat 9am–5pm.

A foodie's delight. Stalls include organic meat and veg, Olvi oils, with their award-winning pestos, west-coast oysters and an enormous variety of cheeses. Plenty of snacking opportunities too, on anything from potato cakes and sushi to raspberry tartlets.

MARKETS

RECORDS

For a city of its size, Dublin possesses an astonishing array of record and CD shops. There are branches of the chain stores HMV in Grafton Street and Henry Street, Tower Records in Wicklow Street, and Virgin on Aston Quay and Henry Street, together with branches of Dublin's own Golden Discs in Grafton Street and St Stephen's Green Shopping Centre. For something more esoteric try those listed below.

Claddagh Records
Map 6, E5. 2 Cecilia St ℭ677 0262.
Mon–Fri 10.30am–5.30pm, Sat noon–5.30pm.
Offers an incredibly comprehensive range of Irish traditional and contemporary recordings, together with racks filled with world music, country, blues and Scottish and English folk music.

Comet Records
Map 6, G4. 5 Cope St ℭ671 8592.
Mon–Sat 10am–6pm, Sun noon–6pm.
Wide-ranging stock of indie, dance and chart music, and a good place to collar the latest releases by up-and-coming Irish bands and to chat about their gigs with the store's owner.

Freebird Records
Map 5, I6. 1 Eden Quay ℭ873 1250.
Mon–Wed & Sat 10.30am–6pm, Thurs & Fri 10.30am–7.30pm.
This basement store, just by O'Connell Bridge, crams an enormous range of new and used indie, rock and metal CDs into its small surroundings. Prices are very reasonable.

Secret Book and Record Store
Map 5, H8. 15a Wicklow St ℭ679 7272.
Mon–Sat 11am–6.30pm, Sun (books only) noon–6pm.

Probably the best selection of rare vinyl in Dublin, with collector items from the Fifties onwards. Mainly rock, folk and blues. Also has a comprehensive secondhand books section.

SHOPPING CENTRES AND DEPARTMENT STORES

Dublin's redeveloped centre contains several impressive shopping centres, the biggest of which is the Jervis Centre on Mary Street, replete with British chains, and the most elegant the Powerscourt Centre, worth visiting for the architecture as much as the retail outlets. Dublin's economic boom is reflected too in the number of revamped department stores, the most stylish of which is Brown Thomas.

Arnotts
Map 5, H5. Henry St ✆805 0400.
Mon, Wed, Fri & Sat 9am–6.30pm, Tues 9.30am–6.30pm, Thurs 9am–9pm, Sun noon–6pm.

The oldest department store in Dublin, recently refurbished. Inside are affordable fashions, for both adults and children, to compete with Grafton Street, plus a large kitchenware department and Manchester Utd and Liverpool soccer superstores (see p.297).

Brown Thomas
Map 4, D6. Grafton St ✆605 6666.
Mon–Sat 9am–6pm, Thurs till 8pm, Sun noon–6pm.

Dublin's most prestigious department store, with the emphasis on quality throughout. Amongst the goods on offer are cosmetics, kitchenware, furnishings and Irish linen, and it has a particularly good range of designer clothing, including Irish labels such as Louise Kennedy and Paul Costelloe, and collections by the likes of Ralph Lauren and Nicole Farhi. A younger, trendy crowd are catered for by Brown Thomas's building on the other side of Grafton Street, BT2.

Clery's
Map 4, D3. 18/27 Lower O'Connell St ℂ878 6000.
Mon–Sat 9am–6.30pm, Thurs till 9pm, Fri till 8pm.
Old department store with a little bit of everything, still serving
customers at a fairly genteel pace, while the city revs up all
around it; clothing generally for older clients, with younger
fashions occupying far less floor space. The small Irish gifts
section has assorted machine-knit Aran sweaters.

Powerscourt Centre
Map 4, D6. Clarendon St ℂ679 4144.
Mon–Sat 9am–6pm, Thurs till 8pm, Sun noon–6.30pm.
Once a magnificent Georgian townhouse (see p.24), this
elegant southside space now provides a handful of outlets for
designer fashions, fine art, a wealth of antiques and some excellent eateries. Light music and jazz in the atrium every Saturday.

St Stephen's Green Shopping Centre
Map 4, D7. St Stephen's Green West.
Mon–Sat 9am–7pm, Thurs till 8pm, Sun noon–6pm.
A temple to consumerism packed with clothing stores chiefly
aiming at the tots to twentysomethings, along with a sprinkling
of inexpensive gift shops. It's also home to Dunnes Stores, with
their comprehensively stocked food hall. The café on the top
floor is worth a stop for its live jazz (Mon–Sat 3–5pm) and
excellent views over the green.

Festivals and events

Dublin has **festivals and events** for sports fans, music, drama and cinema lovers, gardeners, devotees of *Ulysses* or *Dracula* – to name only some of the enthusiasms catered for. Though sports events are the only major thing happening in the winter months, there's something for everyone at almost any time of year. For most events, tickets can be obtained at short notice through the booking service at Dublin Tourism or the venue concerned – but bear in mind that you'll need to book accommodation well in advance (see p.7). What follows is a calendar of the regular major events. For one-offs, consult *The Event Guide, In Dublin* or the tourist offices. Sports events are covered separately in the *Sports* chapter.

MARCH

St Patrick's Day
March 17. "Paddy's Day" sees a parade of floats and marching bands through the centre of Dublin, starting at St Patrick's

Cathedral and finishing at the top of O'Connell Street. Last time round, over half a million people watched the parade, and the pubs were thronged with music and merriment until the wee hours. Such is the enthusiasm for St Patrick's Day that celebrations in 2000 will stretch over four days (March 16–19), with plenty of street theatre and traditional music to accompany the usual pub sessions and parade. For further information call ℡676 3205.

Dublin Film Festival

March/April. A ten-day showcase of the best in home-grown and international cinema, organized by the Irish Film Centre in Temple Bar, who put on screenings in a range of cinemas around the city. For details contact the organizing office at 1 Suffolk Street (℡679 2937, fax 2939; *www.iol.ie/dff*).

APRIL

Easter Rising

Commemorations on Easter Sunday, with a Republican march from the GPO to Glasnevin Cemetery.

Handel's Messiah

April 13. Excerpts from Handel's *Messiah* performed at the site of the old Music Hall on Fishamble Street. The concert is held in commemoration of the world premiere of the piece, which took place here in 1742.

MAY

Wicklow Gardens Festival

Mid-May to late July. Open days at private gardens throughout County Wicklow, the "Garden of Ireland", including

Russborough, Avondale, Killruddery and Mount Usher Gardens (©0404 66058).

JUNE

Bloomsday Festival

A week-long celebration of Joyce's *Ulysses* culminating in Bloomsday itself on June 16 (see box, overleaf). Organized by the James Joyce Centre (©878 8547; *www.jamesjoyce.ie*), the festival includes dramatizations of some of the more accessible episodes of the book, along with a full programme of talks, readings and tours celebrating Joyce's life and times, held in various places around the city.

Festival of Music in Great Irish Houses

Classical concerts at stately homes all over Ireland, including several in the vicinity of Dublin, over nine days in June (©278 1528).

JULY

James Joyce Summer School

Annual event dedicated to Joyce and his works, with lectures, seminars and social events held at Newman House (©706 8480) and the James Joyce Centre (©878 8547), usually mid-month.

Guinness Blues Festival

Usually held over the third weekend in July, this is chiefly a blues festival, but with a dash of soul and hip-hop. Over thirty city-centre venues take part, including *Red Box*, *The Mean Fiddler*, *Whelan's*, *Vicar Street* and the Temple Bar Music Centre, and highlights of previous years have included

Bloomsday

Bloomsday, on June 16, is a unique celebration of a novel, held in the city that it so brilliantly evokes. Joyce's *Ulysses* relates the events of a single day in 1904 (so chosen because it was the day he first "walked out" with Nora Barnacle) with obsessive fidelity to the localities, characters and speech of his native Dublin. As Joyce wrote, "If I can get to the heart of Dublin, I can get to the heart of every city in the world. In the particular is contained the universal." Performances from *Ulysses* take place throughout the day outside the James Joyce Centre in North Great George's Street, and the Bloomsday Lecture at 2pm is followed by a lively walking tour through the inner northside, but for an extensive Bloomsday pilgrimage, you could visit the following:

The Martello tower at Sandycove; the location of "stately plump Buck Mulligan's" ablutions at the start of the novel. Joyce himself spent six tense days here with Oliver St John Gogarty, the model for Mulligan, who later noted, "He is planning some sort of novel that will show us all up and the country as well: all will be fatuous except James Joyce."

Sandymount Strand. A walk on the mudflats in Dublin Bay gave Stephen Dedalus pause for reflection.

7 Eccles Street. The starting point for Bloom's odyssey and the site of Molly's climactic soliloquy; though the house has gone, its front door is preserved in the Joyce Centre on North Great George's Street.

St Andrew's and Sweny's Chemist Shop. On his way into the centre, Bloom drops into Mass at All Hallows Church, now St Andrew's on Westland Row, and carries on to Sweny's on

Lincoln Place (which still exists), where he buys a bar of lemon soap (as one still can).

Glasnevin Cemetery. Paddy Dignam's funeral passed by Trinity, Parnell Square and Mountjoy Prison, encompassing the noblest and grimmest institutions in Dublin.

The Oval and Mooney's. As the *Freeman's Journal* and *Evening Telegraph* offices no longer exist, pilgrims can settle for visiting two pubs mentioned in Chapter 5. *The Oval* on Middle Abbey Street hasn't changed much, unlike *Mooney's* on Lower Abbey Street (now the *Abbey Mooney*). In 1988, a series of fourteen pavement plaques tracing Bloom's route from Abbey Street to the National Library was installed.

Davy Byrne's. Joyce wouldn't recognize this Duke Street pub, which now caters to yuppies and tourists. Nonetheless, it's a fitting place for pilgrims to consume a mustard-and-Gorgonzola sandwich and a glass of Burgundy, in emulation of Bloom.

The National Library. Its great reading room was the setting for Stephen's impassioned speech on Shakespeare.

The Ormond Hotel. A plaque celebrates the hotel's role in the "Sirens" chapter at the end of Bloom's walk along Wellington Quay, and the bartenders wear period costume on Bloomsday.

Olhausen's. Since the brothel quarter vanished long ago, pilgrims can content themselves with a visit to Olhausen's the butchers at 72 Talbot St, where Bloom bought a pig's trotter and a sheep's hoof as a snack.

B.B. King and Robert Cray. Most gigs are free, and there are also talks and workshops (©497 0381; *www.guinnessbluesfest.com*).

AUGUST

Bray International Festival of Music and Dance

Three-day festival held in early August in the seaside resort of
Bray, with street and indoor entertainment involving Irish
dancing and musicians, mummers, Morris dancers and international visiting groups (℗286 0080).

SEPTEMBER

Dublin Fringe Festival

Lively programme of theatre, dance, performance arts and
comedy lasting for about three weeks from late September to
mid-October, and focusing in particular on new Irish writing
and innovative production styles. It's held in venues all around
the city centre, and most tickets are under £10 (℗872 9016;
www.fringefest.com).

OCTOBER

Dublin Theatre Festival

First two weeks in October. Major festival with around twenty
productions, half of which are Irish, held in mainstream theatres around the city. Centralized booking ℗874 8525; information ℗677 8439.

Oscar Wilde Autumn School

An annual celebration of Wilde's life, works and times, with
talks, screenings and performances in Bray (℗286 5245).

Sports

Dublin offers a wide range of participation sports activities for visitors to enjoy, but its real forte is spectator sports (and betting on the outcome): rugby, soccer, hurling, Gaelic football and horse racing are all avidly followed.

The following guide doesn't pretend to be exhaustive, but should give an idea of what's on offer and point you in the right direction for more detailed information.

EQUESTRIAN SPORTS

Equestrian sports are extremely popular in Ireland, with less of the snobbery attached in Britain. **Horse racing** is an Irish passion, as you'll find out if you visit Dublin's nearest large racecourse, **Leopardstown** in the southern suburb of Foxrock (bus #63 or #68). Races are held at weekends throughout the year, the main events being the Dennys Goldmedal Chase in late December, the Ladbroke and Champion Hurdle races on successive weekends in January, and the Hennessy Gold Cup in February. The **Irish Grand National** is held on Easter Monday at Fairyhouse, 25km north of Dublin. Flat racing classics are held at the Curragh, 50km southwest of Dublin (the Goffs Irish 1000 Guineas in May, the Budweiser Irish Derby in

June, the Irish St Leger in September). For current information on race meetings call the 24hr premium-rate line ℂ1550/112218.

Show jumping has more of an elitist image, and the **Dublin Horse Show** at the Royal Dublin Society in August was once the highlight of Anglo-Irish social life. While no longer the focus of diplomatic receptions it is still a prestigious international event, with top riders competing for the Aga Khan Trophy and Nations Cup, and prizes in 88 different classes of jumping and dressage. More than 1500 horses compete, before an audience of 100,000. Though day-tickets might be available, you'd be wise to book ahead (ℂ688 0866). The RDS pavilion in Ballsbridge is accessible by bus #5, #6, #8 or #45.

Polo has a limited following, but visitors to Phoenix Park enjoy watching matches on the Nine Acres polo grounds on Wednesday, Saturday & Sunday during the summer months.

If you'd like to go **riding**, there are plenty of opportunities in the rolling countryside to the south of Dublin. One of the most accessible places is Brennanstown Riding School (ℂ286 3778, fax 282 9590), 3km south of Bray off the Dublin–Wexford road, which offers all levels of tuition and cross-country rides in the glorious Wicklow Hills.

FISHING

Ireland is renowned for its **fishing**, as you can read for yourself in several leaflets published by the Bord Fáilte. The River Liffey has **trout** fishing between Celbridge and Millicent Bridge, 20km from the centre, and there are **salmon** in other stretches of the river. **Sea fishing** is popular off Howth, Dún Laoghaire and Dalkey; it can be arranged at the harbour or through local hotels. Dublin's tackle shops can supply permits, rods, bait and advice.

GAELIC FOOTBALL AND HURLING

Gaelic football and hurling occupy a special place in Ireland, as ancient sports whose renaissance was entwined with the Celtic revival movement and the struggle for independence. The Gaelic Athletic Association (GAA) fostered a network of local clubs that are still the heart and soul of many communities, with political clout in the provinces (see p.127).

Although Dubliners are less keen on either sport (especially hurling), the national stadium for Gaelic games (hurling, Gaelic football, handball and camogie, a version of hurling for women) is at **Croke Park** (©836 3222), near the Royal Canal. Named after Archbishop Croke, an advocate of athletics and teetotalism, it is hallowed by sporting triumphs and the "Bloody Sunday" massacre of 1920 (see p.318). While the stadium may not be used for any sport not played by the ancient Gaels, the GAA have permitted U2 and Live Aid concerts to be held there.

Hurling is said to have descended from a game played by the legendary warrior Cúchulainn. The ball (slíothar) may be hit in the air or along the ground, and caught or carried on the flattened end of the player's hurley stick. It's a game of constant movement and aggression that doesn't permit a defensive, reactive style of play. Dublin is nowhere in the league (whose big boys are Cork and Kilkenny, with Cork the victor in 1999), so the crowd at the **All-Ireland Final** on the first Sunday in September mainly consists of out-of-towners.

To the uninitiated, **Gaelic football** resembles a cross between soccer and rugby. Cork and Kerry are the titans of the National Football League (NFL). The **All-Ireland Final** occurs on the third Sunday in September and has been won by Dubliners on 22 occasions (a record beaten only by Kerry); more people watch the game than any other event in Ireland. Like hurling, it's played right throughout the year.

GOLF

Golf is Ireland's fastest growing sport and a major tourist activity. There are more than twenty private golf courses in and around Dublin, and as many public ones, the majority of them affiliated to the Golfing Union of Ireland. Typical green fees are around £25–30 (more at weekends), usually based on a per day rather than a per round basis. It's wise to check in advance with the club, as fees and the availability of tee time vary. Midweek is generally the best time for visitors. The Deer Park at Howth (℃832 2624, fax 839 2405) is Ireland's largest public golf complex, with five courses ranging from an 18-hole pitch-and-putt course to a challenging par-72, 6678-yard, 18-hole course, and a hotel offering B&B and golf packages. Though non-residents can't book time on the links, it's worth phoning ahead to check how busy they are. Other courses worth trying are the 18-hole Dún Laoghaire Golf Club in Eglinton Park (℃280 1694), or the 9-hole course at Bray (℃286 2484). In addition, there are many short pitch-and-putt courses. For information, contact the Pitch & Putt Union of Ireland, House of Sport, Long Mile Road, Dublin 12 (℃450 9299).

Tournaments occur all over Ireland for much of the year; the biggest is the **Irish Golf Open Championship** in late June/early July.

GREYHOUND RACING

If you fancy a flutter or just a fun evening out, **greyhound racing** requires little experience of betting and draws a lively crowd of Dubliners from all walks of life. There are races most nights of the week throughout the year; admission £4 (children free). The **Shelbourne Park Greyhound Stadium** on South Lotts Road, Ringsend, is easily accessible by bus #3 from Pearse Street, and has a comfortable enclosure for watching the races (Feb–early Dec Mon & Wed 8pm, Sat 7.30pm; rest of year Mon & Sat only). The other venue, **Harold's Cross Stadium**, off Harold's Cross Road, can be reached by bus #16, #16A or #16B (Tues & Fri 8pm; Feb to early Dec also Thurs 8pm).

RUGBY

Lansdowne Road (✆668 4601, fax 660 5640) in Ballsbridge is Irish Rugby Union's holy of holies, where national and international championships take place from January to March. The **All-Ireland Finals** is the climax of the club season, while the **Five Nations Championship** is the showcase for international rugby. All of these matches happen between January and March. Lansdowne Road is also sometimes "borrowed" for international soccer matches.

SOCCER

Although the fortunes of Ireland's national football team are a matter of keen concern for almost everyone, Dublin **soccer** fans are less enthusiastic about local teams. Ireland's national league can hardly compete with the money, allure and success of English football, where Dublin-born players like Liam Brady have achieved international stardom. This explains why the most popular teams among Dubliners are Liverpool and Manchester United (both from cities with a large Irish community), a state of affairs acknowledged by RTÉ, which relays live coverage of top English matches far more often than Irish ones. The city currently has five teams in the League of Ireland's premier division – Bohemians, Shamrock Rovers, St Patrick's Athletic, Shelbourne and UCD.

SWIMMING AND WATER SPORTS

The coastline north and south of Dublin offers ample opportunities for **water sports**. Though the water seldom rises above chilly even on hot days, Dubliners enjoy **swimming** in the sea in summertime, when sunbathers pack the shingle **beaches** at Killiney and Bray, and the sandy ones at Sutton, Malahide and Donabate (all accessible by DART or suburban train). Though the beach at Sandymount is small, it's only 5km from the centre, and near the famous **Forty Foot Pool**.

The other great activity along the coast is **sailing**, with long-established yacht clubs in Dún Laoghaire, Howth, Malahide and Clontarf. Unfortunately, many are members-only, so you won't be able to use the facilities unless you belong to a club with reciprocal membership. Contact the **Irish Sailing Association**, 3 Park Road, Dún Laoghaire (☎280 0239), for details. The **National Sailing School** (☎284 4195) by Dún Laoghaire's West Pier offers courses (from £123) at all levels.

Though the west coast is more rewarding, there are some fine dive spots to the south of Dublin, like **Dalkey Island**. Qualified divers can hire gear (£12–25) or book a half-day's boat diving (£29 all-inclusive) at Oceantec, 10 Marine Terrace (Tues–Sat 9.30am–6pm ☎280 1083; *www.oceantecadventure.com*).

Windsurfing is equally popular around Dalkey and Dún Laoghaire, where Wind & Wave, at 16A The Crescent in Monkstown (☎284 4177), rents gear and offers tuition. If you're less bothered about the setting, you can go windsurfing in the Grand Canal Dock basin at Ringsend (bus #3 from Pearse Street), where Surf Dock (☎668 3945, fax 1215) runs courses and rents sailboards by the hour.

Directory

AIRLINES Aer Lingus, 41 Upper O'Connell St or 42 Grafton St (℃844 4777 for UK enquiries, ℃886 8888 for Europe and transatlantic); British Airways, 60 Dawson St ℃1800 626742; British Midland, Nutley, Merrion Rd (℃704 4259 for enquiries, ℃283 8833 for reservations); Ryanair, 3 Dawson St ℃677 4422.

BANKS Banks are open Mon–Fri 10am–4pm (5pm Thurs). The two major Irish banks are Allied Irish and the Bank of Ireland, with many branches around town. Others include the National Irish and Ulster banks. Most banks have automatic teller machines (ATMs), accepting a variety of cash, credit and debit cards.

BICYCLES Bicycles can be hired from: Bike Store, 58 Lower Gardiner St ℃872 5399; Dublin Bike Tours, 3 Mornington Rd, Ranelagh ℃679 0899; McDonald's Cycles, 38 Wexford St ℃475 2586 and Track Cycles, 8 Botanic Rd, Glasnevin ℃850 0252.

CAR RENTAL Argus Rent-a-Car in the Dublin Tourism Centre, Suffolk St ℃605 7701; Budget, 29 Abbey St Lower ℃878 7814; Dan Dooley, 42 Westland Row ℃677 2723; Thrifty Rent-a-Car, 14 Duke St ℃679 9420.

CARRIAGE TOURS From St Stephen's Green, £20, lasting 30 minutes or longer by arrangement.

DENTIST In the case of dental emergencies, contact the Eastern Health Board, Dr Steeven's Hospital, Dublin 8 ℭ679 0700.

DISABILITY The National Rehabilitation Board, 25 Clyde Rd, Dublin 4 ℭ608 0400, which produces a number of free publications, and the Dublin Tourism Centre both offer advice and information to people with disabilities visiting Ireland. *Be Our Guest*, the Irish Hotels Federation's annual accommodation guide, details hotels and guesthouses that are wheelchair accessible or suitable for people with disabilities with the assistance of a helper. Wheelchairs can be hired for around £20 per week from the Irish Wheelchair Association (ℭ833 8241). If you're travelling by ferry from Britain there are reductions available for members of the Disabled Drivers Association and Disabled Drivers Motor Club.

ELECTRICITY 220 volts, 50hz AC is standard, with three square-pin plugs the norm. All British devices should function normally, though North American ones will require both a transformer and a plug adaptor. Australian and New Zealand appliances will only need an adaptor.

EMBASSIES Australia, Fitzwilton House, Wilton Terrace ℭ676 1517; **Belgium**, 2 Shrewsbury Rd ℭ269 2082; **Canada**, 65–68 St Stephen's Green ℭ478 1988; **Denmark**, 121 St Stephen's Green ℭ475 6404; **France**, 36 Ailesbury Rd ℭ260 1666; **Germany**, 31 Trimlestown Ave, Booterstown ℭ269 3011; **Italy**, 63 Northumberland Rd ℭ660 1744; **Netherlands**, 160 Merrion Rd ℭ269 3444; **Norway**, 2 Molesworth St ℭ662 1800; **Portugal**,

Knocksinna House, Knocksinna, Foxrock ©289 4416; **Spain**, 17A Merlyn Park ©269 1640; **Sweden**, 13–17 Dawson St ©671 5822; **Switzerland**, 6 Ailesbury Rd ©269 2515; **UK**, 31–33 Merrion Rd ©269 5211; **US**, 42 Elgin Rd ©668 8777.

EMERGENCIES Ring ©999 for emergency medical aid, fire services or police.

EXCHANGE There are foreign exchange desks at the airport and Dún Laoghaire ferry port. In town, try American Express Foreign Exchange, Dublin Tourism Centre, Suffolk St (Mon–Sat 9am–5pm) or 41 Nassau St (same times), or Thomas Cook, 118 Grafton St (Mon, Tues, Fri & Sat 9am–5.30pm, Wed 10am–5.30pm, Thurs 9am–8pm); all give fair exchange rates, although the best are usually offered by banks. Account holders with some British banks can withdraw money direct from their own account using a cashcard at an ATM – in some cases free of charge, though it's best to check this with your bank before leaving home. Most ATMs accept Plus and Cirrus. Otherwise, major credit cards, Eurocheques and cards and travellers' cheques are almost universally accepted.

FERRIES Irish Ferries ©661 0511; Isle of Man Steam Packet Co. ©1800/551743; Merchant Ferries ©819 2999; Stena Line ©204 7777.

HEALTH Residents of European Union countries are entitled to free medical treatment and prescribed medicines under the EU Reciprocal Medical Treatment arrangement, provided that a completed E111 form is held (available from Post Offices in Britain and Social Security offices elsewhere). Citizens of most non-EU countries are charged for all medical services including those provided by hospital accident and emergency departments. In all cases, it's advisable to take out medical insurance before travelling. Reciprocal medical agreements may apply between other countries, eg Medicare in Australia has such an agreement with Ireland and Britain, but check the precise terms before departure.

HELPLINES The Rape Crisis Centre ✆661 4911, freephone ✆1800/778888; Victim Support ✆1800/661771; Tourist Victim Support ✆478 5295.

HOSPITALS Mater Misericordiae, Eccles St ✆830 1122; St Vincent's, Donnybrook ✆269 4533; and Beaumont Hospital, Beaumont ✆837 7755. All have accident and emergency departments.

INTERNET CAFÉS *Global Internet Café*, 8 Lower O'Connell St; *Cyberia*, Unit 2, Temple Lane, Temple Bar.

LAUNDRIES Most self-service laundrettes are open Mon–Fri 8am–8pm, with earlier closing on Saturday. Central ones include Nova, 2 Belvedere St; Powder Launderette, 42a South Richmond St; and Wash to Iron, 45 Francis St. For dry-cleaning a central option is Craft Cleaners, 12 Upper Baggot St.

LEFT LUGGAGE There are left luggage offices at Busáras (Mon–Sat 8am–8pm, Sun 10am–6pm), Heuston Station (Mon–Sat 7.15am–8.35pm, Sun 8am–3pm & 5–9pm) and Connolly Station (Mon–Sat 7.40am–9.30pm, Sun 9.15am–1pm & 5–9pm).

LOST PROPERTY For items lost on Dublin Bus ring ✆703 3055; for those left on trains, DART lines (✆703 3633) or Heuston Station (✆703 2102); otherwise contact the police (✆475 5555).

NEWSPAPERS AND MAGAZINES The two national daily broadsheet newspapers, the *Irish Times* and the *Irish Independent*, are produced in Dublin. Its one evening paper, the *Evening Herald*, is part of the Independent group. Sundays see the production of three broadsheets – the *Sunday Tribune*, the *Sunday Times* and the *Sunday Independent*, and the more salacious tabloid *Sunday World*. English daily, Sunday and tabloid papers are widely available – *The Mirror, The Sun* and *The Star* have their own Irish editions. Other European newspapers are available at larger newsagents, such as the O'Connell St branch of Eason's. Dublin's listings magazines are the fortnightly *In Dublin* (£1.95) and the free *Event Guide*. Other magazines to look out for include *Magill,* which focuses on political and economic analysis; *The Phoenix*, political satire; *The Big Issue,* which supports Dublin's homeless; and *Hot Press*, Ireland's left-field and iconoclastic music magazine.

PARKING On-street parking spaces may be hard to find in the city centre. The majority have coin-operated meters, but an increasing number are covered by disc display schemes, with discs available from nearby shops. Theft from cars is common, so it's highly advisable to remove all money and luggage from your car when you park.

PHARMACIES O'Connell's, 55 Lower O'Connell St (℗873 0427) is open until 10pm daily.

PHOTOGRAPHY Most types of film are readily available from pharmacies and specialist camera shops. For rapid developing try One Hour Photo, 110 Lower Grafton St ℗677 4472; 5 St Stephen's Green ℗671 8578; and the ILAC Centre, Henry St ℗872 8824.

POLICE The main Metropolitan Garda station is in Harcourt St ℰ475 5555.

POST OFFICES The General Post Office is on Lower O'Connell St (Mon–Sat 8am–8pm, Sun – stamps only – 10.30am–6.30pm; ℰ705 7000). Another handy post office is situated in St Andrew's St, near the Suffolk St Tourism Centre. Stamps may also be purchased at many newsagents. Current costs for postcards and letters are: Ireland and Britain 30p; other EU countries 32p; the rest of the world 45p.

PUBLIC HOLIDAYS New Year's Day; St Patrick's Day (March 17); Good Friday; Easter Monday; First Monday in May; First Monday in June; First Monday in August; Last Monday in October; Christmas Day; St Stephen's Day (December 26).

PUBLIC TOILETS Public toilets are few and far between and often require a 10p coin for entry. Key locations include St Stephen's Green (west side), most large shopping centres, and railway and bus stations.

TAX Value Added Tax rates vary, but visitors from outside the EU can claim a VAT refund on all goods purchased in Ireland. Ask for a special VAT receipt when you purchase an item – you should then get this stamped at customs in the airport and a cash refund will be given.

TAXIS To order a taxi by phone call Metro Cabs ℰ668 3333; wheelchair accessible cabs are available from Eurocabs ℰ844 5844, if booked one hour in advance.

TELEPHONES Local calls cost a minimum of 20p. Many phones also accept prepaid cards purchasable from newsagents, post offices and from the Telecom Éireann

Telecentres situated at Upper O'Connell St (Mon–Sat 9.30am–6pm) and King St South (Mon–Sat 9.30am–6pm, Thurs till 8pm). These also have several payphones and provide directories, including The Golden Pages. There are also booths at the GPO. For emergencies phone ℂ999; operator services, including reverse-charge calls ℂ10; directory enquiries ℂ1190 for numbers in Ireland, ℂ1197 for Great Britain; ℂ1198 for international directory enquiries; telemessages ℂ196; international operator service ℂ114. The area code for calls to Dublin from outside the city is ℂ01. If dialling from the UK, prefix ℂ00 353 1 to Dublin numbers. To call the UK prefix ℂ00 44 plus the area code (minus the initial 0).

TELEVISION AND RADIO Radio Telefis Éireann (RTÉ) is the national broadcasting company and provides two television channels, RTÉ1 and Network 2. In addition to a host of cable and satellite channels, Dublin's geographical position means that British television channels (BBC1 and 2, ITV and channels 4 and 5) are also available. Similarly, there are three state radio channels, RTÉ 1 and 2 and the classical station RTÉ FM3, together with a national commercial station, Today FM. Dublin also has a number of independent stations, including 98FM, 104FM and Anna Livia.

TIME Ireland follows UK Time. Clocks are moved forward one hour in March and back again at the end of October for daylight saving.

TRAVEL AGENTS USIT (youth/student travel), 19–21 Aston Quay ℂ679 8833; Thomas Cook, 118 Grafton St ℂ677 1721; CIE Tours (Irish tour organizer), 35 Lower Abbey St ℂ703 1888; Trailfinders (long-haul flights), 4/5 Dawson St ℂ677 7888.

CONTEXTS

History

The Vikings

When Dublin Bay was first settled can never be determined, though it may have been as long as five thousand years ago. Although the Egyptian astrologer Ptolemy marked a place called Eblana in his map of 140 AD, major habitation of the area began when **Viking** raiders arrived from Norway in the first half of the ninth century.

Before the Vikings arrived there were two small settlements: Áth Cliath ("the ford of the hurdles"), a fortified enclosure used for trading purposes since the sixth century, which gave rise to the city's Gaelic name Báile Átha Cliath ("the town of the ford of the hurdles") and a monastic site located at the point of convergence of the rivers Liffey and Poddle, an area known as **Dubh Linn** ("dark pool"), from which the city's current English name is derived. It was this latter area that the Norse raiders attacked in 837 and transformed into a port. The *Dubh Linn* settlement became an important trading post for the Vikings; large amounts of amber and silver, as well as artefacts such as a set of weighing scales, recovered from the Wood Quay area and the Viking graveyard near Kilmainham, testify to its importance. The Norsemen having established themselves, *Dubh Linn* became the focus for attacks not only from the Irish, but also from Danish Vikings who had arrived from England in 851. The internal feuding weakened the Viking position, and, when the Norsemen split to follow two different leaders, it ultimately led to their defeat by the King of Leinster in 902, forcing them to withdraw. However in 917 they returned and laid the foundations for a permanent settlement by building wooden houses in the **Wood Quay** and **Christ Church** areas, with the result that, over the next decade, a flourishing town life developed and Dublin's role as a centre of commerce intensified.

The first half of the tenth century saw the Norsemen gradually become Gaelicized, as they intermarried with the Irish and started converting to **Christianity** (the first Viking king to convert was Olaf Cuarán, who was baptized in 943). This, plus the need to defend their settlement, resulted in the Vikings' heightened involvement in internal battles. As well as allying themselves with various factions vying for power, the Norsemen made contact with another Viking settlement in York, who then sent large fleets from England to plunder Ireland anew and precipitated a series of conflicts with the Irish kings that would continue for the rest of the century. The Vikings lost their impetus when the kingdom of York collapsed in 954. In an attempt to counter the threat posed by **Brian Ború**, the Irish High King, they became part of an alliance centred around their former adversary the King of Leinster, but their combined forces failed to prevent Ború from defeating them at the **Battle of Clontarf** in 1014, after which Dublin became a Christian vassal state. The Norsemen were then completely assimilated into the Gaelic world, and with the ensuing **Hiberno-Norse** culture came a great deal of Christian development, particularly under the kingship of Sitric "Silkbeard" IV.

The Normans

The eleventh and twelfth centuries saw the Hiberno-Norse of Dublin become further embroiled in Gaelic struggles for supremacy, which, at the end of the twelfth century, led to **Dermot MacMurrough**, the Ard-rí (high king) of Leinster, fleeing to the court of the **Norman** king Henry II to request assistance in regaining power. In return for his fealty, Henry dispatched a band of mainly Welsh knights under the leadership of **Strongbow**. Dublin was rapidly conquered in 1170 and the following year Henry granted the town a charter and established a court there, opening the way for further migration, mainly from Bristol. The new invaders circumscribed the town with walls, erected Dublin Castle and the cathedrals of Christ Church and St Patrick, along with other churches, such as St Audoen's. Dublin's status as a Christian centre developed rapidly, and during the thirteenth century it became a focal point for pilgrimages, particularly as the reputed *bacall Íosa* ("staff of Jesus") resided in the city.

The Irish rose against subjugation in the early fourteenth century, and Dublin suffered during **Edward II**'s abortive attempt to reconstitute English control. Although the town was seen as the capital of the English colony in Ireland, in reality only a small tract of land was under English jurisdiction and even this area, known as **the Pale**, (from which the expression "beyond the Pale" arises), was vulnerable to attack. Dublin was under constant threat, with major restrictions placed on the movement and entry of Gaels, and the people crammed within the city's walls faced the medieval scourges of plague and fire ravaging other European cities.

The Tudors and the Stuarts

During the late 1400s the English attempted to exercise further control over areas outside the Pale by supporting the stronger Irish lords, most notably the **Fitzgeralds** of Kildare and the Butlers, Earls of Ormonde. However **Henry VIII** reversed this policy when he came to power in 1509, preferring to extend royal control regardless of the Irish families. In 1534 the Fitzgeralds protested by staging a symbolic rebellion against Dublin Castle, led by **Silken Thomas**. It did not last long; the young Fitzgerald could not have anticipated the ferocity of the king's response when he sent over a large army to confiscate all the Fitzgerald lands – he was captured and executed the following year.

Dublin thus became the focus for recolonization, and the town grew once again as a new wave of migrants swarmed in. Henry's **reformation of the Church** resulted in Dublin being declared an Anglican city; in 1537 the monasteries were dissolved (All Saints became Trinity College), the *bacall Íosa* was burnt and many relics and images destroyed. However this period also saw some of Ireland's strongest acts of **rebellion**, with the Irish kings resisting the impingement of their powers. Elizabeth, on taking over the throne, believed that the struggle for supremacy in Ireland was vital to England's security (her fear being that the Spanish would use it as a base to attack England) so she devoted large resources to defeating the rebellion, and it was finally quelled at the **Battle of Kinsale** in 1601. The resulting **Act of Supremacy** established power firmly in London, with legal and official appointments no longer the exclusive right of Sean-Ghaill (Old Irish) but going solely to the Nua-Ghaill, the English Protestant migrants.

In 1633 the reformer Thomas Wentworth was appointed to the position of Lord Deputy and began implementing plans to develop Dublin. Much of his work was undone, however, when Ireland became a pawn in the **English Civil War**, and the capital was half-destroyed as various factions attempted to assert their control (on top of this the plague once again swept through the city). Rebuilding took place during **Cromwell's Commonwealth**, but the restoration of the monarchy in 1660 led to the appointment of the **duke of Ormonde** as Lord Deputy of Ireland and to the resurgence of Dublin. A rapid building programme began, which included the salvaging of Dublin Castle and the start of work on the Royal Hospital at Kilmainham, and the town again became a self-sustaining and prosperous trading entity. The arts flourished and the theatre, first established before the war, was revived.

THE TUDORS AND THE STUARTS

The Williamite Wars

However, another reversal came with the **Williamite Wars**. In 1685 the Catholic King **James II** took the English throne and replaced Ormonde with the Catholic Earl of Tyrconnell, introducing an Act of Parliament that would have ousted Ireland's Protestant settlers. To counteract this "popish plan" the English establishment invited the Dutch prince, **William of Orange**, to take over the English throne, precipitating a series of confrontations between the two sides. The decisive clash, the **Battle of the Boyne** in 1692, saw James and his Irish Catholic supporters defeated by William, who then imposed a set of laws barring Catholics from holding any office of state, voting or buying land. With three-quarters of Irish soil now belonging to Anglo-Irish Protestants or absentee English landlords, a rural migration followed, ensuring that Dublin had a **Catholic majority** by the middle of the eighteenth century. Sectarian violence became commonplace in the city, with regular gang wars taking place, such as those between the Liberty and Ormond Boys (see p.91).

Dublin prospered during the eighteenth century while the rest of Ireland, with few exceptions, sank into extreme poverty. The capital enjoyed its architectural heyday: the **Wide Streets Commission** of the 1750s undertook the gentrification of the city, with a view to transforming it into a European-style capital with boulevards and tree-lined squares (those which so characterize Dublin today); the **Royal Exchange**, the **Four Courts**, the **Custom House** and the west front of **Trinity** were all built around this time; and Plutocrats commissioned their own extravagant townhouses, like **Leinster House** and **Powerscourt House**. While Dublin's Protestant upper-middle classes patronized craftsmen and virtuosi in the written and musical arts (Handel's *Messiah* was premiered by the composer himself in 1742), the aspirations of a rising Catholic middle class were denied.

The Act of Union

Henry Grattan's Declaration of Rights during the parliament of 1782 came close to declaring Irish (or, at least, Protestant Anglo-Irish) independence. The following years saw the establishment of the **United Irishmen**, a movement inspired by a combination of the ideas of the patriot **Wolfe Tone** and the success of the French Revolution (see p.92). Seeking social reform and justice, they were driven underground by the government's declaration of their illegality in 1794. The subsequent revolt of 1798 was suppressed, leading to the 1801 **Act of Union**, which abolished the Irish Parliament and instigated direct rule from London. The cause of the United Irishmen was briefly taken up by **Robert Emmet**, the brother of one of its leaders, when he staged his own attempted rebellion in Dublin in 1803, but this too was crushed (see p.95).

The impact on Dublin of the transferral of power to London was enormous. Although the social whirl continued to revolve around the new vice-regent's lodge in Phoenix Park, it was with the participation of a rapidly diminishing upper class. With Dublin's economic decline, and its population now over seventy percent Catholic, the town became the stage for political ferment and agitation for **Catholic emancipation**. It came in 1829, when **Daniel O'Connell** became the first Catholic MP of modern times, and, after the Municipal Corporation Act of 1840 had declared that city officials could only be elected by ratepayers, he also became Dublin's first Catholic Lord Mayor. However his attempts at securing the repeal of the Union resulted in his eventual trial and imprisonment for sedition.

The Famine, Parnell and Home Rule

The **Great Famine** of 1845–49 had a disastrous effect on Ireland. Almost 1.5 million out of a population of 8.5 million starved to death and nearly another 1.5 million emigrated, mainly to North America. Dublin's slums were already bulging at the seams when the Irish potato crop first failed in 1845 and thousands of refugees fleeing starvation began to arrive, increasing its population to 247,000 by 1851. The workhouses closed their doors, and diseases of deprivation reaped further havoc among those left on the streets. Resentment focused on the failure of the British government to intervene and on the absentee landlords who had continued to profit while remaining indifferent to the suffering of their tenants (ironically a visit by Queen Victoria to Dublin in 1849 passed without incident and was generally seen as a success).

The result of this deprivation was a growing hostility, advocated in particular by the most prominent group of rebels at this time, the **Fenian** Brotherhood, formed by James Stephens and James O'Mahony around 1858. Although the rebellion they staged in 1867 was a failure, many members went on to join the Irish Republican Brotherhood, the organization whose primary focus was on securing **Home Rule** for Ireland: the establishment of its own independent government. The driving force behind this movement was **Charles Stewart Parnell** (see p.114), MP for Meath and president of the Irish Land League, whose objective, as part of the agitation for Home Rule, was "Irish land for Irish people". A breakthrough appeared to be imminent until two officials of the British government were killed in 1882 in **Phoenix Park** by an obscure organization called "The Invincibles" (see p.146). Attempts to implicate Parnell in the crime failed, but when his own long-standing affair with a married woman, Kitty O'Shea, became public knowledge, the Home Rule Party split bitterly and Parnell died not long afterwards in 1891. A year later yet another Irish Home Rule Bill was voted down by the British Parliament, stimulating pressure for reform from all quarters of Ireland.

In 1893, **Douglas Hyde** co-founded the **Gaelic League** in Dublin, using as his model the Gaelic Athletic Association, established eight years previously. Its aim was the preservation of Irish as a spoken language and its success prefigured the Celtic literary revival pioneered by **W.B. Yeats** and **Lady Gregory** and the establishment of the **Abbey Theatre** in 1904. Simultaneously, there was an expansion in the impact of political groups such as **Sinn Féin** and a revival of the IRB (Irish Republican Brotherhood). The focus for political struggle this time, however, became the establishment of trade unionism in Ireland, which was brought to a head by the **great lockout** of 1913, during which Dublin's first "Bloody Sunday" took place, leaving over 200 people injured. The resultant heightening of political activity led to the formation in Dublin of the **Irish Citizens' Army** as a worker's defence force by socialists **James Larkin** and **James Connolly**.

The 1916 Easter Rising and the War of Independence

The increasing pressure for Home Rule seemed to be yielding results, despite threats from Ulster Unionists that they would resist any move towards an Irish parliament, when the outbreak of **World War I** halted proceedings. However, **John Redmond**, leader of the Irish Parliamentary Party, believed the war consolidated his position because he had secured a promise of Home Rule in return for the support of the Irish against Germany; many of the 180,000 Irish volunteers who fought for Britain in the war were committed nationalists hoping to return home to Irish self-government.

However, alternative plans were already being made by a small group of dedicated revolutionaries. In 1916, with the Irish nationalist sentiment "England's difficulty is Ireland's opportunity" rapidly gaining currency in this circle, the move to rebellion increased, and former members of the IRB, younger republicans such as **Pádraig Pearse**, and socialists led by **James Connolly** joined forces to participate in what would become the **Easter Rising** (see p.110). Initial plans for the rising were made for Easter Sunday, but when the leader of the Irish Volunteers cancelled their involvement (due to a confusion), it was postponed until the next day. On Monday, April 24, 1916, only one thousand men showed up, with Pádraig Pearse reading his **Proclamation of the Republic** at the GPO before seizing the building, along with others in the city, including Jacobs' Biscuit Factory and Liberty Hall. After six days of fighting, with 300 civilians, 130 British and 60 republican casualties, the rebels surrendered.

The initial reaction to the uprising by Dubliners was hostile – they resented the rebels for the damage they had caused – but attitudes changed when the leaders of the rebellion were executed. This, combined with a widespread fear that conscription would be extended to Ireland, resulted in a revival of Sinn Féin and overwhelming success in the election of 1918. Instead of taking their seats at Westminster however, the newly elected MPs met as the **Dáil Éireann** in Dublin and declared independence under the leadership of **Eamon de Valera**. One member of the cabinet was **Michael Collins**, who, though he held the nominal position of Minister of Finance, harboured plans for further military action and was seen as leader of the extremist military wing of the Volunteers, increasingly referred to as the **Irish Republican Army**.

In January 1919 the first killings in what became known as the **War of Independence** took place when two members of the Royal Irish Constabulary were murdered in County Tipperary. Two years of fighting ensued against the British, who employed a ruthless paramilitary army known as the **Black and Tans** (because of the colour of their uniform) to oppose the rebels. In Dublin, Collins established his own unit of men ("the Apostles") to track and murder G-men, detectives of the Dublin Metropolitan Police who had detailed knowledge of the actions of the city's republicans (this unit proved so successful that, in December 1919, they almost succeeded in murdering the viceroy, Lord French, in the outskirts of the city). An increasingly ugly cycle of reprisals between the two sides culminated in the city's second "**Bloody Sunday**" on November 11, 1920 when, as an act of vengeance for the murder of fourteen undercover spies by Collins and his team, the Black and Tans opened fire at a Gaelic football match at Croke Park, killing eleven spectators and the captain of the Tipperary hurling team, Michael Hogan.

The Irish Free State and Civil War

Despite the IRA's greatest show of strength in May 1921, when they took over the Custom House and set it alight, the war with the British had taken a severe toll on their resources; on July 9, 1921, de Valera met with representatives of the British government and a truce was signed. Negotiations then ensued to formulate a treaty, and an Irish team headed by Michael Collins and Arthur Griffith was sent to London – Eamon de Valera was conspicuous by his absence. Collins and his team signed the **Anglo-Irish Treaty** on December 6, 1921, and the **Irish Free State** was brought into being. However, it did so at the expense of many of the fundamental tenets of republican ideology; not only did it partition Ireland, but members of the new parliament were obliged to swear allegiance to George V. De Valera rejected the document and, when it was passed by a small majority in the Dáil, he and his supporters stormed out, precipitating the **Irish Civil War**.

The first major military action taken in the Civil War was on June 28, 1922, when Collins' Free State forces shelled the Four Courts buildings being held by republicans (known as the "**Irregulars**"), so destroying the public records office, which had titles and deeds dating back to Henry II. Republican forces followed almost identical tactics to those in 1916, occupying prominent buildings in the city centre, particularly around O'Connell Street, only to be bombarded by the heavy artillery of the Free State Forces. Outside Dublin, conventional resistance from the anti-Treaty Irregulars ended on August 12, when a seaborne force captured Cork city, forcing units to flee to hills in the southwest of the country and enter into a guerrilla campaign (the most notable success of which was the killing of Collins on August 22). Like the War of Independence before it the Civil War descended into a series of bloody recriminations, often involving erstwhile comrades. Acts of violence committed by the anti-Treaty side were countered with the execution of republican prisoners – in all, 77 prisoners were shot in this way by the Free State Forces and up to 12,000 republicans imprisoned before a truce was eventually called on May 24, 1923.

Recent history

With the ending of the Civil War the Free State became virtually a one-party monopoly until 1926, when de Valera split from the defeated republicans to form a new party called **Fianna Fáil** ("Soldiers of Destiny"). Fianna Fáil contested the 1927 elections, achieved a majority in 1932 and proceeded to dominate Irish political life over the next seventy years (though ironically it was the political decendants of the Free State Forces, during a brief period of government, who introduced the **Republic of Ireland Bill** in

November 1948). Fianna Fáil started with the political iso-
lationism of de Valera's economic policy, and then moved to
a more expansionist one, introduced by **Séan Lemass** in
1959. The trend towards participation on the international
stage was further reflected by Ireland's joining of the United
Nations and then the **European Community** in 1972.

The last real celebration of republicanism came in 1966,
on the fiftieth anniversary of the Easter Rising, when the
event was officially commemorated in Dublin by the building of the Garden of Remembrance on Parnell Square, and
unofficially by the blowing up of Nelson's Pillar on
O'Connell Street. Increasing **sectarian violence** in
Northern Ireland had little impact on the people of Dublin,
though there were violent street protests in the aftermath of
Derry's "Bloody Sunday" in 1972, with rioters attacking
and burning the British Embassy, and, in 1974, 25 people
were killed by three car bombs, planted by loyalist paramili-
taries. Despite this, many Dubliners see themselves as post-
nationalist in their politics, reflected in the overwhelming
endorsement in 1998 of removing the articles in the
Republic's constitution which claimed sovereignty over
Northern Ireland.

Architecturally the city stagnated during the post-inde-
pendence period, and a good deal of its Georgian heritage
was destroyed in a glut of **development** in the 1960s,
which one commentator referred to as "post colonial van-
dalism". This period also saw the clearance of many of the
inner-city slums, with former inhabitants being moved to
huge estates in the suburbs, which, with very high levels of
crime, unemployment and, latterly, **drug** addiction, quickly
degenerated. The city's drug problem became an epidemic
in the 1980s, and was finally brought to a head in 1996,
when a campaigning journalist was shot at the behest of
one of the drug barons. This acted as a catalyst for the
police, who subsequently took on those controlling the

drugs trade in the city with considerable success, though high levels of addiction still remain.

Since the early Nineties Dublin has been transformed, with the birth of the much celebrated "Celtic Tiger" – an epithet used to describe the similarity of the Irish economy to the tiger economies of Southeast Asia. One of the results of this economic boom has been a cultural renaissance in Dublin, and in 1991 it was named the European City of Culture. **Regeneration** has been the keynote of the Nineties, spearheaded by the **Temple Bar** development, whose architects sought to express the city's new-found confidence in a modern Irish style. Urban renewal has reversed the trend for people to move out of the centre, with apartments being built in formerly run-down areas, and the city's wealth is apparent from a vibrancy and cosmopolitanism not known to Dublin since its Georgian heyday.

Music

Irish traditional **music** is alive and well in Dublin, and on any night of the week you'll find a session in full swing, impromptu or organized.

Though the west of Ireland continues to produce the best-known exponents of traditional music, Dublin has its own virtuosi of the whistle, the fiddle and the mandolin, and the city has played a major part in the continuation of the folk ballad, notably through **The Dubliners**, who have maintained their impetus for the last thirty years. The Dubliners have been blessed with two powerful singers – Luke Kelly (who died in 1984) and Ronnie Drew – and excellent instrumentalists in Johnny Sheehan (fiddle) and Barney McKenna (banjo). Their spirited and often bawdy performances were to directly influence the London Irish band **The Pogues**, with whom they recorded a wildly explosive version of *The Wild Rover*.

Dublin has had greatest success as a rock city. While showbands roamed the rest of Ireland, pounding out cover versions in shiny suits and with variable accuracy, Dublin experienced its own beat boom in the 1960s. Maybe it was the proximity to Liverpool or perhaps it was all down to an American studying at Trinity College, Ian Whitcomb, whose band Bluesville had a top-ten USA hit in 1965 with *You Turn Me On*. Or maybe it was envy at the success of **Van Morrison**'s Belfast band Them. Whatever the reason, Dublin's music scene began to follow in the tracks of the land across the water. While bands like The Greenbeats and Purple Pussycat are long (and perhaps best) forgotten, there is no doubt that the beat groups formed a fecund spawning ground for Ireland's later success, fuelled by increasing access to pirate radio and the UK's Radio One.

While Donegal-born **Rory Gallagher** was blasting out the blues with Taste, the first Irish rock band to have a real impact, Dublin's own Skid Row set the template for others to follow. The original band featured Brush Shiels on bass (still a luminary of the contemporary scene) and an incredibly young Gary Moore on guitar, later to be replaced by Eric Bell. One of the band's lead singers was Phil Lynott and, while bands like Dr Strangely Strange and Granny's Intentions were twiddling with psychedelia and others like Horslips and Spud were beginning the experiment of amalgamating traditional music with rock, it was the black Dubliner who led the first Irish band to dominate the rock world. Thin Lizzie's first major success was a proto-metal version of *Whiskey in the Jar* (1973), but for many their finest hour was *Jailbreak* (1976), featuring *The Boys are Back in Town*, and a then unique twin lead guitar sound.

Punk hit Dublin in the mid-1970s as visiting British bands played *Moran's Hotel* and other local venues. One local R&B band took special notice and transformed both its image and its music. "We were the first neighbourhood rock heroes to happen in ten years", the singer **Bob Geldof** noted, with typical modesty. His band, The Boomtown Rats, had considerable success with singles such as *Rat Trap* and *I Don't Like Mondays*, before Geldof achieved worldwide fame through his co-organization of Live Aid. But Dublin's punk scene produced a horde of bands like Radiators from Space (with Phil Chevron, later of The Pogues), the Virgin Prunes (with Gavin Friday), the Blades and the Vipers, all of whose influence would be long-lasting, and a certain Larry Mullen stuck a note on his school notice board looking for co-pupils with whom to form a band.

That band, **U2**, released its first album, *Boy*, in 1980. Spin it now, almost twenty years later, and it's possible to discern how this then young band might later become the biggest thing since sliced soda bread. For, despite the recent critical backlash, U2 are still one of the biggest rock bands in the world. Their 1987 album *The Joshua Tree* broke them worldwide and also begat one-time popular Dublin parodists, **The Joshua Trio**. Since then, a series of albums (*Rattle and Hum*, *Achtung Baby*, *Zooropa* and *Pop*) have cemented the band's success, which they have fed back into the city through such initiatives as their own Mother label for new Irish acts.

In the wake of U2's success, a number of other Dublin bands (In Tua Nua, Aslan, Light a Big Fire) were signed to major labels, but though producing stimulating and often innovative music, none achieved lasting success. One which failed even to get signed up was Ton Ton Macoute, amongst whose ranks was a certain **Sinéad O'Connor**. Her Prince-composed solo single *Nothing Compares 2 U* was a massive international hit, bringing a degree of fame which did not always sit pretty on her shoulders.

Other Dublin bands to make an impact include **Hothouse Flowers**, fronted by *sean nós* singer Liam O'Maonlai – who, since the band's split, has recorded with Tim Finn (Split Enz/Crowded House) and Belfast singer Andy White. **Something Happens**, probably the best buskers ever to appear on Grafton Street, produced some wonderful pop, but eventually faded. The quirky **A House**, fronted by singer Dave Couse, have struggled with the perversity of record labels. Both the mellifluous Stars of Heaven and the soulful, if unfortunately named, Fat Lady Sings are no more, but the latter's singer/guitarist Nick Kelly has recently released his own solo album. Gavin Friday continues to appear in a variety of incarnations, and Lesley Dowdall of **In Tua Nua** has recently revamped her solo career. For a while, the success of Alan Parker's film *The Commitments* seemed likely to spawn a whole new era of Irish soul bands; the film's young singer, Andrew Strong, who enjoyed a brief spell in the spotlight and a band bearing the film's name, but few originals, continues to tour. The film's bass player, Glen Hansard, has experienced some degree of success with his band **The Frames**. Singer/songwriters Jack L and Mark Dignam have a loyal local following, as do the young punk band **Bambi**, who form part of the excellent Hope Collective.

Today, you'll still find plenty of young hopefuls plying their trade in places such as **Eamon Doran's** (see *Live Music and Clubs*), but the dominant music in Dublin is dance, and the city has a thriving underground scene, with several dance labels promoting and producing their own artists; notable among these are Influx, who feature Dublin's most celebrated DJ Johnny Moy and have residences in both the *Kitchen* and *Rí-Rá*, Quadrophonic, who also promote at the *Kitchen*, and recently, D1, who showcase at the *Funnel Bar*. (For dance music venues see p.261).

Books

Most of the books listed below are in print and in paperback – those that are out of print (o/p) should be easy to track down in libraries, secondhand bookshops or through book-finding services of the kind offered by Waterstones. Publishers follow each title; first the UK or Irish publisher, then the US. Only one publisher is listed if the UK/Irish and US publishers are the same. Where books are published in only one of these countries, UK, IRE or US follows the publisher's name.

Fiction

Peter Ackroyd, *The Last Will and Testament of Oscar Wilde* (Penguin, UK). Hilarious parody of the tragic artist in exile, and a must for devotees of Wilde's epigrammatic wit.

John Banville, *The Book of Evidence* (Picador; Warner); *Ghosts*, *Athena* and *The Untouchable* (all Picador; Vintage). A selection of novels from the most important Irish novelist since McGahern. His 1989 Booker Prize nomination, *The Book of Evidence*, tells a sleazy tale of a weird Dublin murder.

Samuel Beckett, *More Pricks Than Kicks* and *Molly/Malone Dies/The Unnamable* (all Calder; Grove Press). The former, Beckett's earliest publication, consists of ten tales describing the grotesque existence, marriages and accidental death of his Dublin eccentric, Belacqua Shuah. The latter is a wonderful trilogy of breakdown and glum humour.

Brendan Behan, *The Scarperer* (Queens House, US, o/p). Originally serialized in the *Irish Times* in 1953 under the pseudonym Emmet Street, this slight crime tale roams the bars and police stations of north Dublin.

Maeve Binchy, *Dublin Four* (Arrow, UK). Ireland's (and often Britain's) most popular author's four tales of Dublin life feature flat-hunting in Ringsend and disastrous dinner parties in Donnybrook.

FICTION

Dermot Bolger, *The Journey Home* (Penguin, UK). One of the most powerful of contemporary Irish writers, Bolger set his third novel around the bleak lives of young people in his own native Finglas. *A Second Life* (Penguin, UK, o/p) is an assured novel about a man who, miraculously given a second chance at life, sets out to find the truth about his adoption; and *Father's Music* (Flamingo, UK) is a psychological thriller set in Dublin.

Christy Brown, *Down All the Days* (Minerva; Stein & Day). The author of *My Left Foot* later wrote this flamboyantly styled but hugely enjoyable tale of working-class life in Crumlin in the 1940s and 1950s.

Philip Casey, *The Fabulists* (Lilliput; Serif). A deftly-woven love story and depiction of the lean side of contemporary Dublin in a debut novel which illuminates the inner lives of the powerless.

Ita Daly, *A Singular Attraction* (Poolbeg, IRE). A woman approaching middle age seeks freedom in the post-abortion and divorce referenda Dublin of the 1980s.

J.P. Donleavy, *The Ginger Man* (Abacus; Atlantic Monthly Press). A raucous, rambunctious romp of a book tracing the exploits of Donleavy's semi-autobiographical and dangerously cynical law student, Sebastian Dangerfield, in postwar Dublin; banned for some years in Ireland.

Emma Donoghue, *Stir Fry* (Penguin, UK). A finely crafted lesbian love story from a young Dubliner, conjuring up a delightful image of the city.

Roddy Doyle, *The Commitments* (Minerva; Vintage), *The Snapper* (Vintage; Penguin), *The Van* (Minerva; Penguin), *Paddy Clarke Ha Ha Ha*, *The Woman Who Walked into Doors* (both Vintage; Penguin), and *A Star Called Henry* (Jonathan Cape; Viking Press). Doyle drew upon his experiences as a teacher in his native Kilbarrack to pen his initial hilarious trilogy centred around the exploits of the north Dublin Rabbitte family and written in a

FICTION

vernacular style. The fourth and fifth novels are, respectively, an amusing and moving account of working-class family life which won the Booker Prize in 1993, and a sensitive tale of a woman trying to escape a life of domestic violence. Doyle's latest novel centres on hero Henry Smart, interweaving the violence of early twentieth-century Irish history with his own irreverent humour.

Hugo Hamilton, *Dublin Where the Palm Trees Grow* (Faber & Faber, UK). A fine collection of stories set with equal assurance in Berlin and middle-class Dublin.

Neil Jordan, *The Past* (Vintage; Braziller o/p). Film-maker Jordan's first full-length work is an ambitious account of the troubled first years of the Irish Free State.

James Joyce, *Dubliners*, *A Portrait of the Artist As a Young Man*, *Ulysses* and *Finnegans Wake* (all Penguin). *Ulysses* is Joyce's masterwork, a sublimely evocative account of 24 hours in the intertwining lives of Dublin, Stephen Dedalus and Leopold and Molly Bloom. The story and its characters are loosely drawn from Homer's *Odyssey*, but the style is a breathtaking melange of parody, fantasy, realism and (Joyce's major innovation) stream-of-consciousness. Following its completion, Joyce strove for sixteen years to construct *Finnegans Wake*, a cyclical concoction, following the Vicoesque concept of history as inevitable repetition. Often profoundly obscure, there are passages of great lyricism and humour in its account of the Earwicker family: Humphrey Chimpden Earwicker, his wife Anna Livia Plurabelle, and their two sons and pub in Chapelizod.

Ferdia Mac Anna, *The Last of the High Kings* (Penguin; Talk Miramax). A funny and perceptive look at Irish family life, centred on seventeen-year-old Frankie Griffin, who dreams of escape from the eccentric and chaotic world created by his relatives.

John McGahern, *The Leavetaking* (Faber & Faber, UK). A spare and stark tale of a teacher in a Clontarf national school reviewing his

FICTION

life on the day he expects to be sacked for marrying an American divorcée.

Iris Murdoch, *The Red and the Green* (Penguin; Viking). Dubliner Murdoch rarely wrote about Ireland – this fictional account of an Anglo-Irish family during the time leading up to the Easter Rising is something of an exception.

Flann O'Brien, *At Swim-Two-Birds* (Penguin; Dalkey Archive Press), *The Dalkey Archive*, *The Third Policeman* and *The Best of Myles* (all Flamingo; Dalkey Archive Press). The first is a surreal and fantastically funny concoction of books within books, where characters rebel against their author, Gaelic folk heroes roam and Dublin bars are visited where "A pint of plain is your only man"; the later works (in order) feature St Augustine and Joyce working behind a bar, a man turning into a bicycle as a consequence of molecular transference, and side-splitting extracts from Flann O'Brien's *Irish Times* column, which is an excellent introduction to his off-the-wall humour.

Joseph O'Connor, *Cowboys and Indians* (Flamingo, UK). "Dublin at Christmas was a dangerous town. Too many familiar people, all waiting to jump out of the shadows and wave their latest attitude in your face." Life on the peripheries of Dublin and London with Eddie Virago.

Julia O'Faolain, *No Country for Young Men* (Carroll & Graf, US). Republican politics and its repercussions seen through the eyes of four generations of the O'Malley family.

Liam O'Flaherty, *The Informer* (Wolfhound Press; Harcourt Brace), *The Assassin* (Wolfhound Press; Irish Books and Media) and *Insurrection* (Wolfhound Press; Irish American Book Co). *The Informer* is probably his best-known work, a racy tale of Gypo Nolan, a former Republican, who betrays a colleague to the Garda and is hunted down amongst the slums around the Custom House by his erstwhile associates.

FICTION

James Plunkett, *Strumpet City* (Arrow, UK). A hefty and well-written novel set in Dublin in the years leading up to World War II, extremely popular when it was first published in 1969.

James Stephens, *The Charwoman's Daughter* (North Books, US). Stephens is one of Ireland's comic geniuses; here he delivers a whimsical fairy tale, real rags-to-riches stuff, in turn-of-the-century Dublin.

Bram Stoker, *Dracula* (Penguin; Signet). Stoker woke up after a nightmare brought on by a hefty lobster supper, and proceeded to write his way into the nightmares of the twentieth century.

Francis Stuart, *Black List: Section H* (Penguin). Although mainly focusing on Stuart's experiences in wartime Germany, the early chapters are set amongst the literary salons of 1920s Dublin.

Jonathan Swift, *Gulliver's Travels* (Penguin; New American Library Classics); *The Tale of a Tub and Other Stories* (Oxford University Press). Acerbic satire from the only writer in the English language with as sharp a pen as Voltaire.

Colm Tóibín, *The South*, *The Heather Blazing* and *The Blackwater Lightship* (all Picador; Penguin). Three powerful novels from one of Ireland's finest writers, in particular *The Heather Blazing*, the story of a Dublin judge reflecting upon his life while on holiday with his family.

William Trevor, *Mrs Eckdorf in O'Neill's Hotel* (Penguin). A barmy American photographer flies to Dublin to undertake a study of the said hotel and encounters a bunch of bizarre characters staying there.

Poetry and Drama

Sebastian Barry, *Our Lady of Sligo* and *Plays* (both Methuen). Characters from Barry's family history are central to his plays, all characterized by a rich use of language. Of the latters *The Steward*

of Christendom, relating the story of the Catholic head of the
Dublin Metropolitan Police before the change in regime in 1922, is
particularly compelling.

Samuel Beckett, *Complete Dramatic Works* (Faber & Faber, UK).
Bleak hilarity from the laureate of the void, including his seminal
masterpiece *Waiting For Godot*, and other absurdist treats such
as *Endgame*.

Brendan Behan, *The Complete Plays* (Methuen; Grove Press).
Behan's dramatic works, of which *The Quare Fellow* remains
the most important; with events revolving around a prison
execution Behan draws attention to society's complicity in the
act.

Brian Friel, *Plays: Two* (Faber & Faber). A selection of the Derry
playwright's work, including *Dancing at Lughnasa*, a family drama
which examines the tensions between Catholicism and paganism
in Irish society.

Patrick Kavanagh, *The Complete Poems* (Goldsmith Press; Peter
Hand Kavanagh Press). One of Ireland's best-loved poets of the
rural scene, Kavanagh is perhaps most famous for *The Great
Hunger*, in which he attacked sexual repression in 1940s
Ireland.

Derek Mahon, *The Yellow Book* (The Gallery Press; Wake-
Forest). Highly allusive, sensuous verse belying Mahon's *fin-
de-siècle* disenchantment with the "sado-monetarism" of
Ireland.

Frank McGuinness, *Plays* and *Someone To Watch Over Me* (both
Faber & Faber). The former is a collection of the major works from
McGuinness, one of Ireland's most important playwrights,
including *Observe the Sons of Ulster Marching towards the
Somme*, and the latter an exploration of the cultural resources
that sustain three hostages – one English, one Irish and one
American – in the Middle East.

Sean O'Casey, *Three Plays* (Papermac; St Martin's). Includes the socialist playwright's famous Dublin trilogy *Juno and the Paycock*, *Shadow of a Gunman* and *The Plough and the Stars*, which challenged the revolutionary rhetoric and political orthodoxies of the day.

John Millington Synge, *The Complete Plays* (Methuen; Vintage). Plenty of "begorras" and "mavourneens" in Synge's invented dialogue of the Irish peasantry; his humorous masterpiece *The Playboy of the Western World*, depicting the rebellion of a peasant youth, incited audiences to riot.

Oscar Wilde, *The Complete Works of Oscar Wilde* (HarperCollins). The full emotional range, from the glittering satire of *Lady Windermere's Fan* and *The Importance of Being Earnest*, to the moving verse of *The Ballad of Reading Gaol*, written during his imprisonment.

Books on Dublin

Douglas Bennett, *An Encyclopaedia of Dublin* (Gill & Macmillan, IRE). An assiduously compiled reference book detailing everything you might ever wish to know about Dublin and then some.

John Bradley (ed), *Viking Dublin Exposed: The Wood Quay Saga* (O'Brien, IRE, o/p). Absorbing account of the archeological discoveries made at Wood Quay, covering the political battle for adequate excavation and demonstrating the international significance of the material found.

W.J. Brennan-Whitmore, *Dublin Burning* (Gill & Macmillan, IRE). A vivid and engaging memoir of the 1916 uprising by the Irish Volunteers officer commanding North Earle Street.

Peter Costello, *Dublin Churches* (Gill & Macmillan, IRE). More than 150 churches are described and photographed in this detailed study.

John Cowell, *Dublin's Famous People: Where They Lived* (O'Brien Press; Irish American Book Co). Brief biographies of literati and glitterati.

Maurice Craig, *Dublin 1660–1860* (Penguin, UK). Revised since its original publication in 1952, this is a classic account of the Dublin of Ormonde, Swift and Grattan and the three great eras of the city's development.

Mary E. Daly, *Dublin: The Deposed Capital* (Cork University Press; University of Notre Dame Press, o/p). A comprehensive social and economic anatomy of Dublin's development and decay between 1860 and 1914.

John Graby and Deirdre O'Connor (eds), *Dublin Guide* (Phaidon, UK). Detailed written and pictorial information on all the city's major and less well-known buildings.

Desmond Guinness, *Georgian Dublin* (Batsford, o/p). A photographic celebration of Dublin's Georgian heritage, from grand public edifices to domestic interiors and decorative plasterwork.

Kevin C. Kearns, *Dublin Tenement Life: An Oral History* (Gill & Macmillan; Irish Books and Media) and *Dublin Pub Life and Lore* (Gill & Macmillan; Roberts Rinehart). Two vibrant and stimulating accounts based entirely on the reminiscences of Dubliners.

Joss Lynam, *Easy Walks Near Dublin* (Gill & Macmillan, IRE). An excellent guide to forty walks, including several in the Wicklow Mountains.

Peter Zöller and John McArdle, *Dublin: Portrait of a City* (Gill & Macmillan, IRE). Zöller's award-winning photojournalism is teamed up with McArdle's caustic prose in an attempt to capture the essence of Dublin city.

Irish history, politics and society

John Ardagh, *Ireland and the Irish: Portrait of a Changing Society* (Penguin). A comprehensive and lively anatomy of contemporary Irish society and its attempts to come to terms with a changing world.

J.C. Beckett, *The Making of Modern Ireland 1603–1923* (Faber & Faber, UK). A classic account of the complexities of Irish history.

Terence Brown, *Ireland: A Social and Cultural History 1922–1985* (Cornell University Press, US). A brilliantly perceptive survey of writers' responses to the state of post-revolutionary Ireland.

Max Caulfield, *The Easter Rebellion* (Gill & Macmillan; Roberts Rinehart). This essential account of the events of 1916, originally published in 1963, has recently been revised and reissued.

Michael Collins, *In His Own Words* (Gill & Macmillan, IRE). Extracts from the Irish revolutionary's writings and speeches.

Liam Fay, *Beyond Belief* (Hot Press, IRE). An irreverent and often hysterically funny investigation into the state of religion in modern Ireland, written by a *Hot Press* regular.

Roy Foster, *Modern Ireland 1600–1972* (Penguin). Superb and provocative book, generally reckoned to be unrivalled in its scholarship and acuity, although it has been criticized for what some feel to be an excessive sympathy towards the Anglo-Irish. Not recommended for beginners.

Robert Kee, *The Green Flag* (Penguin). Awesomely assiduous history and masterful analysis of Ireland from the first plantations to the creation of the Free State. Three volumes.

George Morrison, *The Irish Civil War* (Weidenfeld & Nicolson, UK). A powerful collection of photographic images of the Irish Civil War, accompanied by commentary on the origins and causes of the conflict by Robert Kee.

IRISH HISTORY, POLITICS AND SOCIETY

Fintan O'Toole, *The Ex-Isle of Erin: Images of Global Ireland* (New Island Books, IRE). *Irish Times* journalist O'Toole examines the impact of globalism upon Irish society.

Colm Tóibín, *The Irish Famine* (Profile, UK). Tóibín's highly readable and thought-provoking analysis of the 1845–49 famine, which takes an incisive look both at the issues surrounding the failure of the potato crop, and the inadequacy of previous historical accounts of the crisis.

Biography and autobiography

Brendan Behan, *Borstal Boy* (Arrow; David R. Godine). Behan's at times romanticized account of his involvement in the Republican movement and his early years in jail.

Christy Brown, *My Left Foot* (Minerva; Heinemann). Born with cerebral palsy, Brown painstakingly typed out this unsentimental autobiography, published in 1954 when he was twenty-two, focusing on his upbringing in a huge southside family, dominated by the remarkable endurance and character of his mother.

Noel Browne, *Against the Tide* (Gill & Macmillan; Irish Books and Media). Fine autobiography of one of Ireland's most radical ministers, and particularly illuminating on the role of Catholicism in Irish politics.

Tony Clayton-Lea and Richie Taylor, *Irish Rock* (Gill & Macmillan, IRE). Now seven years old, this is still the only decent book available on the subject and much of it is an account of the development of the Dublin music scene.

Antony Cronin, *Dead as Doornails: A Chronicle of Life* (Dolmen Press, o/p; Oxford University Press, o/p), *No Laughing Matter: The Life and Times of Flann O'Brien* (Paladin, o/p; Fromm), *Samuel Beckett: The Last Modernist* (Flamingo; HarperCollins). Cronin's work ranges from his sparkling account of literary bohemia in the 1950s and 1960s via an illuminating biography of Brian O'Nolan (alias Flann O'Brien) to his 1997 analysis of Beckett's life and work.

Ruth Dudley Edwards, *James Connolly* (Gill & Macmillan, IRE). A short, direct biography of the socialist leader, which gathers pace around the time of his relations with Larkin, the 1913 lockout and the 1916 uprising.

Richard Ellmann, *James Joyce* (Oxford University Press, US), *Oscar Wilde* (Penguin; Vintage). Ellmann's wonderful biography of Joyce is a literary masterpiece in its own right. His work on Wilde was, unfortunately, unfinished when he died, but is still an excellent insight into the work of this often misunderstood writer.

Oliver St John Gogarty, *As I Was Going Down Sackville Street* (O'Brien Press; Irish American Book Co) and *Intimations* (Sphere, o/p). Two of the poet and surgeon's accounts, once considered racy, of Dublin in the 1920s and 1930s; the author, much to his own disgust, was the model for Joyce's Buck Mulligan.

Michael Holroyd, *The Search for Love*, *The Pursuit of Power*, *The Lure of Fantasy* (all Chatto & Windus; Random House). Outstanding three-part biography of George Bernard Shaw.

James Knowlson, *Damned to Fame: The Life of Samuel Beckett* (Bloomsbury; Simon & Schuster). This biography, by one of the world's pre-eminent Beckett scholars, makes a good complement to the more anecdotal and gossipy style of Cronin's book (see opposite), which came out at the same time.

Brenda Maddox, *Nora: A Biography of Nora Joyce* (Minerva; Fawcett). This is a hugely enjoyable account of the life of Nora Barnacle, wife of JJ and an absolute treasure in her own right.

Ulick O'Connor, *Brendan Behan* (Abacus; Grove Press). An absorbing and sometimes pathetically touching account of the life of probably Dublin's most provocative dramatist and drinker.

Nuala O'Faolain, *Are You Somebody?* (Sceptre; Owl Books). The best-selling memoirs of *Irish Times* journalist O'Faolain offer a unique perspective on attitudes to women in Irish society.

BIOGRAPHY AND AUTOBIOGRAPHY

Peter Sheridan, *44: A Dublin Memoir* (Macmillan). From an author known more for his plays this is a colourful and moving account of an inner-city childhood in the Sixties.

INDEX

ROUGH GUIDES: Travel

ROUGH GUIDES: Mini Guides, Travel Specials and Phrasebooks

MINI GUIDES

Antigua
Bangkok
Barbados
Big Island of Hawaii
Boston
Brussels
Budapest
Dublin
Edinburgh
Florence
Honolulu
Lisbon
London Restaurants
Madrid
Maui
Melbourne
New Orleans
St Lucia

Seattle
Sydney
Tokyo
Toronto

TRAVEL SPECIALS

First-Time Asia
First-Time Europe
More Women Travel

PHRASEBOOKS

Czech
Dutch
Egyptian Arabic
European
French

German
Greek
Hindi & Urdu
Hungarian
Indonesian
Italian
Japanese
Mandarin Chinese
Mexican Spanish
Polish
Portuguese
Russian
Spanish
Swahili
Thai
Turkish
Vietnamese

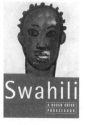

AVAILABLE AT ALL GOOD BOOKSHOPS

ROUGH GUIDES:
Reference and Music CDs

REFERENCE
Classical Music
Classical:
  100 Essential CDs
Drum'n'bass
House Music

World Music:
  100 Essential CDs
English Football
European Football
Internet
Millennium

**ROUGH GUIDE
MUSIC CDs**
Music of the Andes
Australian
  Aboriginal
Brazilian Music
Cajun & Zydeco
Classic Jazz
Music of Colombia
Cuban Music
Eastern Europe
Music of Egypt
English Roots
  Music
Flamenco
India & Pakistan
Irish Music
Music of Japan
Kenya & Tanzania
Native American
North African
Music of Portugal

Jazz
Music USA
Opera
Opera:
  100 Essential CDs
Reggae
Rock
Rock:
  100 Essential CDs
Techno
World Music

Reggae
Salsa
Scottish Music
South African
  Music
Music of Spain
Tango
Tex-Mex
West African Music
World Music
World Music Vol 2
Music of Zimbabwe

AVAILABLE AT ALL GOOD BOOKSHOPS

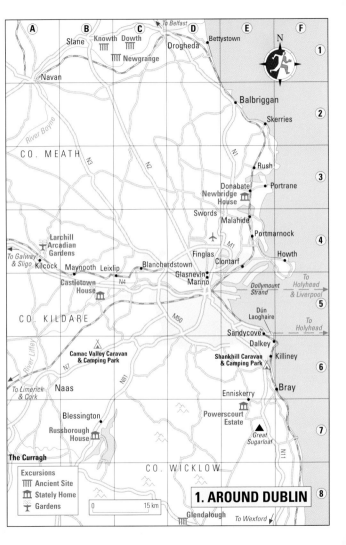

1. AROUND DUBLIN

Excursions

🏛🏛🏛 Ancient Site
🏛 Stately Home
🌳 Gardens

0 ————— 15 km

To Belfast

Ⓐ Ⓑ Ⓒ Ⓓ Ⓔ Ⓕ

Slane
Knowth Dowth
Newgrange
Drogheda
Bettystown ①

Navan

Balbriggan ②

Skerries

River Boyne

CO. MEATH

Rush ③

Donabate Portrane
Newbridge House

Swords

Malahide ④

Larchill Arcadian Gardens
To Galway & Sligo
Kilcock Maynooth Leixlip
Blanchardstown
Finglas
Clontarf
Portmarnock
Howth

Castletown House

Glasnevin
Marino

Dollymount Strand

To Holyhead & Liverpool ⑤

CO. KILDARE

Dún Laoghaire

To Holyhead

Camac Valley Caravan & Camping Park

Sandycove

Dalkey

Shankhill Caravan & Camping Park
Killiney ⑥

Naas

Bray

Enniskerry

To Limerick & Cork

Blessington

Powerscourt Estate
Great Sugarloaf ⑦

Russborough House

The Curragh

CO. WICKLOW ⑧

Glendalough
To Wexford

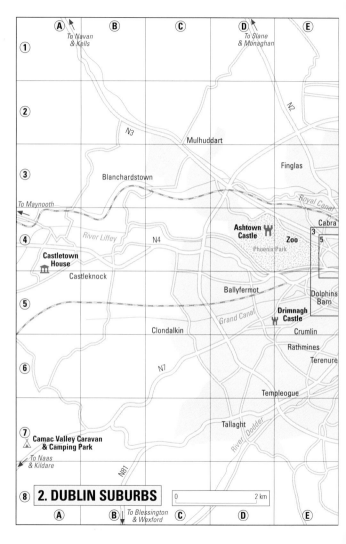

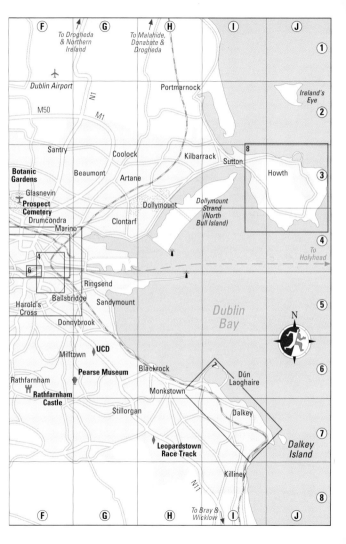

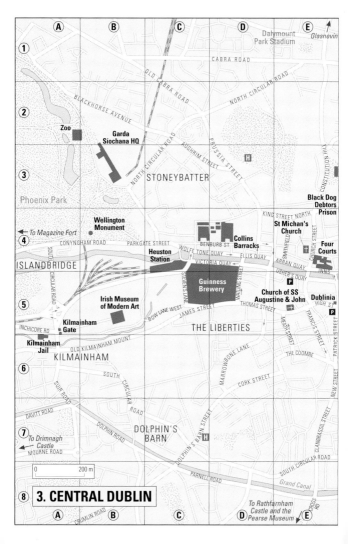

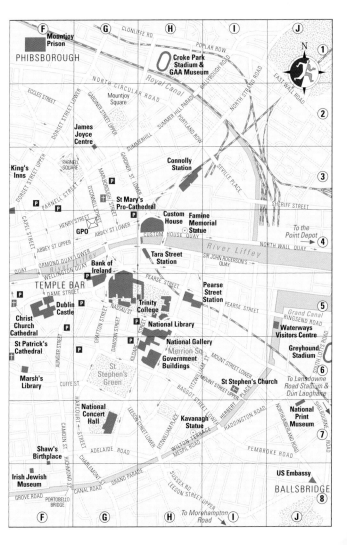

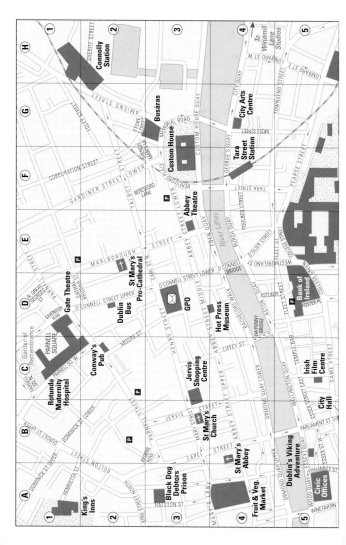

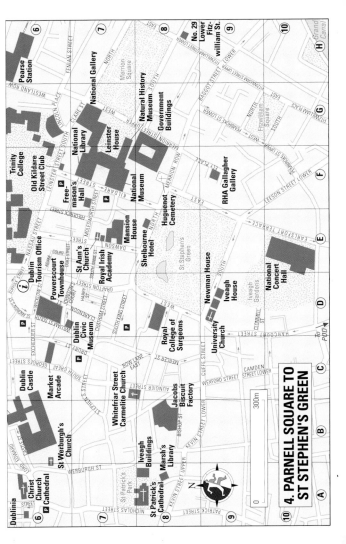

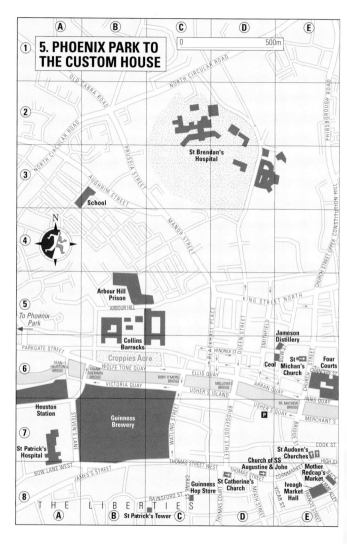

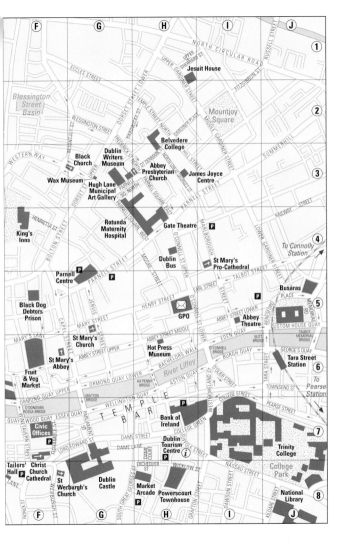

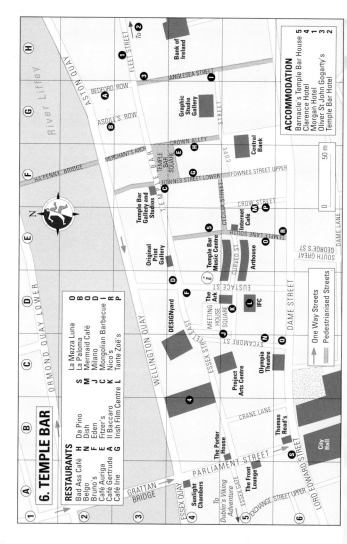

6. TEMPLE BAR

River Liffey

ORMOND QUAY LOWER

HA'PENNY BRIDGE

ASTON QUAY

RESTAURANTS

Bad Ass Café	H	La Mezza Luna	O
Belgo	N	La Paloma	B
Bruno's	F	Mermaid Café	Q
Café Auriga	E	Milano	D
Café Gertrude	A	Mongolian Barbecue	I
Café Irie	G	Nico's	R
Da Pino	O	Tante Zoë's	P
Dish	S		
Eden	J		
Fitzer's	K		
Il Baccaro	C		
Irish Film Centre	L		

ACCOMMODATION

Barnacle's Temple Bar House	5
Clarence Hotel	4
Morgan Hotel	1
Oliver St John Gogarty's	3
Temple Bar Hotel	2

Bank of Ireland

FLEET STREET

To 2

BEDFORD ROW

ANGLESEA STREET

ASDILL'S ROW

Graphic Studio Gallery

CROWN ALLEY

MERCHANT'S ARCH

Temple Bar Gallery and Studios

TEMPLE BAR SQUARE

FOWNES STREET LOWER

FOWNES STREET UPPER

Central Bank

COPE STREET

CECILIA STREET

CROW STREET

Internet Café

Original Print Gallery

Temple Bar Music Centre

CURVED ST

TEMPLE LANE SOUTH

Arthouse

DAME LANE

DESIGNyard

The Ark

MEETING HOUSE SQUARE

EUSTACE ST

IFC

ESSEX STREET EAST

SYCAMORE ST

SOUTH GREAT GEORGE'S ST

DAME STREET

Project Arts Centre

Olympia Theatre

CRANE LANE

Thomas Read's

City Hall

The Porter House

PARLIAMENT STREET

The Front Lounge

LORD EDWARD STREET

ESSEX GATE

EXCHANGE STREET UPPER

To Dublin's Viking Adventure

GRATTAN BRIDGE

ESSEX QUAY

Sunlight Chambers

WELLINGTON QUAY

One Way Streets

Pedestrianised Streets

0   50 m

N

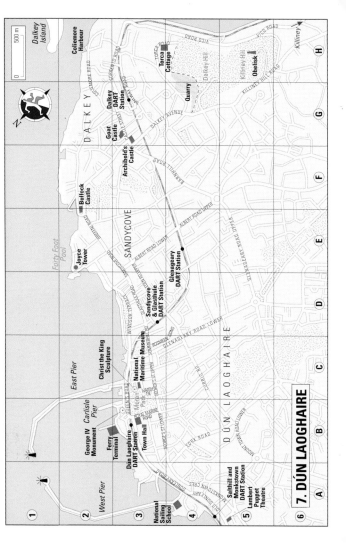

7. DÚN LAOGHAIRE

Dalkey Island

Coliemore Harbour

DALKEY

COLIEMORE ROAD

Torca Cottage

Dalkey DART Station

Goat Castle

Archibold's Castle

Bullock Castle

DALKEY AVENUE

Quarry

SORRENTO ROAD

VICO ROAD

Killiney Hill

Obelisk

KILLINEY HILL ROAD

Killiney

Forty Foot Pool

Joyce Tower

SANDYCOVE

ALBERT ROAD UPPER

ALBERT ROAD LOWER

Glenageary DART Station

GLENAGEARY ROAD UPPER

GLENAGEARY ROAD LOWER

East Pier

Christ the King Sculpture

National Maritime Museum

Sandycove & Glasthule DART Station

West Pier

George IV Monument

Carlisle Pier

Ferry Terminal

Dún Laoghaire DART Station

Town Hall

ROYAL MARINE ROAD

QUEEN'S ROAD

MARINE ROAD

GEORGE'S ST UPPER

DÚN LAOGHAIRE

YORK ROAD

National Sailing School

Salthill and Monkstown DART Station

Lambert Puppet Theatre

OLD DUNLEARY

MONKSTOWN CRES

OLD DUNLEARY ROAD

MONKSTOWN ROAD LOWER

N

500 m

0

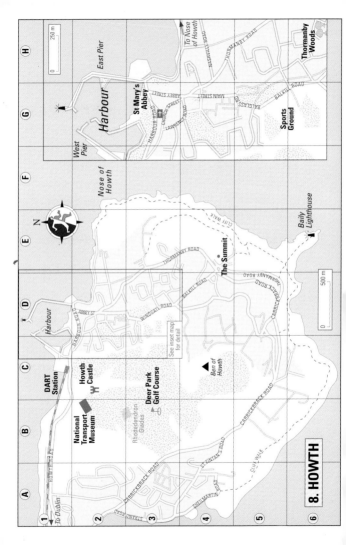

8. HOWTH

Map labels:

To Dublin

DART Station

National Transport Museum

Howth Castle

Harbour

ABBEY ST

Rhododendron Glades

Deer Park Golf Course

Ben of Howth

See inset map for detail

HOWTH ROAD

CARRICKBRACK ROAD

STRAND ROAD

ST FINTAN'S ROAD

CLIFF WALK

SHIELMARTIN

THORMANBY ROAD

WINDGATE ROAD

BALKILL ROAD

CARRICKBRACK ROAD

The Summit

NORMANBY ROAD

CLIFF WALK

Baily Lighthouse

N

Nose of Howth

West Pier

East Pier

Harbour

To Nose of Howth

St Mary's Abbey

HARBOUR ROAD

ABBEY STREET

CHURCH STREET

LAWRENCE ROAD

MAIN STREET

THORMANBY ROAD

NASHVILLE ROAD

BALGLASS

BALKILL ROAD

Sports Ground

Thormanby Woods

0   250 m

0   500 m